Reaching further:
How to remove obstacles
to personal excellence

A handbook for all learners and achievers seeking to reach their full potential; and a resource for teachers, trainers, personal and executive coaches, therapists, and all others who promote personal development.

Copyright 2005 by John G. Hartung, Psy.D.

Published by the
Colorado School of Professional Psychology
555 E. Pikes Peak Avenue #108
Colorado Springs, CO 80903-3612
719.442.0505

For information about permission to
Reproduce selections from this book, write to:

John Hartung
The Colorado Center for Alternative Psychology
215 Crown High Ct.
Colorado Springs, CO 80904

hartung@cospp.edu

ISBN 0-9764638-1-4

Dedicated to those who have taught me the most:
those clients, trainees, and patients around the world
who have enriched me by including me in their lives, and
who have shared their stories of courage and healing.

Contents

Figures

Figures continued

Case examples

Foreword

Attempting to deal with obstacles to personal excellence nearly always takes the approach that one is either impaired and therefore in need of *treatment*; in trouble, therefore in need of *assistance*; or undereducated, therefore in need of *education*. Frequently the obstacles are a combination of some or all of these considerations requiring more than any one book, authority, or professional is able to offer. Such is not the case with this volume, *Reaching further: How to remove obstacles to personal excellence*. Written by a world-recognized scholar in the field of energy psychology, this publication bridges many needs, professional approaches, and specific skill/technique offerings.

The professional will find the book exciting in that Dr. Hartung is not restricted to an artificially traditional approach to the practice of psychology and human services. His blend of traditional and contemporary psychology, clinical and consultative methods, oriental and occidental knowledge, and research/literature based information, brings not only both old and new therapeutic methodology but also a refreshingly new professional permission to practice inside and sometimes *outside* the usual and customary "boundaries" of what is often narrowly defined as psychological services.

Dr. Hartung gives recognition to the demand for professionals who not only "think outside of the box" but who have the courage to practice outside that box, and the professionally demonstrated knowledge and skills to do so. As the author to this forward, and one who has been trained in both traditional and alternative skills and thinking, I have personally experimented with many of the skill models and methodologies in this volume. Recently while giving a workshop to a group of musicians dealing with performance anxiety, I utilized several specific techniques in this book to overcome the obstacles to excellent performance with musicians at a national competition. The competition was fierce, the rewards for success were huge (like scholarships and new instruments), teachers and parents were present, competing colleagues were in the audience cheering and jeering – there was all that goes with the dichotomous wish for success and failure among college age persons. One student in particular, in front of such an audience practiced under my direction several of the techniques in this book and the success was so spectacular in less than one and one half hours that the audience applauded with a standing ovation for the student who at the beginning was so disabled that he could not hold his trumpet without visibly shaking. At the end he was performing with a confidence that was truly astounding (and he won the competition!).

Many more testimonials such as the one above are available. However, suffice it to say here that this book is not a repeat of anything that has heretofore been published for the specific, hands-on practice of psychology and related disciplines. It is not a book for simply reading. It must be used for clinical experimentation, demonstration, and personal application, and offered to other professionals for collaboration in our attempt to put new wine in new bottles for those who thirst for success and excellence. The Colorado School of Professional Psychology offers congratulations to one of its professors, Dr. Hartung, and takes considerable pride in publishing this fine work.

Richard H. Cox, PhD, MD, DMin, ABPP
Provost, Colorado School of Professional Psychology
April, 2005

Preface

The epicenter of the December, 2004, tsunami was at the northern tip of Sumatra, and many people in the Indonesian province of Banda Aceh were killed. Two years earlier I had been in Banda Aceh with a UNICEF-sponsored team teaching trauma strategies that community health workers could use with survivors of the civil war. As of this writing most of our trainees either have not yet been located, or did not survive the catastrophe. In the spirit of solidarity, all profits from sales of this book made by the author will be invested in humanitarian projects that involve training and treatment for persons affected by disasters around the world, whether caused by natural events or by human intention.

I describe a number of exercises, all of which I have tested extensively both for personal use and in professional settings. I have found them to be easy to learn, effective, and safe. They can be explained in different ways so that almost anyone can fit the concepts into terms with which they are already familiar. The exercises are also portable, and can be practiced almost anywhere and at almost any time. If the instructions are followed carefully the exercises should prove to be similarly helpful and safe when used by others. In my experience there is very little risk involved in doing the exercises, whether for one's own use or in treating someone else. Less than one person in about a thousand has reported to me that one or another of the exercises has generated such strong emotion that they could not continue, at least for the time being.

Rare though the risks are, it is nonetheless essential that common sense and respect be shown at all times. The information in the book (as is the case with almost anything in existence) can be used incorrectly, in excess, with ill intentions, and otherwise inappropriately. Here are a few general guidelines to keep in mind throughout the book.

- Those who decide to practice the exercises either for personal or professional purposes must accept complete responsibility for what they do. The author can accept no responsibility for any negative effects that may accrue. If in doubt as to the proper use of any of the exercises, please contact the author prior to trying them.
- Some people who report amnesia for some period in their life, amnesia for which there is no medical explanation, may have experienced events so difficult that they learned to hide those events outside of their conscious memory. Unless you are a professional, do not use the exercises with these persons as some of the exercises could open up those hidden memories and cause the person to relive the original experience. The reliving is called an "abreaction", which in turn can lead to "dissociation" as the person tries once again to put the memories out of consciousness. Refer the person instead to a professional acquainted with the exercises. References can be found in Appendix A.

- The person being treated always has the final say in whether to continue using the exercises or not. If someone says they want to stop, that indeed means *stop*. We always honor the decision of the person being treated.
- If a person does begin to relive a particularly strong memory, stop what you are doing and have the person tap the edge of his or her hand (where you would do a karate chop) until the person feels calm again (see the **sh** points, pages 38 and 39).
- These exercises frequently produce positive changes in medical conditions: I do not, however, recommend that the exercises be used for medical problems by persons not trained in the relevant medical profession, particularly for physical pain and allergies.

As the handbook is field-tested in different countries and cultures, suggestions for improving the content, readability, and cultural sensitivity of the book will be collected for future editions. Readers can contribute to future publications, indicating whether you would like to be recognized for your suggestions, or prefer to remain anonymous. You can contact me directly at:

John Hartung
The Colorado Center for Alternative Psychology
215 Crown High Court
Colorado Springs, CO 80904 (USA)

hartung@cospp.edu

Any person who wishes to reproduce any part of this book for purely personal purposes may do so.

Please contact the author for permission to reproduce the book for any professional use and distribution. This is not a training manual for professionals. While the instructions in the book can be learned easily, trainers and professional therapists will need additional preparation in order to fit the exercises within a broader theoretical and therapeutic context. Additionally, those who wish to use the book for professional purposes are strongly advised to witness the power of the exercises for themselves under supervised practicum experiences prior to treating others. I also ask that you respect any registered titles, and that you recognize the originators of the exercises.

John Hartung
Colorado Springs
April, 2005

Introduction

I begin with two stories about some of the people that motivated me to write this book, and about the kinds of people that I hope the book will serve. (The footnotes[1] are explained in the notes at the end of the chapter).

JoAnne: A career threatened

I had been a psychologist for about 20 years and an executive coach for eight when I met "JoAnne", a junior executive with a biotechnology company. She had asked for a two-hour coaching session to learn about the latest strategies for managing public speaking anxiety. As we began our initial interview she told me about what she had been doing to get free of her anxiety. I was impressed to learn that she seemed to have tried virtually everything that I knew from the field of traditional management practice. She had, for example, gotten into the habit of over-preparing the material she would be presenting, then practiced and rehearsed over and over, using deep breathing exercises and reading list after list of positive self-statements. But her anxiety remained. She also mentioned that two weeks following this interview she would face her company's senior management team to deliver a major report, and feared that her swift career rise was about to derail. I thought I had two choices. One was to admit I knew no more than she about conventional approaches to anxiety reduction and to send her on her way, to another predictable failure. A second alternative, however, was to risk trying out some new and odd-appearing exercises I had been using successfully with my clinical patients for some months. I opted for this choice.

I told JoAnne that her dedication to excellence was obvious. I also said it was regrettable that she had not enjoyed more success after working so hard to overcome her public speaking anxiety. I then said that her experience was similar to what I had seen with people before: there are definite limits to traditional approaches to her problem. She looked quite disappointed and wondered aloud if her problem was hopeless. Our next conversation went something like this:

John: I don't know of anything else beyond what you already mentioned, at least not from the traditional approaches that you obviously already know so well. On the other hand, I've been trying out some new ideas in my clinical practice, some new things that look promising. I've got to say right up front that they are anything but traditional as we think of that word in executive coaching. In fact, they will probably sound strange, if not weird. Let me ask you: how experimental do you feel today?

JoAnne: I'd have to say that I'll try anything at this point. Can you tell me what you're talking about?

John: Let me see how I can put this. Have you ever heard about acupuncture?

JoAnne: Sure. Some of my friends have tried it. Mostly they say it's worked for them. One person had a sore knee. Another used it for a difficult pregnancy. It's an alternative medical treatment, from China I think, or somewhere else in Asia, isn't it?

I told her about how I had recently treated an anxious clinical patient, and how we both had been surprised at the speed and power of the treatment. I then mentioned some of the acupuncture science I was aware of, but JoAnne stopped me fairly quickly, and said she really didn't need any further information. She was clearly motivated to get on with our experiment.

John: Let's start by having you tell me a little about what happens to you when you think ahead to the report you are going to give to senior management. Imagine the scene coming up, and now look around at the senior managers in attendance, and notice what you're thinking about yourself, and how that makes you feel right now.

JoAnne: I usually try to avoid feeling so awful.

John: It's natural to want to avoid feeling bad. But we won't be able to tell if this is going to be of use to you today unless we start with some kind of baseline, then see if things change. So I'm curious to know how you feel right now when you imagine standing up in front of your bosses.

JoAnne: OK, let's give it a try.

John: Imagine ahead to that talk you are going to give in two weeks. Now, let's say you use a scale from zero to ten, where zero means no anxiety whatsoever, and 10 is the worst you could imagine feeling. Where would you rate your anxiety right now?

JoAnne: At least a nine.

I then explained what we would be doing, and then had her tap on several key acupuncture points – under her eye, under her arm, and under her collarbone. I suggested it was a sort of acupuncture, but without the needles[2].

John: OK, breathe, and look at senior management again in your mind. What do you notice?

JoAnne: That's odd. It's shifted somehow. I can still see them, but the feeling is different.

I asked her for a number and she said she felt at about a six. We repeated the same pattern, with some variations as she was reminded of past events that had embarrassed her. I told her this was all normal. After ten minutes she could no longer feel any anxiety when she thought ahead to her presentation. When I asked for a number representing how she felt at the moment. She first said it was at a zero, and then changed that to a one.

JoAnne: It can't be a zero, can it? This stuff has been with me for years. It's been eating at me. I still don't believe it's gone now, even though I really don't feel bothered right now when I think ahead.

We used another 20 minutes to practice further, and I drew her a paper map of the points on her body that she would tap as she rehearsed for the presentation after she had gotten home. We used the remaining time to review her plans for preparing for the meeting: practice a few brief stories to give some life to the statistics she would be mentioning, double check her visual-aid equipment, have a glass of water nearby and remember to drink, practice deep breathing so it would become a habit, and so forth. She seemed to have a good plan.

JoAnne: But will it work? I mean, feeling this way in your office is one thing, but what about later?

John: We've still got some time. What if we worked on the thoughts you have right now about possibly failing. What are you thinking about yourself now?

JoAnne: [Laughs.] That's easy, it's that old notion that I always struggle with, about not being able to believe that I really am standing up and being visible and acting like I've got something to say to the world.

John: So if you put it into words? Begin with 'I' . . .

JoAnne: I . . . can't believe this is me. No, it's more like 'I don't deserve all of this attention' . . .. and maybe 'I can't do this'.

John: Those all make sense, don't they? How about just thinking about those thoughts, notice how they make you feel, and let's go over the acupuncture points again. Or if you would like, I could teach you another technique.

She said she would like to learn even more, so I then demonstrated a strategy called the Tapas pose (which you can view in figure 1 on the next page). She did the Tapas pose several times for a couple of minutes each time. Again, she was able to say that she lowered her anxiety to a "1". She also said that the "1" seemed about right to her – that it might be appropriate to keep some anxiety until she could put into practice what she had learned in our session.

To enhance the positive, she repeated the exercises several more times during our session while saying different affirmations to herself: "Given how prepared I am, I deserve to enjoy myself in my work", and "I want to be successful", and finally, "I can do this."

I suggested that if and when her anxiety and doubts came up again, just to notice it and tap the same points, or use the Tapas pose. I reminded her that she could call me to talk about any of this further, and our session ended.

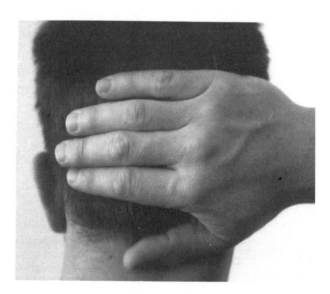

Figure 1. **The Tapas pose that JoAnne used[3]**

JoAnne flew back to her work site about a thousand miles from my office and I did not hear from her for two months. I then received the following email.

4

Greetings,

Thanks for the work you did with me in our meeting a couple of months ago. Has it really been that long? Sorry for being so late in checking in. The presentation that we worked on together went really well. As you probably can guess, I was over-prepared as usual, and since I felt none of that old terror I was really able to be myself – even my jokes went over well. The visual props were good, and I had none of that cottonmouth I had told you about. I didn't even have to change my clothes before dinner that night. Remember how I used to sweat? Senior management was there with tough questions. I don't know if they were more pleased with the information that I could give them or the time I answered one of their questions with, "I don't know. But I'll get back with you by the end of the day with the data." Amazing being able to say "I don't know" without getting that knot in my stomach. After my presentation an HR guy approached me and asked if I would consider being company spokesperson for the next year or so while they launch a new product. Nothing significant, just a promotion, salary increase, and some exotic international travel. Thought you might like to know.

Best regards, JoAnne

The distraught father and son

While in the midst of writing this introduction I had to take an overnight flight from Chicago to Mexico City. I found my seat on the plane, next to a father and his four-year-old son who were traveling to Mexico to visit family. By 1:30 am we were in the air and the flight attendants had switched off the cabin lights so we could sleep. The darkness was far from soothing for the little boy next to me, however, and he began, at first quietly, to murmur "Mommie, Mommie, Mommie". Dad, who seemed to be a splendid parent, stroked his son's arm and spoke to him in a quiet voice. The little boy was not to be comforted, unfortunately, and soon was shouting for his absent mother. Things went from bad to worse. The screaming intensified, and the little boy's worry grew to panic. The poor little fellow eventually threw up all over his father and himself.

I found an airsickness bag, got towels from the washroom, and together we cleaned up our row of seats. Another passenger whispered that there was an empty seat in back of the plane, but by then I had decided to stay in that seat to see if I could offer some help to this now quite distressed father. As the son screamed, Dad turned to me wide-eyed. "Might I help out", I asked. He nodded, and I said the following:

John: *Frequently a little boy will feel better if you gently tap him under the eyes, like this.*

I then tapped myself under my own eyes and guided the father as he tapped the same points under his son's eyes (you can see where to tap the points in figure 2 below).

Figure 2. **The key acupuncture points that the father used for his son's anxiety**[4]

I knew from my clinical work that these points are widely accepted acupuncture treatment points for anxiety and panic, and thought it was worth a try in this situation. The little boy was screaming and jumping around considerably by now and it took the father several attempts to find the exact point under his son's eyes. I continued to tap under my own eyes to show where the points were and encouraged the father to continue. He persisted. My words were largely limited to "Tap real softly", or "A little bit higher", or "That's it, good."

It took about 20 seconds for me to guide the father to the exact location of the acupuncture points under his son's eyes, and about another 20 seconds of gentle tapping for the little boy to become calm. Both the father and I kept tapping for a short time, he under his son's eyes, I under my own. The entire procedure took about 2 minutes. I then told the father and his son that they had done a good job. The little boy looked at me as if bewildered by his ability to be calm without having his mother close at hand. His father mouthed "Gracias". He never did ask me what the tapping was all about – not surprising to me as so frequently people experience the changes that occur with these exercises as being natural and unremarkable.

Five minutes later both Father and Son were asleep, and so they stayed until the flight attendants had to waken them when we arrived in Mexico.

This acupuncture point used here, and the Tapas pose you have already seen in figure 1, are two simple but powerful techniques you will learn in this handbook.

I begin with these two stories because I think the three individuals give a sense of how the techniques can be used in different circumstances. Whether you are an executive looking to move further in your career, or a parent hoping to be more effective in raising your children, or a child who hopes to feel safer when no real danger exists – I believe that you can find useful ideas in this handbook.

JoAnne, and the father and his son, were able to overcome some fairly troublesome problems in a fairly brief period of time. They did not have to explain exactly what had caused the problem, nor spend time uncovering early memories. Earlier in my career I believed that it was necessary to talk for a long period of time to "understand" a problem before any benefit could be expected. These days I am guided by quite a different set of assumptions. Because so much has changed about how we understand the process of change, I also no longer use the word "therapy" to describe the techniques I will be discussing. And because what I will describe seems to be relatively easy to learn, I believe that the proper use of this handbook will allow most readers to be able to resolve a wide variety of issues without the need for other professional assistance. Of course, not all readers will find that these techniques work as fast and as powerfully as they did with JoAnne and the father and his child, but many will. Others will find that they need to repeat the exercises, persevere, and practice before they experience deep and lasting benefit.

How I discovered the exercises

The techniques I used with JoAnne and the father and son are mostly based on the same concepts that guide acupuncture and other treatments that involve the subtle energy running through our bodies. My exposure to acupuncture began in 1981 when I was able to observe the practice of medical acupuncture while on a trip to Shanghai. I thought of medicine as distinct from psychology in those days, and it did not occur to me that acupuncture theory might be applicable to psychological issues.

I studied for my doctorate in psychology at a traditional graduate department, taught at a traditional university, and talked to my patients – in traditional ways. My frustration with psychology as I practiced it in those days motivated me to experiment with new approaches that would work faster, produce results that lasted over time, and have a broader impact on society. In 1993 I had the good fortune to meet several master trainers who had learned to use acupuncture theory for psychological problems, and my professional life was revitalized. I first began to change my clinical practice, and then began more and more to use the same methods in my work as executive coach.

Some of the techniques in this book may appear strange as they are based on acupuncture and other concepts that may not be familiar to all readers. I have found that the best way to become familiar with them is simply to practice them. My emphasis will be on outcome: do they work or not? I have also included some exercises that will seem more familiar since they are already in wide use in many societies. For those readers who would like first to learn about the basic theories and concepts that underlie the more unusual exercises, I recommend you first read Appendix A, and then return to this point in the book. For others – like JoAnne and many of my coaching clients, and like the desperate father in the plane – who would like to get right to the exercises themselves, read on.

My intended audience

I have used the exercises in this book to help my coaching clients, to treat my clinical patients, and to help myself.

I write first for any self-learner who would like to become adept at using the techniques just by reading about them and practicing them for personal development, without having to depend on any other outside assistance. I have personally used each of the techniques that I will describe for my own self-help purposes. The exercises are simple to learn, easy to remember, portable, and when practiced they usually produce immediate benefit – sometimes quite remarkable – for a wide variety of problems and issues. I use "excellence" in the book title as a reference to those persons who would like to eliminate whatever interferes with their reaching their goals, so that they can do their best whether that means inventing a product, teaching a student, raising a family, taking on different career responsibilities, or running a marathon.

A second group of intended readers includes anyone in a mentoring role: executive and life coaches, teachers, trainers, consultants, and therapists. As a coach, therapist, and teacher myself, I have found that being able to teach these exercises to my clients, students, and trainees has been invaluable. I believe that virtually anyone who has chosen to help others in their personal development will find that having these resources in their repertoire will enhance their work. My experience suggests that the book is most likely to be used by coaches and therapists as they work with their clients (instead of directly by clients for self-use). Chapter 10 is written specifically for psychotherapists and coaches.

I was in a coaching session with JoAnne, the executive with the public speaking problem, when I first had the idea to write this book, but have had many other moments when I wondered why such a book was not already available. One of those moments occurred when I was in the plane wishing I could have handed the father a handbook that he could use later. Another was when I was treating a musician, so nervous on stage that she could not play her flute because her lips were so dry. All she wanted, she said, was a simple guide for calming herself while she waited for her cue during a concert. Another moment

8

was with a man who was an excellent and contented middle manager and wanted to continue doing the work he loved, and also knew he could not turn down a promotion unless he could first feel all right about not climbing someone else's arbitrary career ladder. And yet another moment was with a parent whose grown children referred him so that he might learn to "get closer to us" by learning to feel more patient towards them. The defining feature of these and other similar moments was that each person had decided on a direction in life and had found it to be good and meaningful – and now was looking for ways to keep from being thrown off course by anxiety, doubts, irritations, anger, and other nuisances. These were people already aimed in a direction that they liked, and now wanted to feel and act better as they acted on their choices. Each one wanted some kind of portable guide that they could use at different times during a day, as the need arose, so they could remember to keep practicing the exercises and techniques that they found to be so useful.

Clear instructions are necessary but not sufficient

I have taught the exercises in this handbook to hundreds of people, and they and I have found them to be very effective in the vast majority of cases. As more and more people asked me for a handbook that would help them to stay on track after they had terminated their consultation with me, I realized my challenge would be to translate into detailed written instructions what I had been doing and saying in my office. Obviously, having a handbook that one could use alone, without depending on additional outside guidance, could be empowering, as well as more efficient and much less costly. It would be an especially good resource for anyone with a do-it-yourself preference, who valued independence and self-reliance. The question, however, was whether it would be as convincing and instructive as was a face-to-face learning experience.

I sent the first drafts of the book to persons already acquainted with the basic concepts, and to another group of persons for whom the concepts were unfamiliar. I received much helpful feedback and advice, and rewrote most of the original draft extensively, so what you have now is a "field-tested" document that has been widely endorsed. That is to say that those people who actually used the book found the instructions to be sufficiently clear, and the exercises effective.

Some persons asked for a copy of the draft, but then neither read it nor tried out the exercises. This is not so unusual; I suspect many other self-help books have been placed on a shelf unread. This is where the two audiences converge. If you acquired this handbook planning to use it for yourself, and if you actually use it, you will probably benefit from that use.

If on the other hand you doubt, for whatever reason, that you will practice the exercises enough to learn them and to benefit from them, you might consider contracting with someone from the second intended audience – a mentor, psychologist, executive coach, consultant, or someone else in a teacher role who is familiar with the theories and practices described here. Sometimes in spite of our best intentions it is difficult to motivate ourselves or to keep to a routine, even though we know intellectually that doing so would be good for us. Sometimes having another person as a teacher can get us to do something that we will not accomplish on our own. We may need to watch someone else demonstrate a new behavior, and then to coach and encourage us as we do it ourselves. Sometimes simply knowing that someone is observing us, or paying attention to us, can be very motivational.

If you cannot find someone in your geographic area to assist you, you can consult Appendix A where I have included a short (and incomplete) list of professionals who teach these techniques, either in one-on-one consultation or in training courses.

How to use this book

From this point onward the handbook takes on a practical tone. I open each chapter with **the bigger picture** to provide some basic information about specific problems that face those seeking a higher level of competence and performance. I hope to present the problems in a context that normalizes those problems. That is, I want to show first how certain thoughts, feelings, and behaviors have survival value for us at a basic level, and how they are meant to assist us through life. I then will suggest how they can become exaggerated and cause more harm than good, and why it makes sense to work to get them back to a normal and cordial relationship with us.

In most chapters I describe one or two **case examples** of how my clients have used the methods to help themselves. All of the information comes from persons I have worked with, though I have blended information from several persons to protect identities. The problems that these people faced, and the steps they took to resolve them, are factual. I hope readers will find commonality with one or more of these persons. I believe that "achievers", "leadership", and "excellence" can be defined in many in different ways, and I hope this book will reach a wide range of individuals who realize that the definition of individual success and meaningfulness is highly personalized. The exercises I describe are ones I have used with persons in different parts of the world, under varying conditions of stress or economic privilege. Among those reporting benefit have been community leaders in the highlands of Guatemala, Nicaraguan counselors dedicated to confronting violence against women, Asian psychotherapists who labor in refugee camps and tent cities, physicians studying alternative medicine for victims of terrorism – as well as executives of corporations and foundations in various countries. I have even witnessed benefit by psychologists who were once locked into the notion that healing must be painful, long-term, and costly!

Finally, I describe the **exercises** in a way that teaches the reader how to use them immediately, and how to measure benefit. I plan to be very specific, sometimes repetitive, and will give step-by-step instructions on what to do. In chapters one through five there are seven basic exercises listed by priority. To highlight these basic exercises and to distinguish them from other information in the book, I list them as #1 through #7. Some of the exercises will be familiar to the reader, some perhaps not. Where appropriate, I will summarize a complete exercise on a single page so it can be copied for easier use (this was one of the many suggestions I received from my informal "editors", to whom I am most grateful.)

Readers who want to read more about the methods, or about scientific support for what I write, will find **notes** at the end of each chapter, beginning with this chapter. Names of authors, books, and articles mentioned in the notes are then collected in the references section at the end of the book. As mentioned, if you do not find the exercises sufficiently helpful you can consult appendix A for information about professionals who can help further, and additional information about the history and concepts that underlie the exercises.

In chapter one I introduce the basic seven exercises in detail. By beginning with chapter one, you will be able to become familiar with the basic exercises. I mention them again in chapters two through five, though in less detail. If you find the title of a particular chapter to be especially intriguing, you may begin there, then refer back to chapter one for more information on the exercises.

The graphics, drawings and photos are collectively called **figures**, and are numbered in sequence. All of the persons who served as models are family and colleagues, not clients.

Some do's

Do practice, practice, and practice. Trying out a technique once, or even once a week, is not likely to produce much change, any more than jogging once a week will significantly improve your cardiovascular conditioning, or reading a book about leadership will make you a skilled leader.

Do follow the instructions carefully, at least while you are still learning to do the exercises, and repeat them exactly as they are written. Be strict until you know the exercises by heart. The systems described have been tested by hundreds of practitioners with hundreds of thousands of clients. As far as we know, these are the "best practices" to date. There is no need to modify them. Always use common sense and show respect for your client. Never treat anyone that you have not first informed fully about what you plan to do, and always consult with your client throughout any treatment you offer to do.

Do innovate, however, after you have learned the basics of the exercises well. You might try them out with your work group as a brief "relaxation" exercise before a difficult meeting (as some have done). You might lend the book to a colleague who is about to derail because of some personal habits that are fueled by anxiety or anger. Or you might lend it to someone you supervise and offer encouragement and confidential help. You do not need to be a trained therapist either to use or to teach the techniques. However, before you hope to teach them to someone else effectively, it would be a good idea to learn them by using them first for yourself, working through some issues that concern you personally. And as I said, follow the instructions, use common sense, and show the deepest respect for anyone you treat.

Do move beyond *eliminating problems*. Notice that the title of the book contains the words *further* and *excellence*. After you have removed obstacles and resolved difficulties (such as the matter of public speaking or the apprehension I mentioned earlier), continue doing the exercises to help you emphasize the positive, to develop optimism, to dream beyond reality. Life is about more than survival, more than simply relief from symptoms.

Do persevere. Look what happened in my case: I did not "get" the techniques the first time I learned them, and had to repeat my training. I finally experienced the power of the methods, and then became a trainer myself. This area of knowledge can appear quite weird at first, but can quickly come to feel very familiar once we have had a personal experience of the value of these deceptively simple exercises[5].

Eliminating the negative, enhancing the positive

This book has the dual focus of eliminating those obstacles that hinder personal achievement and excellence, and enhancing positive personal qualities[6] that will help in achieving one's goals. Implicit in the title is the assumption that people using this book have already developed serious and practical skills that they need in life, in their professions, in their relationships. What I have found in my work, however, is that many individuals with highly developed skills keep those abilities under wraps, as it were, often appearing to be much less capable than they really are. In such a case the individual is likely to have unfinished business in the form of self-doubts, anxiety, grief, anger, and so on – which in turn become obstacles that interfere with their reaching their full potential. The issue, then, is not so much a matter of developing even more skills, but in freeing up those they have already been developing. A slight variation of this is when individuals have the *aptitude* to learn new skills, but for reasons of low self-esteem, fear of failure, and related handicaps, are not realizing their full potential.

To explain these kinds of limits people place on themselves I often use a metaphor that virtually everyone in Colorado Springs (where I have lived for 30 years) understands immediately. Outside of our city, in clear view 300 days a year, there appears 14,000-foot Pikes Peak. In an annual marathon some 1,000 men, women, and children run, walk, and hike the 14 miles to the top. Another 1,000 complete the round trip.

I ask my clients to imagine a runner in exceptional physical and mental condition preparing for the run. Surrounded by friends, carrying just enough water to stay hydrated, the runner can take on the task of climbing the mountain with a sense of confidence, excitement, and even enjoyment. If, however, the runner were then to put on a backpack containing some 10 pounds of cement blocks, it is not likely that all of the practice and conditioning and self-care would prove to be very beneficial. If the load were increased to 40 pounds, the runner might not reach the top of the mountain at all.

Many of the people I work with, and perhaps many of the readers of this book, seem similar to the runner with a backpack. They have prepared themselves well by becoming educated and skilled in what they need to reach their goals, by learning to listen and teach and empower, by exercising patience and perseverance as they assume additional responsibilities, by learning how to organize and set priorities, and generally by continuing to improve themselves according to the changing demands of their life. Too often, however, they also wear metaphorical backpacks, not necessarily carrying an intolerable weight, but with "extra baggage" from the past. And generally the baggage, like the cement blocks, has no present function and is at best out of date, even if it did have some purpose once upon a time.

The dual purpose of the exercises is to remove the negatives (i.e., lightening the metaphorical backpack bit by bit), and to replace them with positives (in the form of personal strengths and assets).

In part one of the book I describe strategies designed to reduce the negatives, that is, to lighten the load that otherwise skilled and motivated people carry with them. The backpack may contain old memories of failure, or anxieties about taking on the unknown, or anger about real or perceived slights. Whatever the issue, at least in so far as I discuss them, I will describe exercises to reduce the impact of old baggage so that it does not continue to interfere so much with one's pursuit of personal and professional goals.

In part two the focus is on enhancing the positive. In that section you will find additional examples for feeling, thinking, imaging, and behaving positively. This short handbook, then, can help you to resolve what interferes with success and to enhance positive internal resources.

Given my experiences over many years and with many individuals, I am confident that this handbook can be used to compliment more traditional programs, such as those dedicated to management and executive development[7], athletic and fitness training, public speaking, active listening – in sum, almost any area of training designed to give a person the skills required to be successful in a chosen field.

In this regard, before your proceed further you might like to read about other persons who have benefited from using the exercises described in the book. In addition to what you just read about JoAnne with her career concerns, and about the father who wanted to help his son to become less anxious, you can also find stories about:
- other leaders on pages 83, 115, and 116;
- a scientist on page 68;
- a professional athlete on pages 164 through 166;
- medical applications on pages 184 and 185;
- managing jet lag on page 138; and
- stressed out students on page 22.

Notes to the Introduction:

1. These footnotes in the text refer to notes at the end of each chapter. In the notes I refer to authors and writings for those readers interested in further information on a topic. These are linked in turn to the original sources in the **references** at the end of the book. The year in parentheses after a name refers you to the publication date.

2. I suggested it was a sort of acupuncture, but without the needles. I describe the use of acupuncture points on pages 36 through 47.

3. Figure 1: The Tapas pose that JoAnne used is described on pages 28 through 35.

4. Figure 2: The acupuncture points that the father used for his son's anxiety are discussed in chapters 3 and 10, and in Appendix A.

5. The adage, "Physician, heal thyself", is relevant here. Using the techniques routinely for our own improvement can remind us of their power, and can increase our credibility when we introduce the techniques to our clients. The focus of chapter 9 is on using the exercises for self-care and as part of a routine.

6. Chapters 7 and 8 deal with strategies for enhancing the positive. The ever-increasing focus on positive psychology is a welcome antidote to the stereotype that we psychologists are interested only in pathology, symptoms, and problems. For a start, you might read Seligman (1990, 2002), who is a former president of the American Psychological Association, and Csikszentmihalyi (2000), known for his elaboration of the concept of "flow." These two introduced an entire issue of a journal dedicated to a scientific overview of positive psychology (Seligman & Csikszentmihalyi, 2000). Also see Aspinwall & Staudinger (2003) on the psychology of human strengths, Lopez & Snyder (2003) on positive psychological assessment, and Peterson & Seligman (2004) on character strengths and virtues.

7. The book by Lombardo and Eichinger (*4th edition or later*) is the best example I have read of the kinds of practical and concrete skills that are traditionally taught to what we commonly think of as high achievers. The authors have worked with the Center for Creative Leadership (CCL), the world's largest open enrollment leadership program and widely recognized for the quality of its programs. These kinds of more traditional leadership training mesh extremely well, in my experience, with what I will be describing. The traditional approaches are also limited, however, both in terms of efficiency and effectiveness, which is why I think something like this book and something like their book would be best used in combination for leadership training. Also consult the CCL website, www.ccl.org

Part One: Managing and overcoming obstacles

In this first section we will look at obstacles or barriers to excellence, and at some of the innovative methods that have been shown to help remove those.

We begin with a look at stress (chapter 1). I then separate stress into two distinct emotions, anger (chapter 2) and fear or anxiety (chapter 3). People who seek to achieve more will frequently report that they are preoccupied with ongoing sadness and depression (chapter 4), as well as memories of failure and other traumatic experiences (chapter 5) that interfere with self-realization. I end this section with some simple techniques for managing sleep problems and the ever more commonly reported jet lag (chapter 6). In chapter one I introduce the seven exercises that will be repeated in different forms in chapters 2 through 5. These are the most effective and efficient I have discovered in my work in different countries and under varying cultural conditions. To distinguish them from other information and lists in the book, I will introduce each with the # sign.

#1. deep breathing
#2. TAT
#3. EFT
#4. tapping shortcuts
#5. leading with your heart (cardiac coherence)
#6. the Butterfly Hug
#7. physical activity

Chapter 1: Reducing stress

The bigger picture

Those who study the effect of stress[1] on human beings tell us that stress is a normal human experience. Though we may consider stress to be always negative, it can actually be for better or worse. The word "stress" by itself does not tell us much. It suggests that in some way a person became mobilized to respond to a challenge or test, but doesn't tell us whether the challenge was reasonable or not, or whether the person had a positive or negative experience. In an attempt to shed more light on a complex topic, two alternative words have been suggested. "Distress" was already in use to reflect the negative, but as no single word existed for positive stress, one had to be invented. By adding the Greek prefix for "good", *eu*, the word "eustress" was formed. If the reader has never heard of this word, it may be because the prejudice remains. We still easily assume that stress is always a negative experience.

Some stress, as we now know, can actually be very positive. The fact that we have bodies and minds (or more accurately "bodymind") that can respond to stress at all has merit. If we never felt stress, or did not deeply experience being challenged by life, we would not invent, look for problems to be solved, or care much about higher levels of achievement and performance. This relationship between stress and benefit is depicted in figure 3.

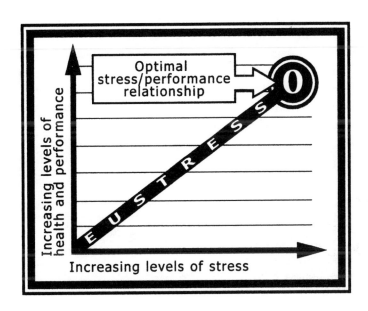

Figure 3. **The positive relationship between stress and performance**

Up to a certain point, then, the greater the stress, the greater the benefit (in terms of motivation, performance, achievement, meaning, health, etc). The *eustress* diagonal implies that increasing stress can be good. This relationship between stress and positive benefit continues only to a certain degree, however, and after reaching its optimal point the reverse relationship begins to occur, as depicted in figure 4.

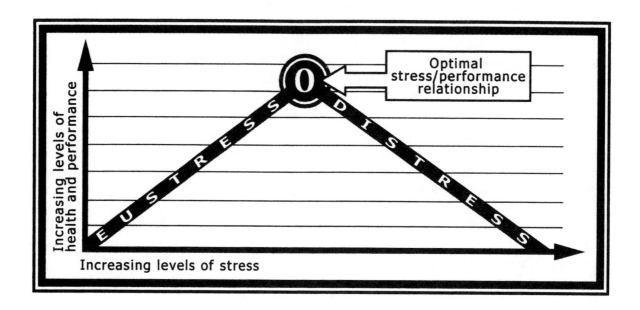

Figure 4. **The relationship between stress and performance**

On the left side of the graph we still see the *eustress* gradient. Notice that the lowest levels represent very low stress and also very low performance. Most people would probably say that if they feel no stress at all, they are also at risk to be apathetic or lazy. Some minimal level seems motivational for most people. As stress then increases, so does the sense of energy and motivation. The upward diagonal represents this relationship, and is where we are more likely to experience various positive conditions that accompany and are facilitated by stress: achievement, performance, invention, creativity and innovation, curiosity, fulfillment, pleasure, accomplishment, joy, and meaning.

As we move further to the right, to the high point of the curve, performance and stress become more and more positively associated. At the highest point is implied the optimal relationship between stress and performance, and it is at this point where we may experience a special kind of concentration and focus, and may lose track of our sense of time and self. It is here where we may feel most challenged and inspired, and where we may transcend ordinary consciousness. Let me list a few of the benefits of stress, which is to say "positive" or "optimal" stress, or *eustress*.

18

Some effects of positive stress or eustress

• On an emotional level: joy, well-being, resilience, forgiveness, positive motivation, passion, a sense of direction and control.

• In our thinking: "I can." "I'm deserving." "Life is worth the effort." "I am worth the effort."

• Social/behavioral: energy and activity, efficiency, attentiveness, higher performance, assertiveness.

• At the physical level: health and well-being, deep and efficient breathing, relative freedom from the pain caused by stressful behavior and thinking such as headaches and tension.

At times we may find ourselves purposely migrating to the left of the highest point, (the *O*) where challenge and performance are both lower. This may be telling us that while there are times to achieve, there are also times to relax, to consolidate, and to regroup. Life does not require that we always be at our maximum performance level. However, if we remain too far to the left too much of the time, we may find that we again lose motivation and begin to feel bored or otherwise unchallenged. Flowing back and forth within this area seems to be where most people prefer to be.

When stress levels go too high, continue for too long, or in some other way out-pace our ability to adjust and respond adaptively, eustress eventually becomes *distress* – as represented by the diagonal line moving to the right of the optimal point and moving downward. Just as the upward slant implies that some stress can be good and increasing stress can be better, the downward slant implies that excessive stress can produce the opposite effect. If we remain excessively stressed even for a short period of time we can become irritable and inefficient, and probably lose our sense of joy and pleasure. If we continue to be excessively stressed, the wear and tear on our body and mind can produce all sorts of additional problems. Even longer, and we can experience the absolute loss of motivation people call burnout, or the debilitating condition we call post-traumatic stress, which implies that some upsetting events continue to haunt us even as time passes and the events become more and more distant memories. Let me offer a short and very incomplete list of what can happen with excessively high levels of stress, that is, the kinds we call *distress*:

Some effects of negative stress[2]

• On an emotional level: anxiety, depression, irritability, anger, joylessness, confusion, lack of motivation, a sense of losing control. (These issues will receive special attention in this book.)

• In our thinking: "I can't." "I'm permanently damaged." "Life is not worth the effort." (Ways to correct thinking errors will also be described.)

• Social/behavioral: inactivity resulting from fatigue, inefficiency, distractability, lower performance, aggressiveness. (Using the techniques in the book to resolve feeling and thinking difficulties can also help to improve behavior.)

• At the gastrointestinal level: peptic ulcers, ulcerative colitis, irritable bowel syndrome, indigestion, and heartburn. (While our focus will not be medical, it is not at all uncommon for persons who practice the techniques in this book to report improvements in physical health. This comment also applies to the remainder of this list.)

• Cardiovascular effects include hypertension, migraine headache, Raynaud's disease, possibly coronary artery disease.

• Respiratory disorders include allergies and hay fever, bronchial asthma and stress-activated hyperventilation.

• We can also include cases of tension headaches, inflammatory joint disease, rheumatoid arthritis, eczema, and psoriasis. Recent studies have also suggested that those persons who get "stressed out" easily may be more susceptible to Alzheimers. The list could continue.

The point is that optimal stress, which is to say positive and motivational eustress, can become distress is it continues too long or at too high an intensity, and can wear and tear on the body and on the mind (or better said, the "bodymind").

The highest point on the curve is where stress takes a turn and produces lower rather than higher performance (along with the other results noted). This high point depends not only on the intensity of external stressors, but also on the individual who is experiencing the stress. Each of us carries through life a combination of nature (genetics) and nurture (life experiences) that determines how well we will cope with challenges and threats, and what it will take for us to weaken and be hurt by stress. This point varies a good deal, which helps us to understand why two persons experiencing the very same negative event (for example, an earthquake or an assault) may report very different reactions. Wherever that point of change happens to be for each of us, it is useful for us to know our limits, and where our optimal levels are. Optimal stress can make us hardy, resilient, and stronger, as if inoculating us to future challenges. We achieve best when we fluctuate around the optimal levels.

What can we do when we find ourselves in the over-stressed side of the curve?

Stress management in the old days

If we go back to prehistoric times, we find that our ancestors often took rather simplistic but quite effective steps to manage stressors. Sociobiologists note how early stressors were frequently life threatening: a saber-toothed tiger might appear suddenly, for example. Those humans who would naturally become startled and put on alert, who would feel an automatic and immediate surge of chemicals rushing through the body, had an evolutionary advantage. Among these, those who could then fight back – or at least run swiftly – were able to enjoy another day, have families, and pass on their genes. The so-called fight-flight response[3] generated by the very useful startle response, along with the very useful emotions of anger and/or fear, describes this evolutionary concept. Even though our environment has changed considerably since then, we have bodies that respond as they did thousands of years ago.

Stress management in the new days

Modern stressors, whether or not they are life threatening, can produce a body-mind reaction similar to what people instinctively felt eons ago. Today just facing an angry boss, being at the receiving end of road rage, or losing a job can also startle us, cause chemicals to rush through our bodies, and generate anger and fear. We feel on the alert, as if facing a life and death threat. Even before we have assessed at a logical and rational level the true danger posed, our primitive limbic-emotional brain may have already mobilized our body to fight or to flee. Fortunately for society, most of us have learned to keep our feelings under control most of the time. We don't punch a waiter for being slow, and we don't flee to the mountains to avoid criticism – not that it would do much good as the criticism might well accompany us in our memories. Unfortunately for the mobilized body, suppressing anger and fear has a way of churning up our insides. It hardly seems fair that we can experience stress so similar to what our ancestors felt, while the simple options they had (fighting or running) are no longer available to us.

I am struck by how societies mimic the older days to deal with this dilemma. Virtually every organized sport, for example, looks to me like a fight and/or flight response – whether we are striking a ball or puck, or racing toward or away from someone on skates or bicycles. Sports seem to be one of modern humanity's way to drain away some of the anger and fear that accumulate during the course of an industrialized day.

Do sports help? Considerably so, which is why I will include physical activity as one of the recommended exercises. Sports are not sufficient, however. In any case, not everyone has the time or interest or skills necessary to go through the physical motions that might mimic the fight and flight actions. It is not always practical to put on a pair of tennis shoes and run out of a boardroom or away from a screaming child. There is also disagreement as to whether being a spectator at sporting events helps our situation or exacerbates it. There is quite a lot of evidence that teens who use violent video games, for example, actually become more, rather than less, aggressive.

Case example: stressed out students

Many people who report feeling "stressed out" seem to be "hot responders", that is, people who characteristically overreact to minor irritants and pressure. How can you tell if you are one of these persons? Let me describe what I used to do when I talked about the topic of stress in an abnormal psychology course at the University of Colorado.

I would ask for a volunteer after explaining exactly what I was going to do: to simulate a threat and a response to threat, the volunteer student would hold his or her hand in a bucket of ice water for one minute. We would take a brief medical history of the volunteer to cover the same precautions I encourage in this book. The hypothesis was that the volunteer's body would react as if it had been thrown into a freezing and potentially life-threatening environment. Students would discuss the various chemical, hormonal, electrical, and electromagnetic variables, and I always happened to find a medically trained student to conduct some basic measures of blood pressure and heart rate (both of which rose during the experiment).

What interested us next was how long the volunteer would need for blood pressure and heart rate to return to the normal range. We found interesting differences. Invariably, persons who returned slowly to normal would talk about how they "knew" they were "hot responders" generally, or how "the adrenaline rush could last for a really long time". Those who returned quickly to normal, on the other hand, reported how "little things don't usually bother me", or "I'm pretty laid back." We called these "cool responders".

We then would conduct a second experiment, one closer to modern life. After having blood pressure and heart rate measured, a student would then perform the very simple task of counting back from 100 by 7's over the course of one minute. That was the extent of the second challenge. But how curious it was to notice that a student's response to this innocuous test would so closely parallel the response to the real threat of being in a freezing environment. Some students responded in "hot" mode, while others showed less physical arousal. Students easily learned the lessons of the class. It was fairly obvious that while it is adaptive to go on alert and to mobilize body resources when faced with a true danger (freezing to death), it makes little sense for the body to react in a similar way when all that a person is doing is counting backwards from 100 over the course of a minute with no real consequence for success or failure. Yet many of us somehow come to believe that every little trivial test in life poses a danger to our integrity. Habitual overreactions are not only a waste of time. There is also unnecessary wear and tear as the body reacts as if it were in danger, even though it is not.

To complete this case example: using the exercises that come next can be helpful in these situations on several levels. First, they can help us to recover more quickly after we have faced true threat and danger (which is why I have taught the techniques to 100's of victims of natural disasters, accidents, and personal assaults). Secondly, they can help us to distinguish better between real and imagined threat (which is why I teach them to university students). And finally, they can teach us to become "cool responders" who respond in a more adaptive and measured way to life's daily demands.

For future reference

Attention has been given recently to an alternative stress response called the "tend and befriend" option[4]. While both men and women sometimes affiliate and look to support from others when under stress, in general women do so more than men. A possible evolutionary explanation for this response is that while fleeing from a predator may be adaptive for males, running away may not be tenable for a nursing mother, or one who is taking care of infants. Research into the concept of tend and befriend was only recently initiated.

There is also preliminary evidence that affiliation in response to stress is healthy for our bodies. Those who seek social support at work – especially during high stress moments – may lower their blood pressure, for example[5]. In one study, men benefited most when they felt supported by co-workers, whereas women found support from direct supervisors to be the more important stress reducer.

Perhaps by the time the second edition of this book appears more will be known about this possible gender difference in stress responding, along with implications for managing stress. Meanwhile, I am forced to rely on the "fight or flight" paradigm that has dominated stress theory for the past 50 years.

The exercises

Here again is the list of the 7 basic exercises:

> #1. deep breathing
> #2. TAT
> #3. EFT
> #4. tapping shortcuts
> #5. leading with your heart (cardiac coherence)
> #6. the Butterfly Hug
> #7. physical activity

Whether traditional and innovative, they all meet these four criteria:

- efficiency (the shortest time required to do the exercise);
- efficacy (the most benefit reported);
- stability (the most lasting results, and/or the degree of ease of repeating the exercise to re-experience the benefit); and
- safety (posing the least likelihood of negative side-effects for the consumer).

23

In this chapter I will describe the exercises at length and in special detail. In other chapters in part one I repeat the exercises, and the descriptions will be less detailed.

You may do these exercises alone or with a companion. If you do them with someone else, I recommend that both of you go through the same steps. You can work on two different issues, each of which might be personally meaningful to only one of you, or you can both focus on a problem relevant to both of you. A third option is for both persons to focus on something that only one of you is wishing to resolve. In this case, the second person says the same words as the person who is working on a problem. This is the way I conduct these exercises with my professional clients; I find that accompanying the other person proves to be especially beneficial to my client (and beneficial to me as well). As an example, when JoAnne tapped the meridian points on her body, I tapped the same points on myself, and when she said, "My anxiety and fear…", I repeated the same words she used, "*My* anxiety and fear." As you can imagine, working as a couple requires that each person care about the other and be in a compassionate and noncompetitive mood.

I strongly recommend learning these skills in the company of another person. If you have access to a coach, therapist, or other professional guide, you will pick up additional nuances that experts notice while working with so many persons.

Learning with a trusted colleague who is initially unfamiliar with the exercises is also recommended. The instructions in the book were written so that simply reading them will describe what one does to perform the exercise correctly. Additionally:
- respect your partner at all times, telling exactly what it is you will be doing and allowing the partner to stop doing it at any time;
- demonstrate the exercise when you are in the role of teacher to show your partner how the exercise looks and feels;
- observe and give feedback, whether your partner is doing the exercise correctly or incorrectly, as we can learn from both kinds of experiences;
- take turns so that each partner is both teacher and student, and work on real issues that are significant for each of you, thereby normalizing the experience while benefiting personally.

If you cannot find a partner, consider practicing in front of a mirror or with a video camera, and/or audiotape the instructions for yourself.

Stress reduction exercise # 1: Deep Breathing[6]

While it may sound odd to teach someone how to do something as automatic and natural as breathing, it is equally odd to observe that many people do not take full advantage of what deep breathing has to offer. Often I will ask a distressed patient or coaching client to show me how he or she breathes by saying: "Hold your hand on your stomach, inhale, and tell me what happens with your hand. Now exhale, and notice what happens." Frequently the person will say, I don't feel anything – which means they are breathing too shallowly for air to get to their diaphragm. Others might say that their stomach expands when they exhale, and deflates when they inhale – exactly the reverse of what should occur. This simple question can be a quick and useful way to diagnosis a problem with what is one of the most powerful, portable, and easy-to-enhance stress-reduction tools we have: breathing.

Caution:

We can resolve problems with how we breathe fairly simply. However, some persons are so *unaccustomed to breathing deeply and relaxing* that they may actually feel worse, at least initially, when they start to relax. It appears that at least some of these persons think they are safer if they remain in a fairly constant state of alert or startle response. When they feel relaxed, they may think that they are less able to respond to dangers and threats and hence feel even more anxious. If you try the exercise I am about to describe and notice that your heart rate increases, that your muscles tense and feel painful, or that you seem to be getting frightened or anxious, *stop doing the exercise*. The feeling of relaxation might be shutting down your distractions and allowing you to pay attention to something that you have been ignoring or denying. Some people, for example, work hard and stay active and preoccupied so that they do not have to pay attention to disturbing thoughts and feelings. Becoming more relaxed and less defended against your feelings may bring to your awareness memories of failure or disappointment that you have been storing away, or may remind you of harm that you have caused or that has been done to you. In this sense being distracted and preoccupied may have served a purpose. Go slowly or stop if deep breathing seems to break down your defenses too quickly. If you notice feeling more disturbed than peaceful, start instead with exercises #2, #3, or #4 to eliminate some of the troubles that are being uncovered. Then try this exercise again.

Given these caveats, the following instructions are an example of how deep and diaphragmatic breathing can be practiced. If you practice this exercise habitually, it can help you to maintain composure and calm even when you find yourself being constantly bombarded by stressors.

• **Inhale**, through your nose if possible. As you breathe in, think of the air as the source of your vital energy: the word "inspire" also means to "inhale." Your abdomen should first move out as you inhale, then your chest should expand, in that order. Rest your hands over your naval so you can feel your abdomen moving. You may also notice that your collar bones rise with a deep breath.

Duration: 2 to 3 seconds or until you can expand your stomach, lungs, and chest without discomfort. Count "one-thousand-one, one-thousand-two, one-thousand-three" as you inhale.

• **Pause**. Allow the lungs to remain inflated. A pause is especially effective in slowing hyperventilation, reducing dizziness, managing fatigue, and relaxing stomach cramps. Holding one's breath can slow heart rate, and generally reduce tension and anxiety. Experiment with your pause. Again, be careful not to cause muscle pain; do not overdo the pause especially if you have stomach tissue injury.

Duration: 1 to 2 second maximum.

• **Exhale**. Slowly exhale. Place your hands on your chest and abdomen so that you can better feel the muscle movements and so you can become more aware of your normal breathing pattern.

Duration: 3 seconds.

• **Pause**. If you feel light-headed, stop the exercise.

Duration: 1 second.

• **Repeat the sequence** for several minutes provided you can do so without pain or light-headedness, or other unpleasant experience. Repeat the entire exercise 10 to 20 times daily. Do so in the morning, afternoon, and evening until you master the skill and it becomes an automatic habit.

A Spanish psychiatrist with whom I occasionally co-train has found that some people can better guide their breathing if they visualize a box, with each side representing one of the four steps in deep breathing. In the example below, the long arrow on the left side (step one) represents a two- or three-second inhale; the top a one-second pause after the inhale; the longer arrow in step three a two- or three-second exhale; and the final arrow in step four a one-second pause after the exhale. Some people will feel relieved to notice that the top and bottom of the box are shorter, and that they do not need to pause for very long.

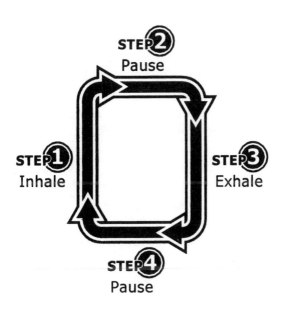

Some clients report that once they have re-learned to breathe deeply, simply thinking about taking a deep breath begins to cause them to relax noticeably. It appears that the *thought* about breathing becomes a cue for the physiological relaxation response.

This breathing exercise may be easier to do if you first practice any of the next three exercises, which will help to eliminate some of the worries and preoccupations that can keep us feeling stressed and short of breath.

Stress reduction exercise #2: TAT®[7]

I have used and taught TAT thousands of times around the world and virtually everyone has reported that it has helped them to ease or eliminate a wide variety of problems. So far no one has ever told me that using the pose caused any continuing negative side effects. At times a person will feel worse after first using TAT, but this experience has been neither very serious nor long lasting, and has not caused any of my clients or students to stop using TAT.

The acronym TAT stands for Tapas Acupressure Technique, invented by my respected colleague Elizabeth Tapas Fleming, an acupuncturist and psychotherapist. I have observed her work with clients in the US and in Mexico. She has given permission for me to reproduce her method. For more details on TAT: [http://www.tat-intl.com].

• TAT pose

The pose is doing by placing both hands on the head. If you feel uncomfortable or fatigued, you can change the position of one hand for that of the other. Tapas believes that the basic energy points involved in the pose are central to healing, and that holding this posture briefly can resolve many of life's problems.

One hand is placed over the back of the head where the visual cortex of the brain is located. Tapas believes that holding a hand there can help to heal memories of past negative events, bringing them up to date as it were.

The middle finger of the other hand rests on the forehead. This finger covers part of the frontal cortex of the brain, where common sense and advanced human reasoning are located. The remaining two fingers of that hand cover two acupuncture points useful in the treatment of trauma. The index finger and pinkie can either float or rest on the face.

Now refer to figure 5 on page 29. With one hand, *lightly* touch the tip of *the thumb* to the area 1/8 inch above the inner corner of your eye.

With *the fourth finger (ring finger)* of the same hand, *lightly* touch the tip of the finger to the area 1/8 inch above the inner corner the other eye. *Both fingers are now on either side of the bridge of your nose.* **Be careful not to touch the eyeball!**

Place the tip of *the middle finger* of the same hand at the point midway between, and about ½ inch above, eyebrow level. *You now have all three finger tips lightly touching the three points.*

Now *place your other hand on the back of your head*, with the palm touching the head so that the thumb is resting at the base of the skull just above the hairline. The palm cradles the back of your skull. *Both hands should be resting gently. No pressure is necessary.*

Figure 5b. **TAT pose, front and back views**

29

• How to define and measure the problem to be treated

First begin with a statement of what is troubling you. I recommend you write this out. Spend some extra time so that you can describe it as best you can. Examples might be, "My nervousness just thinking about all the work I have to do," or "I feel so distracted by the meeting I just had with my boss", or "This pain in my stomach as I think about the pressures of my job," or "How will I ever get everything done in the house today?"

Then measure how troubled the statement makes you feel. I recommend using a scale from 0 to 10, where zero means "It doesn't bother me at all" and 10 means "That's the most troubled I can imagine feeling." Write out the scale, then circle the number that best represents how you feel now[8].

0   1   2   3   4   5   6   7   8   9   10

• TAT exercise

Tapas suggests that the very first time you ever do TAT, you do the TAT pose with your attention for one minute or so thinking of this statement,

"I deserve to live and I can accept love, help, and healing." [TAT pose]

You then focus on the problem you would like to resolve, measure it 0 to 10, do the TAT pose a minute or two, measure on the 0 to 10 scale again, repeat the pose, and continue treating and measuring until the problem has gotten better. Tapas reports that she has taught people to use the technique effectively in this way for a wide variety of problems, including these: allergies (the original use for TAT), traumas, fears, and bad attitudes (e.g., "People are all bad" or "I can never save money").

She recommends not using the pose for more than 20 minutes per day.

Sometimes using the TAT posture will initially worsen an upsetting problem. This may be because the two fingers near the eyes are on acupuncture trauma points and may stir up traumatic memories. For example, you might begin with a 7 and quickly notice it has moved up to a 9. This is a choice point: either continue until the intensity of the problem lessens, or stop using the posture for a period of time. It is normal for some problems to increase in intensity at first because you may first become more aware of the extent of the problem, and only then begin to solve it. This is especially likely if you have been ignoring or avoiding or distracting yourself from the problem. If the increase in intensity is tolerable, you may choose to continue with the posture until the intensity lessens after the initial increase. You can then take a break, notice any new awareness or insights, then resume the posture. I recommend taking a new 0-10 measure each time you stop. Continue in this way until you get to a zero, or until you feel like stopping for a while.

If using the TAT pose aggravates your problem, say the following statement and hold the pose for another minute:

"All parts of me are willing and working to make positive changes that are for my highest good." [TAT pose]

If your problem gets worse instead of better, you can stop using the pose and try one of the other exercises that follow on pages 36 to the end of the chapter. As simple as the TAT pose may appear, it can be quite powerful in "loosening" up hidden or repressed thoughts, feelings, sensations, images, even behaviors. You might tell yourself that "there is no rush" and remind yourself that it is normal and human to have unknown memories, and to be unaware of certain aspects of ourselves. Sometimes using one of the other exercises will chip away at what we have hidden away within ourselves so that there is less to open up, and less intensity to experience when we use TAT at a future date.

• TAT advanced instructions

Tapas also discovered that many problems are complex and multi-layered, and that many of her clients seemed to need to work through certain general themes in order to resolve a specific problem. I have listed those themes below, with some of my own modifications to simplify the instructions. You do not need to accept that all of the themes are literally true about you. It is sufficient simply to consider them as possibilities. You can try this advanced model if the first instructions do not help you as much as you had hoped.

Some people find it helpful to write down their experience after each time they do the TAT pose. This can be particularly helpful if you are working on complex issues that bring up insight after insight, or open layer after layer of emotion for you. If you are working with another person, you can tell that person about what you experience.

If doing TAT for the first time, hold the TAT pose for a minute or so while you keep your attention on this statement:

"I deserve to live and I can accept love, help, and healing." [TAT pose]

You may find it helpful repeat the TAT pose while saying this statement to request permission from yourself to begin to heal:

"If it's time for this to heal now, then let it be so." [TAT pose]

Then follow the next 7 steps. If it helps you to observe changes more easily, write down the number from 0-10 that represents how much the problem bothers you, and write down new numbers after the intensity of your experience changes.

As you follow these advanced instructions, *think or say* anything written in the form of a **"bold statement"** in quote marks. I find it better to say these words out loud.

Whenever you see **[TAT pose]**, hold the TAT pose for a minute or two, and then drop your hands, and notice what happened. You can also hold the pose until you notice a shift in how you feel or think. A shift could be a sigh, a sense of relaxation, not being able to focus on the situation any more, the hands automatically coming out of their position, subtle energy shifts in the body, or simply a sense of peace.

1. First put your attention on the problem. **[TAT pose]**

2. Put your attention on the opposite condition. For example, if you were thinking about how terrible it would be to lose your job, now think about getting another job, or finding a silver lining in having to change jobs. If you are working on a traumatic memory, say, "It's over, I'm OK and I can relax." **[TAT pose]**

3. Say one of the following: **"All the origins of this problem are healing now."** or ... **"God** (or whatever name you use)**, thank you for healing all the origins of this problem." [TAT pose]**

4. Say one of the following statements: **"All the places in my mind, body, and life where this has been a problem are healing now." [TAT pose]**

There are other ways to say this, for example: **"God, thank you for healing all the places in my mind, body, and life where this has been a problem." [TAT pose]**

5. Say one of the following: **"All the parts of me that got something out of having this problem are healing now." [TAT pose]**

Or: **"God, thank you for healing all the parts of me that got something out of having this problem." [TAT pose]**

6. Say the following: **"I forgive everyone I blamed for this problem, including God and myself." [TAT pose]**

I have found that this statement is offensive to certain persons who follow a particular religious creed. If it sounds sacrilegious, change it until it fits you.

7. Say the following: **"I ask forgiveness of everyone I hurt because of this problem." [TAT pose]**

Take a final 0-10 rating. See if there is a difference between this number and the original number. Notice any changes in how you feel, think, or imagine. At this point you can choose to stop for the day or repeat any of the steps again. Some persons choose to repeat the steps until they feel free and at peace. Sometimes a person will find one of the statements to be particularly meaningful, as if it touches the core of a personal problem. That statement alone might be worth repeating along with the TAT pose.

You can do the TAT pose for up to 20 minutes a day. You might also find that it is better for you to use it less, for example only 10 minutes a day. When you are doing the activity, drink several glasses of water daily to hydrate yourself.

This is an easy exercise to read into a tape recorder. Read slowly as you time yourself. Read step #1, for example, then pause for about 15 seconds, then say, slowly, "It's OK to drop my hands now. I'll take a few more seconds now to notice what shifted." Then wait another 10 seconds or so before continuing reading into the recorder. With this timetable you can read the first 9 steps in about 15 minutes. If as you play it back you find your own voice is less soothing than you would like, ask a friend with a soft voice to do the recording. The friend will change "I" and "my" to "you" and your".

● **Doing the pose for another person**

If you wish to use the TAT pose with someone else, place your hands as indicated in the following photos. The first shows how to place your hands for an adult. The main difference is that you will touch the point on the bottom of the skull with your little finger instead of your thumb. Use a light touch.

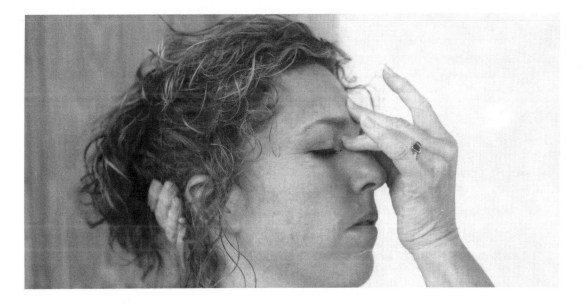

Figure 6. **TAT pose when performed by another person**

33

When doing the pose for children, you do not need to place your fingers exactly on the acupressure points but can cover all of the points simultaneously with the palms of your hands, as indicated. Use a light touch.

Figure 7. **TAT pose for children**

• Phone consultation using TAT:

Many of my clients find it sufficient simply to hold the TAT pose, pay attention to the problem they want to resolve, and then notice changes in how they feel or think. When someone calls me by phone for an emergency technique in a moment of anxiety or rage or other unpleasant experience, I usually will talk them through the pose and ask them to hold it while focusing on their problem. My phone-call clients invariably will report feeling better within minutes, without having to repeat any of the special statements on pages 31 to 33. There are various ways to use the short form. On the next page you will find a single page of instructions plus a photo of the TAT pose.

• The TAT short form:

Hold the TAT pose and say simply, "My problem." Hold the pose for about a minute or so, and pay attention to your feelings, thoughts, and sensations as they float by like clouds in the sky. You can also continue the pose longer until you notice some shift in how you feel or think. You may find it helpful to write down your experiences if you are working alone. Repeat as needed.

Some people will report that they begin to feel worse. Think of this as good news, as you are getting to the root of your problem. Your choices are to continue until you feel better, or stop and use one of the exercises I describe next.

If positive thoughts and feelings begin to appear spontaneously, say something like, "These new feelings", and continue the pose for another minute or so. Whenever you find yourself going in a positive direction, continue going there for a while longer.

If you wish, you can photocopy this page as a short form to use when you find yourself in a plane, at your desk, or at the kitchen table.

Figure 8. **TAT, short form**

35

Stress reduction exercise #3: EFT
("Emotional Freedom Techniques")

Exercises #3 and #4 are based on the work of psychologist Roger Callahan, who developed a popular form of energy psychology called TFT (or thought field therapy). Callahan's approach is described in exercise #4. EFT, a simpler version of TFT, was developed by one of Callahan's students, Gary Craig[9].

• The meridian sources for the EFT energy points

EFT involves tapping or touching certain energy points on the body. These points are based on the concepts of acupuncture that I mentioned in the introduction. Acupuncture is recommended by the World Health Organization and is reimbursable by many insurance companies, but still seems strange to many people. I will attempt to explain acupuncture indirectly by using a metaphor from electric power lines; for this idea I am grateful to a professional electrician I once treated using EFT.

In most neighborhoods we can see the power lines that transport electricity, usually strung on utility poles. Hanging on some of these poles are gray tanks, called "step-up transformers". These transformers, strategically spaced, recharge the electric current from time to time so that it continues to flow through the copper wire. Without the transformers to move it along, the current would eventually stop because of the resistance in those wires.

We can think of the subtle energy current in the body in a similar way. There is a line of energy that runs through the body, much as electricity runs along power lines. This energy line in the body can be separated into 14 segments or "meridians", each one associated with one of the body organs. On each of these meridians are special energy points that act much like tiny step-up transformers: when stimulated, they recharge the energy current so that it keeps flowing along the meridian line. The number of points varies: one of the meridians has only 9 points; another has 67. There are 361 points in all.

Acupuncture involves inserting a thin needle into (or stimulating in some other way) one or more of these 361 energy sites or "acupuncture points". It is now known that an acupuncture needle, when inserted and twirled, generates endorphins around the site of the acupuncture point, and in turn produces the healing of various physical and emotional problems. When a needle is inserted in an area where there is no known acupuncture point, no such endorphin production occurs – which is one way to show that the points in fact do exist[10].

In EFT we stimulate those same energy points, not with needles, but with a tap or touch, with one or more finger tips or the palm of a hand. The tapping or touching produces benefits similar to those of acupuncture, so we assume similar endorphin production occurs with EFT (though the actual mechanism of change is still unknown).

Fortunately we do not need to stimulate all 361 acupuncture points in order to produce healing on a psychological level. Instead, generally only one key point on each of the 14 meridian points needs to be tapped or touched in order to increase energy flow along the entire meridian segment. These 14 key points are precisely the ones we use in EFT.

If you jump ahead for a moment to page 38 you will find a drawing of the key points located on the body of a rather muscular fellow, intentionally drawn that way to show exactly where the points are with respect to muscles and ribs. Two of the meridian lines run up along the center of the body, and the key points for these are under the nose and under the lips. The other 12 meridians are bilateral and the key points for these are found on both sides of the body. (There are also several other points I will explain later.)

I will finish this introduction to the meridian system by describing one of the meridians to show how the key points are located. In Figure 9 on this page you will notice the first few points on the energy lines that compose the "bladder meridian" in Chinese medicine. The two lines of the bladder meridian begin at the inner point of each eye, therefore called bladder-1. The next points on the two lines, bladder-2, are at the beginning of each eyebrow. Bladder-3 is higher up on the forehead, and so on. If we followed the entire lines, we would proceed over the top of the head and down the back on either side of the spinal column where the lines split temporarily, finally ending on the little toes, where bladder-67 can be found. If you were to connect all these dots or energy points you would draw the two bilateral bladder meridian lines, each with its different energy points.

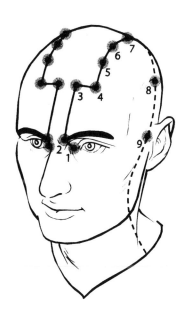

Figure 9. **Some points on the bladder meridian**

Generally speaking, the *first or last points* on any meridian line are the key points, which means that they alone can energize that entire meridian line. In the case of the bladder meridian, the first point is inside the eyes (written as *ie*), where bladder-1 is located. However, most people use *tapping* of the energy points, so I will recommend using bladder-2 (where the eyebrows begin, hence written as *eb*), because tapping bladder-1 could cause eye damage. In this case, the second point works as well as the first.

EFT is used by thousands of persons around the world, and preliminary research supports its effectiveness. You can now study pages 38 and 39 and begin to practice EFT to see if it will be useful for you.

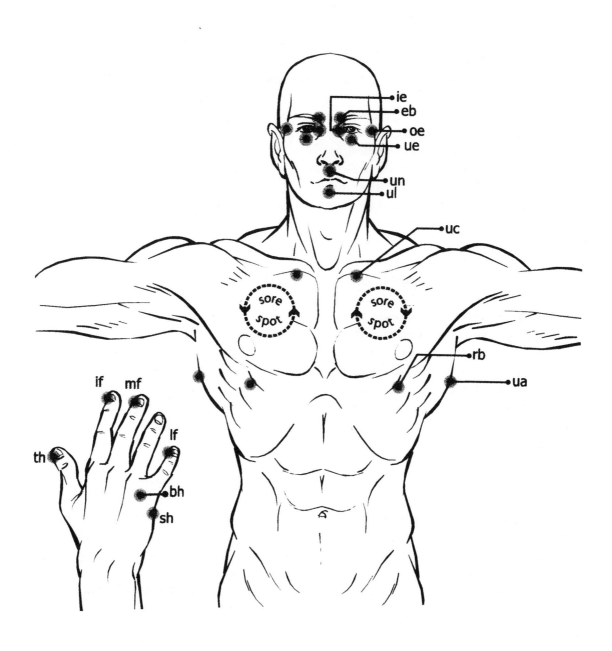

Figure 10. **The acupuncture points used in EFT**

• **Key to the 14 EFT points** (this key refers to the body map on the facing page, p. 38.)

(1) ie = *inside* corner of each *eye*, near the tear ducts. Be careful not to touch the eyes themselves when you use these points. If you use **ie**, *use only touch to stimulate the point, do not tap!*

    eb = this is an alternative way for stimulating the first point, which is found on the inside ends of both *eyebrows*. You may tap or touch **eb**.

(2) oe = *outside* of the *eyes*, on the temple, just beyond the bony ridge around the eyes.

(3) ue = *under* the *eyes*, on top of the bony ridge under the eyes.

(4) un = *under* the *nose*, just above the lips.

(5) ul = *under* the *lips*, in the indentation above the chin.

(6) uc = *under* the *collar bone*. First find where your collarbones protrude, where the bones stick out noticeably, about 2 inches (5 cm) apart. Two inches (5 cm) is about the distance between these two arrows: →   ←. Then go down a half-inch (1 cm) and you will be on the **uc** points, which are just below the collarbones, just above the first ribs, and to the side of the breastplate.

(7) ua = this is a point about a hand's width *under* the *armpit*, or about 4" under your armpit on the side of the body. You touch it when you cross your arms and hold your hands on the sides of your body.

(8) rb = *rib*; if you hold all four finger points vertically, with the little finger touching the lowest rib, then the index finger will be roughly on the proper meridian location, which is on the 3rd rib, on a line directly below the nipple of each breast. Some women may find it uncomfortable to tap this point. In this case, hold your fingers lightly under each breast on the ribs, with the index fingers under the breasts and the other three fingers directly downward. (Tapping inside the knee can also serve for persons who do not wish to tap under the breast).

(9) th = *thumb*, on a point where the thumb nail curves. See the figure to tap the correct side of the thumb nail. To stimulate this point you can touch both the nail and the skin with the index finger of the opposite hand.

(10) if = *index finger*; this point is on the same side of the finger as is the thumb point.

(11) mf = *middle finger*, on the same of the finger as the index and thumb points.

(12) lf = *little finger*; if you hold your hand palm down, then this point and the previous 3 points will all be on the side of the fingers closest to your body.

(13) sh = stands for the *sides* of the *hands*. If you bend your hand and look at your palm, you will see a line running to the side of your hand. The wrinkle of skin that is formed on the side is approximately the location of this point.

(14) bh = this stands for *back of the hand*. You find it between the bones of the little finger and ring finger on the back of the hands, just off the knuckle. You can also tap or touch the channel between these bones with all four finger tips, with the little finger tip tapping between the knuckles of the little and ring fingers and the other 3 fingers further toward the wrist. In this case the tip of the ring finger is roughly on the **bh** point.

Figure 11. **Key to the EFT points**

39

Before going through the EFT steps, practice finding these points, using the key on page 39. The acupuncture points are tiny so stimulate the exact location. If you are only "near" the point, you may not notice any effect. Use a mirror or ask a companion to help you find the points. You might make errors at first. I used to tap the **uc** points too widely, for example, until Michael Reed Gach reminded me they are only 2 inches or 5 cm apart (see Michael's acupressure books in the references). Thanks, Michael.

If you need a bit more motivation to try this out, you might consider that there are many people around the world who make a very good living teaching other people EFT, and using only EFT in their healing practices. The next page essentially contains what these practitioners do. Gary Craig's website [http://www.emofree.org] has more information.

● **The steps in the EFT exercise**

Using figure 10 on page 38 and the key on page 39, complete the following steps:

1. Measure the intensity of the problem:
First think about the issue or problem you want to work on, and get a number from 0 to 10 that represents how stressed you feel, with 10 being "the most stressed-out I could imagine". Write the number down on a sheet of paper.

2. Massage the sore spots while saying the affirmation 3 times:
The heart pumps blood to keep it circulating. The lymph system has no equivalent pump, and the lymph fluid needs to be pushed around in other ways to keep it flowing, and to help keep the immune system healthy. In step 2 we will be pushing lymph fluid, and in the process stimulating the energy system that accompanies it. Basically this step involves preparing the energy field for the tapping or touching in step 3.

Using the figure on page 38, locate the sore spots. With your right hand reach over to your left shoulder and chest area and press down with you fingers until you find a sore spot. Move your fingers around while pressing, and consult the figure on page 38 to find the correct location. This is where a lymph drainage area is located, called the "neurolymphatic reflex". Once you have found it, follow the arrows on page 38, and make a clockwise circular movement while pushing down with your fingers on the sore spot. Do the same with the left hand over the right side of the chest, but do a circle in the opposite direction. Follow the arrows to be sure. You may feel pain when you do these movements, which is a sign that you are on the spot and that your lymph system may be in need of massaging.

As you make firm circular movements, say the following statement: "*I accept myself deeply and completely even though I have this problem of . . .*" (and here you mention your problem: e.g.; "even though I feel this stress", "even though I am upset", etc.)

Say this statement *three times* as you do the vigorous circular rubbing.

3. Stimulate the energy points:

There are 2 easy ways to stimulate the points: tapping or touching.

• Tapping

If you choose to **tap**, think first about your problem and then tap each point 7 to 8 times with the index and middle fingers of your hand before moving on. You can tap only one side of your body or both sides. Here is a list of the points for tapping:

eb, oe, ue, un, ul, uc, ua, rb, th, if, mf, lf, sh, bh.

• Touching

If you prefer to **touch**, which many of my clients choose to do, simply touch each point with the index finger (or with the index fingers and middle fingers together if you can) and breathe once as you do so, then move on to the next point. The points are the same as for tapping except for on very important difference: the eye brow (**eb**) point that you tap first changes to a point located at the inside corner of each eye (**ie**). The eb and ie points are equivalent energetically. *Tapping* on the **ie** point is *not* recommended as the tapping could injure the eye. However, *touching* the **ie** point does not pose such a danger.

The touch list is, then:

ie, oe, ue, un, ul, uc, ua, rb, th, if, mf, lf, sh, bh.

Whether you tap or touch, try to pay attention both to the problem and to any changes that you notice. If you feel a tingling, a sensation, or a "shift" of any kind whatsoever, make a mental note of the point you were stimulating. Each point has to do with a special emotion, which will be discussed later in the book.

4. Do the following "9 brain balancing procedures":
These procedures consist of doing 9 different simple activities while **continuing to tap or hold the bh (or the back-of-the-hand) point**.

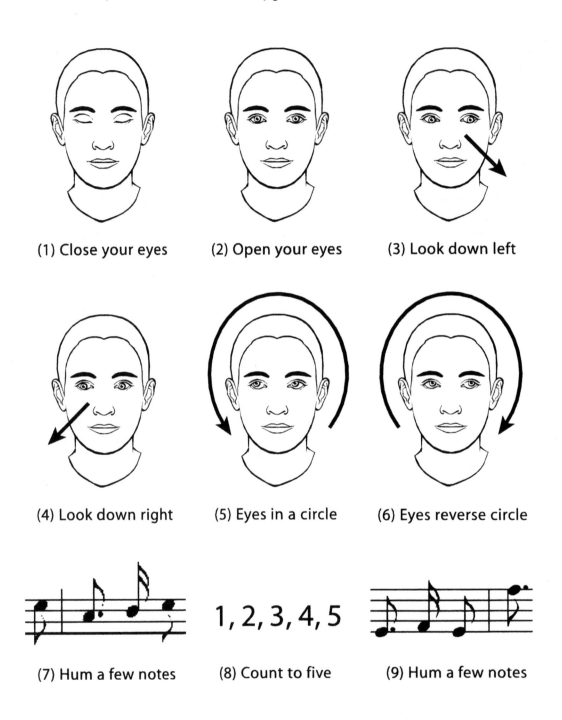

(1) Close your eyes   (2) Open your eyes   (3) Look down left

(4) Look down right   (5) Eyes in a circle   (6) Eyes reverse circle

(7) Hum a few notes   (8) Count to five   (9) Hum a few notes

Figure 12. **9 brain balancing procedures**

These 9 procedures appear to balance the brain by involving both hemispheres in alternation (for example, looking to the right involves the left hemisphere, while looking to the left involves the right hemisphere; humming a tune is generally a right brain function, while counting is left brain).

5. Repeat step 3:
Whether you tap or touch, do a complete re-stimulation of each of the points. Remember that if you tap, start with the eyebrow point (**eb**); if you touch and breathe, start with the optional inside-the-eye point (**ie**). In either case, continue with this sequence:

oe, ue, un, ul, uc, ua, rb, th, if, mf, lf, sh, bh.

6. Measure the problem again:
It is very important that you take another reading on how intense the problem or issue feels to you. Write this number down as well. Notice any change.

7. Repeat EFT as necessary or desired:
If the number is not going down, repeat steps 3, 4, and 5. Then take another measure. Repeat again as necessary.

8. Trouble-shooting:
If the number goes down for a while, then stops moving and is not a 0 or as low as you would like, massage the sore spot again as in step 2. As you massage, say this affirmation which is slightly different from the earlier one:
"*I accept myself deeply and completely even though I **still have some** of this problem.*"
Then repeat steps 3 through 6 again. Often this affirmation along with massaging the sore spot will shift the energy system so that you can continue resolving the problem further.

9. The eye roll as an optional step:
After the intensity of the problem falls and you get to a 1 or 0, you often can increase your positive feelings simply by slowly rolling your eyes from floor to ceiling while tapping the **bh** point of one hand. Start this by holding your head level and looking at the floor. Then, while tapping the **bh** point, slowly raise your eyes upwards to the ceiling. Take 7 to 10 seconds to raise your eyes to the ceiling and keep tapping **bh** as you raise your eyes.

Also consider using this last step all by itself during the day to relieve yourself of little stresses. I will repeat this suggestion in the next exercise.

EFT short form. I was asked by one of my client-editors to reproduce the entire EFT sequence in a one-page summary that can be photocopied. The short form with the figure of the EFT points can be found on page 44.

1. First think about the problem to work on; write a number, 0 to 10.

2. Rub the sore spots in a circle and say 3 times: "*I accept myself deeply and completely even though I have this problem of . .*" (state a problem).

3. Then stimulate each of the points while thinking of the problem. **If you tap**, use the index and middle fingers, & tap 7-8 times on each point – on one side of your body, or both sides: **eb, oe, ue, un, ul, uc, ua, rb, th, if, mf, lf, sh, bh.**

If touching, change the first point: **ie, oe, ue, un, ul, uc, ua, rb, th, if, mf, lf, sh, bh.**

4. Do the "9 brain balancing procedures" **while continuing to tap bh.** (1) close eyes, (2) open eyes, (3) look down left, (4) look down right, (5) move eyes in a circle, (6) move eyes in opposite circle, (7) hum a tune for about 3 sec., (8) count to five, and (9) hum a tune for 3 more sec.

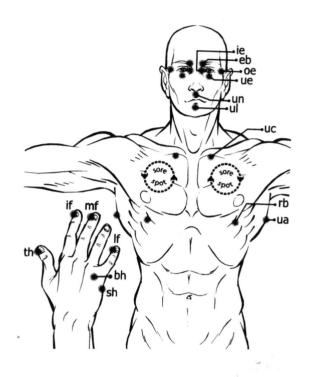

5. Whether you tap or touch, re-stimulate each of the points listed above.

6. & 7. Measure problem 0-10. If the number is not going down, repeat steps 3, 4, and 5. Then take another measure. Repeat as many steps as are necessary for you to feel better.

8. If the number goes down but not as low as you would like, rub the sore spot again as in step 2, but this time say: "*I accept myself deeply and completely even though I **still have** some of this problem.*" Repeat steps 3 through 6 again.

9. The eye roll as an optional step. When you are at 1 or 0, **slowly** roll your eyes from floor to ceiling, all the while tapping the bh point of one hand. Keep your head level.

Figure 13. **EFT short form**

Stress reduction exercise #4: Tapping Shortcuts

Roger Callahan, PhD,[11] is a clinical psychologist who discovered the power of tapping acupuncture points for psychological problems. He once treated a person so phobic to water that she had difficulty even bathing in a few inches of water. After trying all the traditional therapies he knew, he asked his patient to tap under her eye – knowing that this point had to do with the "stomach meridian" and was related to fear and anxiety. The patient, after struggling for years to overcome her hydrophobia without success, immediately began to feel relief. Follow-up for many years thereafter indicated that her fear of water never returned. (For those who read the case studies in the introduction, this stomach point was the same one I suggested for the father whose son was so anxious on the plane.)

Callahan continued to study the other 360 meridian or acupuncture points on the body. He also experimented by asking patients with specific problems to tap certain points until he was able to isolate the most potent points for selected problems. For example, for patients such as the woman described above, he found that using two other points in addition to the under-the-eye point would be even more effective in curing a phobia. Obviously, tapping three key points would be preferable to tapping all 361, and eventually Callahan was able to discover similar "recipes" or "shortcuts" for a wide variety of problems. You can find a more complete list in appendix A.

For now, let us look at the shortcut that Callahan discovered for stress. I have modified it slightly to fit my experience in using it. Pages 46 and 47 face each other. You can refer to the two pages together to practice the three acupuncture points for reducing stress.

For many of my clients I recommend practicing this short protocol by **touching** the points instead of tapping. This allows you to practice the technique whenever you find yourself stressed but in a public space where tapping might seem rather odd, but where you could touch the same points without becoming obvious about it.

Let me mention three short examples where my clients have used this short form.

• A man is waiting to introduce himself to a new group of people. He feels increasingly distressed as it gets closer to his turn.
• A woman approaches a podium. The audience is still arriving, and she realizes she will have to wait before beginning her speech. She feels increasingly stressed.
• Stuck in traffic with two colleagues, you realize you will be late for a meeting and can do nothing about it. Your hands and brow feel tight as you realize the delay is triggering that old habitual tension.

In each of these cases, the individual gently held his/her index and middle fingers to the key points while breathing once each time. And in each case the person noticed the stress melting away. These are true stories, and they have been repeated many times.

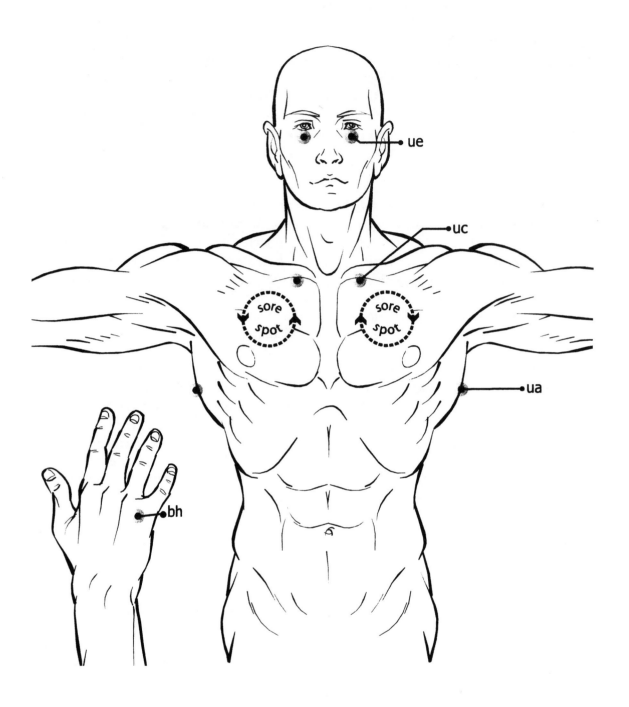

Figure 14. **Tapping shortcut for stress reduction**

46

While consulting the map on the facing page, follow these steps:

1. Think about what is bothering you, and how it is bothering you.

2. Think of the number that represents how upset or stressed you feel, 0 to 10.

3. Tap about 10 times under the eye with two fingers. This is the **ue** point on page 46. Tap on the ridge of bone under the eye and also just below that point. Continue tapping in this area about 10 times. **NOTE: You can touch each point and breathe once if you prefer this to tapping.**

4. Then tap about 10 times (or touch and breathe) on the point on **the side of your body**, approximately 4" under the armpit (**ua**).

5. Tap under the collarbone about 10 times (or touch and breathe) on the **uc** point.

6. Take another measure on the 0 to 10 scale; if there is no change, massage the sore spots. To do so, vigorously rub the sore spot areas as you say three times, *"I accept and love myself deeply and completely even though I still have some of my problems and my limitations."*

7. Then repeat the tapping routine (or touch and breathe) above, i.e. **ue**, **ua**, **uc**.

8. Do the nine brain balancing procedures on page 40 (*while tapping* the **bh** or back-of-the-hand point of one hand, do these 9 procedures: close your eyes, open your eyes, look down to the left, look down to the right, move your eyes in a circle, move your eyes in a circle in the opposite direction, hum any tune for about 3 seconds, count to 5, and again hum any tune for about 5 seconds).

9. Tap about five to ten times again on the **ue**, **ua**, and **uc** points.

10. Take another 0 to 10. If still not 0, or where you would like it to be, repeat all or portions of the above exercises again until you feel as relaxed and as stress-free as you would prefer.

11. Finish with the eye roll described on page 46: (Start by holding your head level and looking at the floor. Then, while tapping the **bh** point of one hand, slowly raise your eyes upwards to the ceiling. Take seven to ten seconds to raise your eyes, continuing to tap **bh** as you raise your eyes).

Some clients choose to carry this protocol with them so they can practice this short routine for stress reduction. Feel free to photocopy pages 46 and 47 as a guide for your practice.

Stress reduction exercise #5:
Leading with your heart

We read more and more about the relationship between stress and our hearts. It appears now that exaggerated and continuous stress may contribute more to heart disease than even a poor diet, lack of physical fitness, or genetics. Stress strains our heart, causing it to pump fuel into our muscles and organs in the form of sugars and fats. It is as if the stress tells the heart to prepare our muscles to fight against or run from threats that so often exist only in our minds. Since we do not fight or flee, the fats and sugars are not burned, but rather accumulate in our systems. This is all relatively bad news.

Here is the good news. Instead of allowing distress to dominate your heart, you can teach your heart to overcome distress. The exercise I describe next will allow you to do that. This is an exercise based on folklore and natural healing, and it has been used and taught in various forms for thousands of years because people say it works. In the past few years, science has caught up to traditional practice and we can now say that this exercise has been scientifically validated. In addition, it is now possible to purchase software[12] that allows you to watch changes in your heart's rhythm as you do the exercise. Indeed, many people already do so in the comfort of their home or office, using their personal computer screens to display this astonishing biofeedback.

Sometimes I will use biofeedback computer displays during the trainings I conduct to show trainees how they are able to control heart rate variability. Let me tell one story about how modern technology and traditional healing practices can be combined.

I was teaching the basic exercises in this book in a country where I thought technological resources were limited. Just down the street, for example, an enterprising couple was selling goats' milk – from their herd tethered on the sidewalk. Nonetheless, a physician in the training group mentioned that he had just purchased heart coherence software, and after lunch he arrived with his laptop. A trainee volunteer agreed to be connected to the software via a finger sleeve, which measured the volunteer's heart rate. The rest of the group watched the computer screen while the volunteer carried out a very simple assignment: to focus on a memory of gratitude and love. Meanwhile, her companion sat nearby and "sent" positive thoughts in her direction.

The next graphs give a rough idea of what we observed. Initially the heart rhythms of the volunteer appeared very choppy and chaotic (see the left graph). Shortly after the volunteer and companion began to focus on their assignments, the volunteer's heart rate began to smooth out, and after about a minute the computer screen registered a decidedly different rhythm (right graph, representing what is generally called "heart coherence"). The rest of the trainees were noticeably awed. Skeptics began to revise their suspicions of the values of "folklore". Some of the "traditionalists", for example those who noted the similarity between what we were doing and the ancient tradition of the charkas, asked me how they could purchase the software we were using.

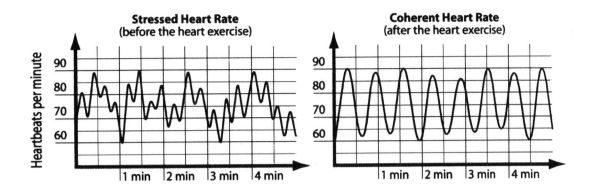

Figure 15. **Heart rhythms indicating stress or coherence**

The heart rhythms on the left, which our volunteer initially exhibited, have been shown to accompany stress, anxiety, depression, and anger. The rhythms on the right, which she was able to generate very quickly (with the assistance of her partner) accompany calm, peace, improved thinking, alertness, increase in joy and pleasure, and effectiveness. A growing body of scientific research supports all of these conclusions[13].

If you doubt your ability to control the beating of your heart, and your ability thereby to manage your stress, you can purchase the heart coherence software and can watch this process of self-control while at home or at your office desk. A recent article in a national newspaper profiled corporations that purchase such devices for their managers and other employees. This use of an external and "objective" measure is also useful for persons who have difficulty detecting changes in their heart or other bodily responses. You can begin by watching you heart rate changes on the screen, and with practice learn to recognize in your body what the computer screen tells you about the subtle energetic changes that you can choose to produce within yourself.

Thousands of studies support the premise that we can regulate our physiological processes – from heart rate to blood pressure to body temperature. My comments here are a very modest introduction to that literature, and to our possibilities for self-regulation.

I have studied various form of this exercise at different times and under different circumstances. Beginning on the next page I describe the one I have found easiest to understand and to practice.

• While seated in comfortable chair, in a quiet room, cover your heart with the palm of your right hand. Hold your hand there, lightly touching your chest, for a minute or two. Continue breathing normally. Some people prefer to hold their hand closer to the center of their chest. This position can also produce a positive effect.

Figure 16. **Holding the right hand over the heart or chest to produce heart coherence**

• As you focus your attention on what you feel under your palm and fingers, let yourself think of a specific time or place where you felt gratitude or love. The studies done to date indicate that reflecting on these two experiences produces the strongest heart coherence. Some people will feel gratitude and love when they think about the face of someone they love – perhaps a grandchild, a friend, or a pet. Others will prefer to recall an experience when they had a "personal best" moment in a sport or other accomplishment. Some may choose to reflect on an instant of awe-inspiring natural beauty – a sunset, mountain mist, desert cactus in bloom, an ocean shore.

50

It is easy to get off track at this point. You may find that your attention shifts automatically into protest or doubt, or some other negative thinking that distracts you. Such distractions will also cause your heart rate to look more like the stress graph. If this happens, first tell yourself that this is normal. Then simply take your attention back to what brings you gratitude and love. Practice until gratitude becomes more natural than negative distractions.

• Notice how the rest of your body responds. Many people will notice a spontaneous deepening in their breathing. Others may become aware of the beating of their hearts. Some may feel lighter. You may also notice that some parts of your body, such as your forehead, begin to feel cooler, while others, such as your palms, feel warmer. If you use one of the computerized devices mentioned in the following **notes**, you can watch changes in your heart rhythm on the monitor. Otherwise, you can learn biofeedback simply by tuning in to your body directly.

• After a minute or two you are likely to experience a kind of balancing or "coherence" in your heart rhythm. This consists of a growing regularity in your heart rate (HR). A healthy, coherent HR is constantly changing from slower to faster frequencies, called heart rate variability (HRV)[14].

• If this is "all" you accomplish, you can notice positive changes in the stress you might have been feeling, or in how you might be thinking more positively, then celebrate and smile. Some individuals prefer to continue, so with the other hand they touch some part of their body that seems to be asking for assistance. It might be a tension or burning in your stomach, or a tension in your neck, or any other of the many possible stress reactions. Let's say that your stomach has been churning ever since your boss shamed you in a conference. In this case, you would cover the area in your stomach with the palm of your left hand, keeping the right hand over your heart. What you will now be doing is "entraining" the stomach energy, that is, training it to get into a rhythm with your heart. Again, this is not just conjecture, but can be measured if your have the proper technical device. Hold the position until you notice a shift in your stomach.

• Some people will want to take a break from time to time to contemplate the changes they are experiencing, or even to write in a log a note about some new insight or memory that appears spontaneously. The posture of the two hands then can be repeated until the person feels an acceptable level of well-being.

• Others might want to connect energy that the heart hand generates with energy centers in the rest of the body. The following figure shows approximately where five other significant energy centers can be found in the body.

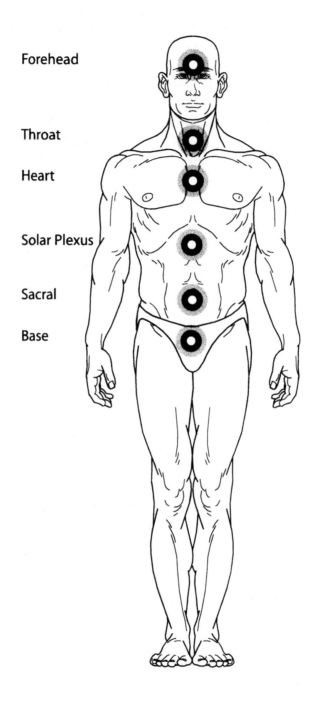

Forehead

Throat

Heart

Solar Plexus

Sacral

Base

Figure 17. **Six energy centers within the human body**

There are various ways to understand these energy centers. They appear to coincide, for example, with areas in the body found to contain unusually high concentrations of receptor molecules. These phenomena, reported by neuroscientist Candace Pert at Georgetown University, refer to areas where peptide molecules are particularly active[15]. In more traditional terms, they appear to overlap with the chakras that one of my trainees mentioned in the story above (and which you can read about in Appendix A).

How to connect your heart with other energy centers

A powerful way to utilize heart coherence is to connect the energy of your heart to the other energy centers in your body. Because the heart generates more measurable than any other part of the body, we can utilize the heart's power to bring harmony and coherence to other organs and muscles.

• First you follow the exercise described on pages 50 and 51 to bring your heart into coherence or balance. As I mentioned, you can either do this subjectively, or purchase a biofeedback device from one of the companies mentioned in Appendix A to watch your heart response on a computer screen.

• Once your heart rhythm is in coherence, continue holding one hand over your heart, and place the other hand lightly on the top of your head. The top of the head is not one of the major energy centers on figure 17, but the brain does produce its own measurable energy and many people report that this initial connection between brain and heart is an excellent way to begin this procedure. Hold your hands over their respective sites for about a minute or two or until you feel a shifting or change in how you feel. Keep your attention on gratitude, love, and appreciation.

• While keeping the primary hand over the heart, move the secondary hand over the forehead, again holding both hands in place for a minute or two or until you sense a shifting.

• Continue to follow this procedure, with the primary hand over the heart to connect with the balanced heart energy, and the secondary hand over the remaining energy centers (throat, solar plexus, lower abdomen, and genital area).

• Finish the procedure with your hands at your sides, breathing deeply and noticing the harmony in your body. You may also imagine how the energy rhythms of your heart would look if you watched them on a computer screen – the undulating waves that we saw in the right hand graph on page 49.

Stress reduction exercise #6: The Butterfly Hug

Two of my good friends, Lucina (Lucy) Artigas and Ignacio Jarero, live in Mexico City where they head up the Mexican Crisis Intervention program called Amamecrisis. In 1997, following the devastation caused by Hurricane Pauline, they traveled to Acapulco to work with the families left homeless and traumatized. Lucy soon found herself in a quandary: 200 children had shown up to seek her psychological assistance. She had expected perhaps a dozen, and had planned to treat them with a new trauma-healing technique called EMDR (for Eye Movement Desensitization and Reprocessing) that she had been using successfully in her clinic. However, EMDR was to be used only on a one-on-one basis. How could she use the technique correctly with so many children?

EMDR seems to work by stimulating first one side of the body, then the other (hence, one brain hemisphere and then the other), in a continuing alternating fashion. Lucy reasoned that the children could tap their own bodies bi-laterally to produce results. Necessity being the mother of invention, she asked the children to cross their hands over their chests and to tap, first with one hand, then the other. The children seemed more enthusiastic when Lucy called the activity the "Butterfly Hug". Long story made short: the method worked splendidly in helping the children to feel calm and comforted, even as they stood in the midst of fallen palm trees and other detritus of the disaster.

The Butterfly Hug has been used with victims of natural disasters in several countries[16]. Of interest here is how it can be used to reduce stress. I begin with a picture of the Butterfly posture. Your finger tips touch ½ inch (1 cm) below the collarbones, about 2 inches (5 cm) apart, the space between these arrows: →   ←. These are the **uc** points already described on page 39.

Figure 18. **The hand positions for the Butterfly Hug**

The procedure for reducing stress using the Butterfly Hug is as follows.

- **First a word of caution**. EMDR is generally conducted under the supervision of a trained psychotherapist. The reason: often we find that a person affected by a disaster or other critical event has stored away memories of similar events in the past, events which have never been resolved. The apparently simple Butterfly Hug at times will open us to our stored memories, causing us quickly to feel overwhelmed by the combined stress of both recent and early traumatic experiences. The same can be true with stress. Sometimes the stress we feel is nothing more than tension left over from a particularly demanding task or interpersonal encounter. In other cases, however, stress represents a habitual mismanaging life's demands, and what we feel at any given moment may actually be the tip of the proverbial iceberg – and may release months and even years of accumulated and unprocessed stress and anger. If your stress feels like this, you may find using the Butterfly Hug will actually increase your feeling of upset. Please stop using the technique if that occurs, and instead refer back to the earlier exercises in this chapter.

- With this cautionary comment in mind (and if you choose to continue with this exercise), focus on your stress, cross your hands and begin tapping slowly, first one side, and then the other. Tap with your right hand over your heart, and with your left hand tap the left side of your chest. Do only a few taps, then stop, breathe deeply, and reflect on your experience. You will notice that your right hand is in the position recommended for producing heart coherence, so you can rest with your hands remaining on your chest. If you feel the same or better, resume tapping, again only for a few seconds.

- Some people find it useful to use the 0 to 10 scale to monitor any changes. Others may prefer simply to observe changes in their breathing or feelings. Continue until your feel closer to the way you would like to feel.

- As mentioned, this simple procedure may remind you of other times where you felt similarly stressed, and may increase your sense of distress. There is no guarantee that you will be able to finish what you start once old memories enter your awareness, so the wisest option would be to stop the tapping and use exercises 1 through 5 described above.

- Lucy now recommends that tapping be done on a specific energy point that is located on the EFT map under the collarbones and just to the side of the sternum or breastplate. In this way you can combine the bilateral stimulation with a meridian point and perhaps notice a more rapid and more positive benefit.

- Many excellent professionals practice EMDR. If for any reason you do not feel comfortable using this technique on your own, you can find information in Appendix A regarding professionals trained in EMDR.

Stress reduction exercise #7: Physical activity

Physical exercise is another effective way to reduce and prevent the excessive kind of stress response we can call distress. Some people find it useful to distinguish between activities that resemble a "fight" (e.g., chopping wood), and those that seem more like "flight" (e.g., running, bicycling, cross country skiing). It is surprising how many sports seem to combine both the fight and flight response: softball, hockey, tennis, touch football, hockey, and so forth. It is recommended that you attend to both lower and upper body conditioning, and that you do aerobic conditioning to increase your heart rate.

The benefits of regular exercise are now well known. Not only does it help to correct physical problems such as high cholesterol, diabetes, and high blood pressure, but it has distinct mood and cognitive advantages as well, such as the ability to boost higher-level thinking and to combat depression and anxiety[17].

Always begin with a medical check-up, and continue to take precautions when you exercise. For example, when performing aerobic activities, consult a HR chart to determine what range you should be in for your age. Note that these are averages: a very fit person and a relatively unfit person may disagree on the HR range suggested. HR recovery following physical activity will also vary with level of fitness. Fitness trainers and researchers suggest that after you complete a physical workout your HR should be within the recommended range for your age, *and then should have dropped by 12 beats after you have rested for one minute*. Other recommended principles are these:

• **Make exercise purposeful and fun**. For the past 20 years of data gathering, fitness statisticians have noted that only about 10% of the people in the US are active enough to achieve fitness gains, and 50% or more of those who begin supervised exercise programs drop out. Much of the drop out rate likely occurs because there is insufficient reward pleasure in the activity itself. More people would maintain their schedule if it were more fun, or intrinsically purposeful. Some researchers recommend that we try to hook our exercise back into a meaningful activity, such as walking the dog, playing a sport with our children, or biking to work.

• **Make exercise a regular part of your life, and also be flexible**. Exercise can be scheduled just as work and social activities are. On the other hand, given that the nature of so many people's schedules requires that we be ready to change them on short notice, it is also important to be flexible. Traveling is a particularly serious disruption for many people these days, and may require that we walk stairwells rather than obsess over how to get in an hour's workout in a gym.

• **Respect the introversion – extraversion continuum**. Some fitness experts make a blanket recommendation that we "exercise with other people" to feel support and to add interest to fitness. This attitude does an injustice to a true introvert who might be better off exercising alone, using that time for solitude, to feel energized, and to think through pending thoughts and problems. An introverted manager who combines exercise with team building might fulfill neither goal, while an extravert will probably enjoy exercise more when exercising with others.

• **Consider multi-tasking**, where at least one of the tasks is inherently pleasurable. One client of mine went to a health center with his wife and son to have time with his family, to lose weight, to take out his frustration and anger, to feel better mentally and physically, to have time for himself away from work, and to increase his productivity when he returned to work. He actually did not like exercising, and if that were his only purpose, would not be likely to exercise at all.

It can be especially difficult to maintain an exercise routine while traveling, so I try to combine several purposes. Walking back to my hotel from a training site, for example, can be a way to exercise, enjoy my solitude, and look at the sights in a special way. The basics required are comfortable clothes and shoes, a map drawn up by a local friend who knows the safe walking areas, the address of the hotel in case I run late, and cab fare. On a recent training in the Andes a local team member suggested we bicycle across the equator, and on another occasion guided me up a volcano – while we debriefed the course we were conducting. Opportunities are often overlooked unless we search for them.

• **Stretch**[18], before and after your workout. Stretching can be soothing on several levels. Generally, it is recommended that we: stretch slowly; stay relaxed; breathe naturally; hold a stretch for 5 to 15 seconds; then release the tension. Bouncing and causing pain are to be avoided. You decide on which muscles need stretching. Some people stretch with a fitness ball, others with an inversion table (which needs to be used with caution, especially if there are medical risks such as glaucoma). You also might consider using the muscle tension exercise described next so that you can notice how stretching and relaxing produce difference experiences, both physical and mental.

There *can be* a positive relationship between exercise and heart coherence.

When persons with heart coherence engage in rigorous exercise, their heart rates continue to show the smooth rhythm of coherence and synchrony that we saw in the "after" graph on page 49, only at a higher elevation on the heart rate chart. Persons who work out with anger and stress, on the other hand, would also show higher rates of heart activity but with the characteristic choppy and chaotic appearance that we saw on the page 49 on the "before" chart.

Other possibilities

Any of the exercises described so far – besides being helpful in eliminating undesirable images, thoughts, and feelings – can be used to strengthen and enhance positive alternatives. Chapter 8 is dedicated to this concept of "performance enhancement"[18].

I would be remiss if I did not mention self-hypnosis[19], meditation[20], prayer[21] and spirituality as other approaches many people practice and report as beneficial in reducing their experience of maladaptive stress. Those familiar with the works of Ken Wilber (2000, 2001), who is one of the more highly respected living philosophers, may be interested in how he views the value of meditation in the development of leaders.

There are many books on stress reduction and relaxation based on the treatment methods called cognitive therapy[22]. These essentially ask the participants to make positive self-statements in the hope that they will eventually talk themselves into new ways of thinking, feeling, and behaving. I used to practice this approach myself and cannot be too critical, except to say that now it seems rather slow and only modestly effective. However, if you find these approaches helpful, I will encourage you to consider using them *in conjunction with* the exercises I described, particularly TAT, EFT or the tapping shortcut, the heart coherence method, or the Butterfly Hug. I believe you may well find what you had been doing before will be accelerated and generally enhanced.

I neither recommend nor discourage the use of pharmaceutical aids/medication. Very few of my clients through the years seem to have needed psychiatric or psychotropic medication to reduce stress once they got into a habit of using the techniques in this chapter, but the decision to take or refuse medications for stress is a personal choice.

More and more people are consuming natural herbal stimulants[23] to increase their energy levels. These stimulants, unfortunately, can produce effects that might feel like a negative stress response, and a person who feels unpleasant stress and who also consumes one of the following might wonder if there is a cause-effect relationship between the two:

Cola (*Cola acuminata*)
Ginkgo biloba
Ginseng
Gotu kola (*Centella asiatica*)
Guarana (*Paullinia cupana*)
Ma huang (*Ephedra sínica*)
Yohimbine (*Pausinystalia yohimbe*)

Other herbal remedies may have calming effects. As the benefit from using these remedies is sometimes unproven, I do not list them here.

We probably all believe that our diet can affect our stress levels for the better or for the worse. There is not space in this book to cover food and drink generally, so I will simply make this comment to remind the reader of this important variable, and suggest consultation with an enlightened nutritionist for further information. As this book went to press, I noticed new titles promoting foods that contain large amounts of peptides, and promising to increase both the sense of well-being and longevity through diet. I also recommend chapter nine in the excellent book by David Servan-Schreiber (2004).

If you seek "tend and befriend" opportunities, particularly when you feel stressed, you already understand the value of social support and nurturance. You do not need to be an extravert, by the way, to find comfort and healing with others.

How to measure your progress

Most of us are comfortable using numbers and other quantitative values to measure various things in our lives. Car efficiency is measured in miles per gallon, cardiovascular health according to LDL and HDL levels, national prosperity in terms of GNP or GDP. We then use the numbers as an indication of how well a particular intervention is working: exercise and dietary changes will, we hope, lower LDL and HDL, for example. The desired direction for some numbers is variable. Sometimes we want our blood pressure to go up, sometimes down. The numbers are meant to give us an objective check on how we experience or perceive things to be. For example, high blood pressure is called a silent killer precisely because we cannot feel it accurately.

I would like to encourage a similar use of quantitative measures along with the exercises in this book so that you can have a relatively dependable way to determine if the exercises are working for you or not. Relying only on how you *feel* can give an inaccurate reading, and may discourage you from continuing.

I will reprint the simple 0 to 10 scale. The zero refers to a complete absence of a problem. The ten indicates the maximal problem possible, or even imaginable. Please write it out before you start using any of the exercises; take a second or third or fourth measure during your routine; and finish with a final measure. Here is the scale again:

No problem   0   1   2   3   4   5   6   7   8   9   10   Maximum problem

Whether the issue to be measured is anxiety or fear of failure or anger or agitation or doubts about yourself, the concept can be measured. Since the measure depends on your subjective rating, you need not be concerned about meeting some standard other than your own personal one, and you do not need to add one more norm to your life based on how "every one else" thinks or feels or acts.

In later chapters, where I speak of accentuating the positive, you can adapt this scale to measure positive changes in your life.

I continue to be surprised by how many of my clients are skeptical of rapid change and as a result second-guess the impact of the exercises. One person may arrive saying "my problem is at an 8". Even though we may then have a successful session, the person may say that "nothing happened." I may ask for a new number and be told it is now a "1". I will then share my confusion: "From 8 to 1 and you say nothing happened?"

Another person may notice some change and report a six, but say the problem is pretty much the same. I might then say, "You went from an eight to a six in a few minutes, which looks like a 25% change. Yet you say there is nothing really different."

In my experience these kinds of reactions do not so much reflect defensiveness as incredulity. Many people are unable to *feel* change (in spite of our belief that we can or should). Others are not used to changing so quickly, and so will doubt their rapid improvement. Still others seem to lack confidence in their ability to change, and their self-doubts, or hopelessness, show up in their denial of change. Using some kind of objective measure of how we are changing, such as the 0 to 10 scale, can give helpful feedback and motivate us to go further.

One way to ensure you are measuring changes is to use repeated measures, and to review all of the ratings and comments you made upon completing your routine. In figure 19 is one example of a work sheet for keeping track of the results of your exercises.

◆ ◆ ◆ ◆ ◆ ◆ ◆ ◆ ◆ ◆ ◆ ◆ ◆ ◆ ◆ ◆

Date: _____ Problem or issue: _____
(You may write here anything that you can measure objectively or subjectively, such as your heart rate or blood pressure, "how stressed" out you feel, how much you feel like leaving an upsetting situation or a relationship, and how anxious or angry you feel.)

My experience with my problem before beginning the exercise:

Circle the number that best fits your experience at this moment: 0 1 2 3 4 5 6 7 9 10

What I did to work on the issue:_____
_____(exercise, breathing, tapping, etc.)

My self-rating at the second measurement: 0   1   2   3   4   5   6   7   8   9   10

What I did next: _____
_____(another exercise)

My self-rating at the third measurement: 0   1   2   3   4   5   6   7   8   9   10

(Repeat exercises and measures as necessary).

My self-rating at the end of the exercise: 0   1   2   3   4   5   6   7   8   9   10

◆ ◆ ◆ ◆ ◆ ◆ ◆ ◆ ◆ ◆ ◆ ◆ ◆ ◆ ◆ ◆

Figure 19. **Example of a personal work sheet**

Case example: Managing stress through homework

Some people prefer to track their progress throughout a day. For example, one manager sought my assistance so he could organize his time better, learn to let his boss's criticism "roll off my back," feel better when in public, and "stop feeling miserable." I taught him to use TAT and EFT, and he practiced both as needed between our sessions. At first he used TAT and EFT after the fact, that is, when he was already feeling upset. Eventually he used them to prepare himself for an event that he might predict could overwhelm him, and learned to take those events in stride when they happened.

To summarize his experiences between sessions, he brought in a log he had kept, with dates, time of day, some information about context or situation, how he felt on the 0-10 scale before and after an experience, and again how he felt after practicing TAT or EFT.

He would write, for example, that he was at a "staff mtg.," "feeling nervous with shallow breathing," and rate it an "8." His notes would then indicate that he practiced TAT and felt at a "4" afterwards. He also wrote conclusions for himself, in this case: "Must rehearse better for presentations, listen better".

As a second example, he once wrote that he had a "Debrief with boss" which left him "ashamed" at a "7." He then did EFT in his office and felt at a 0 afterwards, concluding that "Realized I had done better than boss said, no need to add criticism."

As a third example, he wrote that he did both TAT and EFT in "Preparation for staff luncheon," that he was at a "2" or "1" throughout the luncheon. As he imagined entering the staff dining room and feeling much of the anxiety that usually awaited him, he would then use the exercises to lower his anxiety. When the event actually took place, he noticed he was looking forward to it more than he had before. He concluded afterwards that it was all right to "Plan ahead for these times."

He also practiced deep breathing along with TAT and EFT and eventually noticed that simply taking a deep breath at times when he noticed his anxiety rising would usually begin to relax him immediately.

He also reported that he began to use his time better, after discovering that some of his disorganization had been a kind of self-sabotage. I asked him what he had done to make that happen. He said he thought it had to do with saying to himself statements such as "I deserve to be successful" and "I'll keep doing what I can to do a good job", while doing the TAT pose or tapping the EFT points. I could not, of course, disagree with his hunch. When our four-session contract ended, he said he was still unaccustomed to smiling so much at work, and that he had not known how strong his voice sounded.

Notes to Chapter One:

[Consult the **references** for further information on books and authors mentioned here]

Footnote 1. stress … distress … eustress. The pioneer in stress studies was the innovative and brilliant Hans Selye. He introduced the concept of eustress in his 1974 book, and wrote many follow-ups, including one in 1976. His original writings are still worth reading. A good summary of the stress literature can be found in Everly & Mitchell (1999) and Everly & Lating (2003). Everly is one of the pioneers in the field of critical stress management which produced techniques used around the world by emergency workers. For those interested in biochemistry, any up-to-date introductory psychology text will describe how the body responds to stress.

2. See Everly & Lating (2003) who wrote about the effects of negative stress. The topic is also covered in the popular media.

3. The fight-flight response also includes the "freeze" response as an option, though this is not considered so relevant for this book. Also see Everly & Lating (2003) or an introductory pschology text book.

4. Shelly Taylor (2000, 2002) has studied the "tend and befriend" response to stress.

5. See the article by William A. Karlin and colleagues (2003), published in the journal *Psychosomatic Medicine*.

6. The deep breathing instructions described can be found in Everly & Lating (2003).

7. TAT is registered. Please note this if you teach TAT or use the technique to treat others. Tapas Fleming (1999) offers friendly and instructional courses to medical practitioners and psychotherapists as well as to persons not formally trained in the medical or psychotherapy fields. Her website is http://www.unstressforsuccess.com, and the email address is tapas@unstressforsuccess.com. I also included her training manual in the bibliography. The manual contains further details about the TAT technique I describe.

8. The 0 to 10 scale is based on the work by South African psychiatrist Joseph Wolpe (1969), whose pioneering book is still interesting to read. The scale is in wide use by therapists, though Tapas Fleming no longer employs it in her work. She prefers to teach her clients to attend to how they feel and to notice shifts in their bodily experiences.

9. Gary Craig modeled EFT (Emotional Freedom Techniques) after Roger Callahan's TFT (Thought Field Therapy). I described EFT first because it offers a single set of instructions, instead of the more complex variations ("algorithms") one needs to learn in TFT. Nonetheless, I find the TFT algorithms to be useful (as do many other practitioners around the world) so I also included them as exercise #4. Both Craig and Callahan train

nonprofessionals as well as professional therapists in their methods. Further information on EFT can be found on http://www.emofree.org. Information on TFT can be accessed at http://www.tftrx.com and in the following books: Callahan (1985, 1987a, 1987b); Callahan & Callahan (1996); Callahan & Perry (1991); and Callahan & Trubo (2001).

10. Various hypotheses have been proposed to explain how energy flows through the meridians. In a research study conducted by DeVernejoul, Albarede, & Darras (1985), radioactive technetium was injected into acupoints of patients and the uptake of this isotope was traced by gamma-camera imaging. It was noted that the technetium migrated along classical acupuncture meridian pathways for a distance of 30 centimeters in four to six minutes. This was the basis for a theory offered by Rubik (1995) who likened meridian lines to mechanical pipelines through which energy flows. See also Feinstein (2002) and Pomeranz (1987) for overviews of the subject.

In appendix A, in the section on acupuncture, you can find references to other studies that support the existence of subtle energy, in this case the meridian system.

11. I refer the reader to the book by Callahan & Trubo (2001), should you like to study from the master of TFT. As already mentioned, Callahan teaches his course to nonprofessionals, both in vivo and through a home study format. Fred Gallo's books (Gallo, 2000, 2005; Gallo & Vicenzi, 2000) contain further clarification of the Callahan method, and are recommended. In his method called EDxTM, Gallo uses more than the basic 15 or so meridian points that I recommend in this book, but many fewer than the 361 available. I agree with his view that some people will not benefit if they limit themselves to the basic meridian points, and also that it is only rarely necessary to employ all 361. I also recommend the book by Lambrou & Pratt (2000). Greg Nicosia (http://www.thoughtenergy.com) was instrumental in making TFT available to the wider public. Greg teaches his own system of energy psychology with a lively combination of theoretical stimulation and practical application.

12. See Appendix A for information on how to find software to measure heart coherence.

13. For information about the scientific benefits of maintaining heart coherence, see Barrios-Choplin, McCraty, et al. (1997); Luskin & Reitz (2002), McCraty (2001), and McCraty, Barrios-Choplin, et al. (1998).

14. Increased heart rate variability (HRV) has been correlated with lower mortality risk (Tsuji, Venditti, et al., 1994); decreases in depression (Rechlin & Weis, 1994); and other factors (Stys & Stys, 1998). These gross measures of HRV may be even as predictive of physical and psychological health as is the more harmonic variability implied in heart coherence. It appears that the shortcut tapping techniques described as exercise #4 in Part One of this book produce increased HRV (Pignotti & Steinberg, 2001). The exact benefits that accrue from this relationship is unclear (Herbert & Gaudiano, 2001) and deserves further study.

15. Candace Pert's book on the *Molecules of Emotion* (1999) describes her search for peptide molecules, and her "discovery" in the process of the probable neurophysiological sites of the ancient chakras. More interesting still are two audiocassettes from Sounds True (Pert, 2000), noted in the references section. Also see appendix A for further information about heart coherence and the charkas.

16. The history, supportive research findings, and description of the Butterfly Hug can be read on the web site for the Mexican Association for Interventions in Critical Incidents: http://www.amamecrisis.com.mx/articulo/06_apendice_c.htm. The Butterfly Hug has been used effectively in a number of situations where clinical and research goals were combined. Jarero, Artigas, Mauer, López-Cano, & Alcalá (2000) describe their original model for working with victims of natural disasters. Other groups describe their adaptation of that model to various patient populations. Wilson, Tinker, Hofmann, Becker, & Marshall (2000) did a field study with Kosovar-Albanian children living in a refugee camp; Korkmazler-Oral & Pamuk (2002) report on their work with earthquake victims in Turkey; and Fernandez, Gallinari, & Lorenzetti (2004) have written about an intervention with school children traumatized by an airplane crash.

17. I have collected the information on physical exercise from many sources, and for many years, and find similar information reported in the popular press (no longer limited to fitness magazines) and Sunday newspaper supplements. The book by Kate Hays (1999) describes the use of exercise in conjunction with psychotherapy. Sport and exercise psychology are discussed by van Raalte & Brewer (2004).

18. For several decades Bob Anderson from Boulder, Colorado, has been a popular proponent of stretching. The latest edition of his book by that title (Anderson, 2000) now includes stretching exercises for snowboarding, mountain biking, even sufferers of carpal tunnel syndrome, as well as for the more traditional sports of swimming and running.

19. An early and still good description of self-hypnosis was written by Alman & Lambrou (1983). There are many options now, and I suggest you shop around until you find one that you like both for the text and for the illustrations.

20. The positive effects of transcendental meditation have been documented by Farrow & Herbert (1982) and Benson (1996). Meditation is becoming more and more mainstream. I have health coverage with a company that now sponsors classes in yoga, massage, Tai Chi, and aromatherapy, as well as meditation. The Mind and Life Institute sponsors research into the results of meditation, including the Tibetan Buddhist practices of the Dalai Lama) from the perspective of cognitive neuroscientists (http://www.mindlife.org). See also Davidson & Harrington (2001) on the linkage between science and meditation.

21. Many studies have been done to measure the effects of prayer on a wide range of physical and emotional problems. In many of these studies (though not all) prayer was shown to have *caused* positive benefits. One reviewer of the work to date is Larry

Dossey (1993), who in my experience has a balanced, scientific, and humanistic approach to the subject. Of particular interest to me was Dossey's description of how widely and differently prayer can be defined, understood, and practiced, and still produce healing effects with ill patients.

22. For information on cognitive therapy approaches to stress reduction and relaxation, you might begin with *The Relaxation & Stress Reduction Workbook* by Davis, Eshelman, & McCay (2004, 5th ed.). In addition to more traditional cognitive approaches such as thought stopping and the refuting of irrational ideas, there are chapters on meditation, autogenics, and visualization.

23. For further information on natural herbal stimulants consult the *Physicians' Desk Reference for Herbal Medicines* (2001, 2nd edition). In this book, the authors summarize research findings for 600 herbs and over 100 health conditions.

Chapter 2: Anger and Type A personality

In chapter 1 we visited the concept of stress, which I tied in with fight and flight. If you haven't already read that chapter, it might be useful to do so before continuing.

The bigger picture: fight

Now I focus on the fight side of the fight-flight response[1]. Most of us would probably agree that the fight response, when appropriate and adaptive, can be a legitimate way to protect ourselves and others from threat ("tend and befriend" being another possibility). Social scientists point out that appropriate anger can spur an entire culture to change for the better, as happened with the civil rights movements of the 1960s and the earlier movement for women's suffrage. Although there appears to be no single definition of constructive anger – experts say it varies according to situation and context – psychologists are examining how it can be of value in intimate relationships, work interactions, and political expressions. It also appears that when people learn to discuss their angry feelings with a calm solution focus, health benefits accrue.

When our fight response becomes exaggerated, however, it can become counterproductive – a threat to others and a cause of wear and tear on our own bodies. Recent research shows that highly hostile men are more likely to have an immune system protein that is associated with several risk factors for cardiovascular problems[2]. In this sense hostility can produce the same types of arterial injury and heart disease that result from smoking, high blood pressure, obesity, and high cholesterol.

For many years two extreme ways of dealing with anger – venting or suppressing – were in vogue. Venting or purging oneself of negative emotion is still promoted by those who subscribe to the so-called "catharsis" theory of emotion. On the other extreme were those who taught containment: counting to ten is still one of their popular techniques. It now appears that both those who always vent their anger *and* those who always suppress their anger increase their health risks[3]. Additionally, among those who always vent their anger, hostility and aggression actually seem to increase, rather than to diminish as the catharsis proponents would predict.

It appears at this stage of scientific inquiry that the most significant health risks associated with anger involve some combination of these five elements: ill-will towards others; verbal aggression; a tendency toward causing physical harm; remaining angry for relatively long periods of time instead of taking action and releasing anger; and taking the extremes of either venting or suppressing anger.

67

Much of this recent science confirms the concept of "Type A". The Type A person is someone constantly on the lookout for threat, and whose body and mind are ready to respond aggressively to the threat. Irritable, impatient, pushy, and driven, Type A persons seem unable to set their engines on idle, and are thought to be at risk to wear out their bodies prematurely, particularly through heart failure[4].

The exercises I list in this chapter can reduce the intensity or duration of our irritability and anger, modulate our fighting or aggressive behavior, and improve our physical health. To use parallel concepts, a Type A can learn to become a "Type C", a term that might describe a "recovering Type A". Type C persons are able to translate threats into challenges, and soften high energy and ambition so that their behavior becomes more pleasing both to themselves and to those around them. These types might also be energetic and driven, as is the Type A, but their energy feels friendly to others, and their anger quickly dissipates. In the process they see opportunities for collaboration as well as competition.

In my experience, Type A persons do not customarily seek help because of a spontaneous insight into their dysfunctional behavior and its impact on others. More usually they continue their habits until someone else gives them feedback about their impact – feedback that indicates, under no uncertain terms, that the Type A's behavior is self-sabotaging, insufferable, unacceptable. Frequently, the feedback suggests the Type A is about to derail – be it on a job, in a relationship, or in some other important way. "Do something about your anger, or else", is likely to be the ultimatum from a frustrated spouse or boss.

I would like to exemplify these concepts, and introduce some of the treatments approaches, by telling a short story of a man who was misinterpreted as being a basically rude and angry supervisor, but who was using anger and aggression to cover up his more fragile feelings. I do not know how typical he is, but he does remind me (and perhaps the reader) of other individuals who seem to ride rough shod on others as a way to cover their own inadequacy and fears. While this does not make their behavior any more tolerable to an outsider, it may allow us to appreciate the complexity of human behavior, in this case how a person who has lost hope in the possibility of his changing can produce the most unpleasant of facades to keep himself from feeling vulnerable.

Case example: the misunderstood scientist

I was once consulting with a group of scientists who were in training to become managers in a biotechnology company. One of the participants, "Tomas", had been particularly belligerent and disruptive for the first half of the week-long training course, and I was asked to pull him aside to see what might be done to help him and his group.

I only had a couple of hours so I told him immediately that I, the team trainers, and his own peers were very concerned about him, and that his irritability was widely perceived as disrespectful and critical. He was defensive for a few minutes, so I let him talk, then suggested that whatever his reasons, it seemed to me he was doing a lot more potential damage to himself than to anyone else.

He finally said that for a year or more he had been seriously stressed by a series of life-threatening events, and that just two months prior to this training he had been diagnosed with a serious medical problem – exacerbated if not caused by the stress he had been feeling. "I don't have any idea what I can do about it", he finally confessed. In his despair he had chosen to keep it all to himself, and admitted he was surprised at how this terrible secret had been showing up. Yet he admitted that his belligerence and negativity had also been obvious at work, where those who had known him for most of his career were surprised at his "sudden change in personality." I told him that I thought he showed great courage telling me about his experience, and decided to take a risk with him:

John: I wonder if you recall when I introduced myself the other day that I said I wear two hats, one as executive coach, the other as trainer of trauma specialists. I'd be willing to tell you about my other hat. The role I play there may be of more use to you than traditional coaching, but I'll warn you that it may seem pretty odd. Especially to you as a scientist.

Tomas: What do I have to lose?

John: Let me begin by telling you about the studies that Candace Pert conducted at Georgetown University . . . [and I continued].

Tomas: Sounds fine to me. In my work I'm amazed at how often we discover, in quotes, some new technological advance only to be told later that the practice had been done in some other country for years – even though people were not able to explain why what they were doing worked. We give it a kind of legitimacy, which is really different from saying we invented it.

John: OK. The test, of course, will be in whether you notice anything from practicing some exercises I can teach you. I can't say what might happen, but in my experience these simple techniques usually produce at least a relaxation response. Do you have any objections to that?

Tomas (laughing): My doc has already said I am stressing my heart and probably aggravating my condition. So I doubt learning to relax will do anything but good.

John: I haven't seen any negative side effects from using these techniques for some years, so I can't say that I have any concerns either. But just to be even safer, let's work slowly, and let me show you a way to self-measure what you might be feeling. If you're ready, let's start by having you think about something that has been bothering you. And on a zero to ten scale, where zero means you're not bothered at all and ten is the worst you can even imagine, how upset do you feel right now?

Tomas: *I'd have to say that I'm mostly bothered by the doc's diagnosis of my heart problem. It's scary. I bolt awake at night wondering when I will die. Even now it seems that I can feel my heart pounding. It's at least a '7' right now on your zero to ten scale.*

For the next 20 minutes we did both the TAT and EFT exercises, while he thought about his heart and his fear of dying. As so often happens, he shifted from that to other memories. His level of distress went up as new aspects of his problem came to light, but he persisted with the exercises and he eventually was able to report a "zero" on the scale. He said he was simply amazed at his experience, and he then asked me if we could also work together on a flying phobia that had originated after a light plane crash several years earlier. In another 10 minutes of work on his phobia with the same two exercises, TAT and EFT, he was able to get to a one. Our two-hour coaching session ended on time.

In the remainder of the course, he took on leadership roles in several role-plays, and carried them out fairly well. Most importantly to him, his colleagues told him they appreciated the effort he was making in the course. He left feeling that his heart was working better, on several levels.

The exercises

You will find that most of the exercises I introduced in chapter one will be repeated here as anger reduction strategies. Deep breathing, exercise #1, assists with optimal human functioning for just about every human activity other than a true emergency. Exercises #2 through #5 follow subtle energy theory, which predicts that disruptions at an energetic level accompany most of the disturbances we experience in life (including those produced by anger) and correcting those disruptions helps to produce balance and health once again. Exercise #6, the Butterfly Hug, will be recommended here with reservations because of the risk that it can open up other memories related to anger. Physical exercise, #7, is a fine traditional way to reduce certain negative emotions.

Many of the traditional approaches to stress management are helpful. If angry college students can reduce their anger simply by doing relaxation exercises and learning coping skills (and they can), we can expect an even greater benefit and more rapid response when we complement those traditional methods with the exercises that follow.

Anger reduction exercise #1: Deep breathing

Review pages 25 and 26 for the procedural steps for deep breathing.

It is mostly true that you cannot be angry and relaxed at the same time, and deep breathing is a powerful tool for creating the relaxation response. Physiologically speaking, breathing puts into operation a nervous system called the "parasympathetic". If you feel at times as if your anger is overpowering you, or getting out of control, the most immediate and natural step might simply be to notice you breathing – you are likely to find that you are breathing shallowly, quickly, and inefficiently – and then simply slow and deepen your inhalations. (If you also could do the TAT pose or tap some key EFT points, you would probably notice your breathing growing even more rhythmic and calming.)

I repeat the graph that some individuals find helpful as they practice deep breathing. In particular, those persons who feel nervous when they are asked to pause and hold their breath (either on the inhale or even more likely on the exhale) can notice with this graph that the pause period lasts for only a second.

Each side of this box represents one of the four steps in deep breathing. In the example below, steps one and three show longer arrows indicating that the inhale and exhale can last 2 to 3 seconds. Some people will feel relieved to notice that the top and bottom of the box are shorter, and that they do not need to hold their breath for very long following the inhale or exhale.

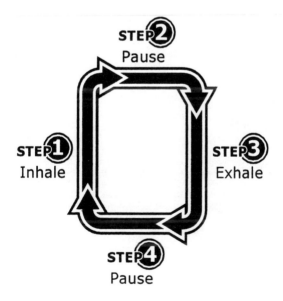

Anger reduction exercise #2: TAT

This is one of the two exercises that proved so powerful for the scientist I described in the case example above, and which has been so useful to other persons who had trouble managing their impulsive anger. Follow the same procedures as outlined on pages 28 through 34. You may also photocopy the one-page short form for TAT below. Because anger so often is a cover for other more fragile emotions, I would encourage you not to be too surprised, and not necessarily to stop the TAT procedure, in the event that while you are working with TAT you notice that your begin to recall other memories that cause you to feel emotions other than anger, such as loss, sadness, or disappointment. These unpredicted experiences may also bring a lump to your throat or tears to your eyes. While you can certainly opt to stop doing TAT and to stop feeling, you might also consider such an experience to be fortunate for you as it will be a chance to remember what you had forgotten, and perhaps allow you to develop new insight into why you have been so driven, so irritable, so combative and argumentative, or so aggressive. You might reflect on the experience of the scientist who was using anger to keep from feeling something else.

Figure 20. **TAT short-form for reducing anger**

Anger reduction exercise #3: EFT

EFT is the second exercise that my coaching client in the example found so helpful. Anger can be a very complex emotion, and sometimes the best approach to an energy treatment is to tap *all* the emotional points on the body, which EFT should cover. Be particularly attentive to any of the EFT points that cause a particularly meaningful shift for you. You might keep tapping on that point longer to add continuing stimulation to your energy system. Remember that you can also simply *touch* each point during the length of one breath, which makes it less obvious if you do EFT in public. Memorize the points that are especially useful for you for future use. You may review the EFT protocol on pages 36 through 43, and then photocopy the one-page short form below. With practice, many of my clients prefer to carry with them only the picture of all the points, which they tap or touch during the day as necessary.

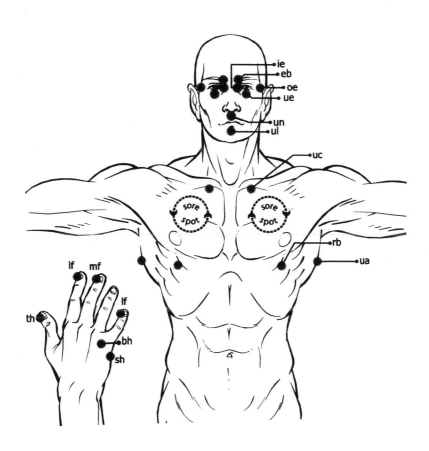

Figure 21. **EFT short form for reducing anger**

73

Anger reduction exercise #4: Tapping shortcut

You may find while doing exercise #3, EFT that certain points do not seem to help much and can be eliminated, while others are particularly powerful and should be stimulated. In this way you may discover a tailor-made tapping shortcut. You might also try the shortcut I describe next. Many persons have found this procedure effective in reducing feelings of anger and rage. Refer to this figure as you follow the instructions on the facing page.

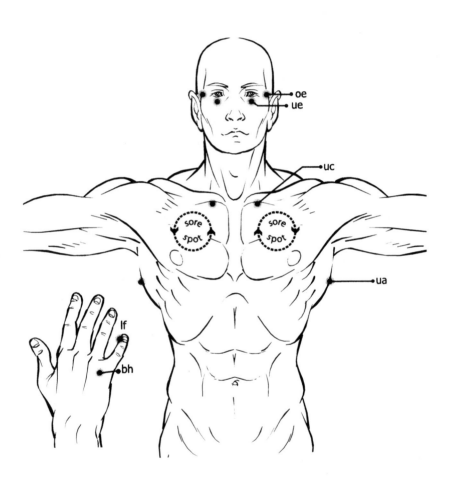

Figure 22. **Tapping shortcut for reducing anger**

• Think about what is causing you to feel angry, irritable, or enraged. Notice how you feel. Think of a number from 0 to 10 that represents how angry or irritated you feel.

• Find the sore spots (more detailed directions are on page 40) and massage them in the direction of the arrows while saying three times: "I accept and love myself deeply and completely even though I have this anger and other problems."

• Then stimulate the following points, either by tapping 7 to 8 times on each point, or touching and holding each point for the duration of one breath.

Begin with the **oe** point on the temples (outside the eye), just behind the ridge of bone surrounding the eye. While you tap or touch, say: "I extend myself with forgiveness. I extend myself with love. I extend myself with forgiveness and love." Then tap or touch the **ue** points under the eyes; the **uc** points under the collarbones; the **ua** points under the arms; **uc** again; and finally the **lf** points at the curve of the little finger nails. As you tap or touch these **lf** points, say the following: "For the sake of my own self-control and peace, there is forgiveness in my heart – I am at peace and in control – Reason and wisdom are within me." My clients also find it extremely helpful at this point to forgive certain persons with whom they know they are angry. If you can think of someone in your life that you are angry at, continue tapping or touching **lf** and say the following: "I forgive you [here you say the person's name, such as "Dad", or "Jerry", or even "You, God" . . .] because I wish to be at peace."

• Do the nine brain balancing procedures on pages 42-43. While tapping the back of one hand (**bh**), do these 9 procedures: close your eyes, open them, look down left, look down right, eyes in a circle, eyes in a circle opposite direction, hum any tune for 3 seconds, count to 5, and hum any tune again

• Tap or touch all the points again as above: **oe** (while repeating the statement), **ue**, **uc**, **ua**, **uc** again, and **lf** (while saying the statement). Repeat if you would like.

• Take another measure on the 0 to 10 scale; if there is no change, do the sore spot massage on page 40, this time saying, "I accept and love myself deeply and completely even though I *still* have *some* of this anger." Repeat all of the above. If you do not get to a zero on the scale, use exercises #1, #2, #3 or #5.

• If you get to a 2 or 1, you can try to lower the number to a zero with the eye roll: while tapping the back of one hand (**bh**), very slowly raise your eyes from floor to ceiling, keeping your head level.

As mentioned, you can notice whether one point or another seems particularly calming or meaningful for you, in which case you can continue tapping or holding the point for as long as you wish. If this shortcut does not work, try exercises #1, #2, #3, or #5.

Anger reduction exercise #5:
Leading with your heart

In some languages the same word is used for "anger" and "heart", with this implication: chronic anger can stain and rust our heart, but a loving heart can also heal and remove anger. It appears more and more than we can choose the direction of this cause-and-effect relationship. On pages 48 through 51 I described a very simple exercise for "entraining" and empowering your heart. It involves placing your hand over your heart to bring your heart rate into a synchronized and coherent rhythm, and may be one of the most effective exercises for handling anger. I suggest you practice the exercise exactly as it is described there.

After you have completed the steps outlined on pages 48 through 51, you can refer to pages 52 and 53 for ideas on how to connect your heart's coherence to some other part of your body that is not yet coherent. Anger often produces strong sensation in some special part of our body, such as the neck, shoulders, stomach, or face. If this strong sensation continues even after you notice that your heart rate has already begun to feel more balanced and coherent, you can use the heart's energy to connect with and to soothe the energy frequencies of the remaining sensation of anger. Because the heart's energy is stronger than that of other organs or parts of the body, you can expect that your heart coherence will gradually train the rest of the body (in this case, the area where you still notice an angry sensation) to come into line with more optimal physiological functioning.

To make this connection happen, keep one hand over your heart and place the other heart over the place where anger seems to have produced tension or pain. Hold both hands in their respective places for several minutes, pay as close attention as you can to the feeling you experience under each hand, and notice any changes that occur. You may feel a slight relaxation in a muscle, or a tingling, or a warming or cooling sensation – all signs of healing of your anger. You may also notice that you begin to recall, visually or not, specific scenes from your life, perhaps a time of having forgiven or having been forgiven. And you may also notice that certain thoughts occur to you rather spontaneously, such as "I can appreciate myself", "I can appreciate differences", "I prefer love to anger." If and when these changes occur to you, remain with them for a few minutes more, with your hands in their respective places, until you are ready to face the challenges of life with your renewed spirit. Remember that it is normal to become distracted and to let negative thoughts drift into consciousness. Simply notice when this happens, and intentionally take your attention to memories of gratitude and love.

If you doubt you have the power to effect these changes, check for scientific support for this exercise in the notes[5].

Anger reduction exercise #6: The Butterfly Hug

Begin by reviewing pages 54 and 55 where the Butterfly Hug is described. Be careful when using this exercise for the purpose of reducing anger, as it can sometimes stimulate other related memories that could cause you to feel even more angry – sometimes a great deal more. This is particularly true for adults who tend to have stored away relatively numerous unresolved memories. Children do not seem so susceptible to this risk, particularly when they use the Butterfly Hug under professional supervision.

You can begin the Butterfly Hug by noticing your anger, rating it on the 0 to 10 scale, then doing only one or two alternating taps to each side of your chest, first one side, then the other, then the first side, then the second, then stop. Check to see if your anger has changed, and if it diminished or increased, and how much. If you noticed that your anger suddenly surged, perhaps the process of bilateral alternating tapping poses a liability for you. Please keep in mind that perhaps 5% of my clients who use the Butterfly Hug *while thinking forgiving and loving thoughts* report that they begin to feel upset rather than peaceful, particularly when they first begin. If this happens to you, I would suggest using exercises #2 (TAT), #3 (EFT), #4 (Tapping Shortcut), or #5 (Leading with your heart).

If on the other hand the gentle tapping, first on one side and then on the other, *reduces* your feelings of rage, upset, irritability – or whatever the form of anger that you feel – you might consider that your anger is relatively isolated and is not connecting with other old memories that could exacerbate your anger, memories of when you felt threatened or treated in some other way that led to an angry feeling. In this case, continue gently tapping as above. The advantage of the Butterfly Hug is that it appears to stimulate communication between the two brain hemispheres, which in turn can help you to integrate important experiences that up to that point have been disassociated from one another. In my experience, integration of our various memories and experiences is always preferable to their being disconnected.

Some clients at this point will tell me that they do not *feel* forgiving, and I say: this is not an attempt on my part to talk you into anything. If you are not ready to forgive, you will not forgive, and that is all right with me. What we are doing is simply raising the issue of anger and forgiveness at an energetic level, and then having you focus on the issue.

This explanation permits the person to experiment with the issue of forgiveness while leaving options open. I believe this is better than trying to talk someone into forgiving based on some preconceived notion that forgiveness is always preferred, appropriate, and timely. Incidentally, when I offer this explanation, most persons do report that they feel more forgiving and less angry after doing the procedure.

Anger reduction exercise #7: Physical activity

Physical activity has already been presented on pages 56 and 57. Some would say that the best forms of exercise for a person hoping to reduce his anger are those that simulate the fighting response. You can experiment to see if this is true for you. Kicking or hitting a tennis ball, soccer ball, squash, or baseball; chopping wood; and pounding nails have all been mentioned as feasible options, as they all give the appearance of simulating an aggression action. Other activities that give the appearance of aggression without involving physical exertion (such as throwing darts) would seem less likely to meet all the conditions of this theory. However, you can experiment to see what is true for you.

Again, because anger can be so complex, some angry persons are also likely to notice that a "flight" kind of activity serves better for them, and bicycling, swimming, or jogging may help to reduce the kind of stress that they associate with anger. Experiment.

I have read varying opinions about the value of weight lifting in this regard. Some say that weight lifting without aerobic activity can increase blood pressure, others that it can have a relaxing effect. It may be another matter of individual personality differences at play here.

Physical activity can also trigger memories that can *increase* an angry feeling. One of my coaching clients reported that he would become angered every time he went jogging, particularly when he was alone and allowed to daydream without distraction. For some reason, he said, running reminded him of various times when he had been humiliated or shamed, and he would return from a run sweating with rage. I taught him TAT and EFT, and he began to stop during his runs when he felt angry, would do TAT and EFT for a few minutes, and then resume running when his anger subsided. He reported that not only did his anger diminish over time, but that he began to understand his reasons for having justified feeling that way.

By the way, were there a guaranteed benefit accruing from the bilateral mechanism involved in the Butterfly Hug, one might have guessed that simply running (one foot forward and touching, then the other forward and touching) would have lowered his anger over time, but he did not report such an experience. In this case, as throughout the book, I encourage you to trust only what you personally find to be true. For the same reason I offer nine (or more) strategic options for your consideration.

Other considerations

The exercises just described – besides being powerful in eliminating negative feelings, thoughts, and images – can also be useful in strengthening and enhancing positive alternatives. Chapter 8 is dedicated to this concept of "performance enhancement".

It may be obvious that using alcohol or other mind-altering chemicals can exacerbate angry reactions. It is one of those peculiar paradoxes: a person takes a drink to control, perhaps to forget about, angry feelings, but then the drink takes the person, as the old saying goes, and the angry feelings become more controllable than before.

In addition to alcohol counseling, chronically angry people often report benefiting from taking an anger management course to understand what makes them tick, and to learn how to handle strong emotion. The course may also help participants to learn a softer form of angry response called assertiveness.

Are the courses enough? In my experience, they are often helpful but not sufficiently so because they tend to focus on ways to control and contain strong negative emotions rather than teaching ways to prevent and eliminate those emotions. However, the courses *along with* the practice of the exercises in this book can be extremely helpful, as the exercises are meant to take us to the cause of the problem and to eliminate the strong feeling when it arises.

Notes to Chapter Two

Footnote 1. For further reading on the fight-flight theory and on anger generally, you might consult the January and March, 2003, issues of the *Monitor*, a publication of the American Psychological Association. In those reports you will also find 16 references on the science behind this theme. These articles describe not only how hostility and inappropriate anger wear down our bodies, but also how they wear down our relationships and our sense of personal well being. Also see Bill Moyer's *Healing and the Mind*, (1993), which is the companion book to the PBS TV series by the same title.

2. Hostility is among the best predictors of heart disease in men. See the article by Suarez, Harlan, Peoples, & Williams (1993).

3. See articles by Stoney & Engebretson (2000), and by Finney, Stoney, & Engebretson (2002), on the negative effects of either always venting *or* always suppressing anger, and Davidson, MacGregor, Stuhr, Dixon, & McLean (2000) on constructive verbal expressions of anger.

4. Rosenman and Friedman coined the phrase in their book, *Type A behavior and your heart* (1974).

5. You may access www.heartmath.com or purchase the book by David Servan-Schreiber's (2004) for further information about and scientific support for the concept of heart coherence.

Chapter 3: Recovery from stage fright, phobias, and other fears

In the same way that anger (chapter 2) parallels the fight side of fight-flight, so fear accompanies the flight side[1].

In its adaptive and natural form, fear can be life saving. If we can outrun a mugger, the fear that propels us would certainly be said to have a survival value. It has also been shown how phobias have a survival function. For the most part phobias seem to be exaggerations of a normal fear to stimuli or events that could harm us. There are many people who develop phobias that keep them far from a cliff (acrophobia), from possibly poisonous insects (arachnophobia), and from the threat of drowning (hydrophobia) or suffocation (claustrophobia). Hardly anyone, on the other hand, develops phobias to grass, to shoes, or to books – which are presumably not inherently dangerous.

Certain fears that seem to have no purpose in adult life may once have served an important function in childhood. An adult's fear of authority figures may now be out of date, but when it first appeared it might have protected the child from a physically more powerful and violent parent. An intelligent and educated adult's fear of success may seem peculiar until we learn that it was once a way to shield the child from being bullied and ostracized. And fear of failure in a person with a long history of success may be left over from a time when the child was shamed and publicly humiliated for making mistakes.

Adaptive fear protects us. Maladaptive fear can cause us to isolate ourselves from the delights of the world, and to avoid challenges that could bring us experiences of personal power and accomplishment. But precisely because this kind of fear is maladaptive – that is, because it has no real function or purpose in the present – it can be unlearned. The exercises in this chapter have been shown with many individuals to be effective in eliminating those feelings of fear that are no longer necessary, or never were necessary.

Case example: The manager about to derail

You already read in the introduction about the protagonist of this story, JoAnne. She was the junior executive who sought help for overcoming her extreme nervousness when facing senior executives. The question of long-term counseling was out of the question, as she was scheduled to speak to the board of directors the following week. While I had been using the energy techniques with my clinical clients for many months, I remained reluctant to try them out with my coaching clients, who had sought me out for consultation and advice, not psychotherapy. However, given that JoAnne seemed to feel such an urgent need to resolve her problem, I took what I thought would be a risk in talking about such unusual ideas to a person I had stereotyped as overly conventional.

I began by trying to place acupuncture theory into notions that I assumed would be more familiar to her, and was somewhat surprised when she said that my explanations about receptor molecules and acupuncture were unnecessary. She said she had called me because she had heard about the coaching I do, and said she didn't need me to convince her that what I had to say was legitimate. Her question was more about whether I thought we had enough time for her to get anything accomplished before the board presentation.

There were several themes in JoAnne's story that I have seen repeated in this work.

• Relatively few people report strong skepticism about the techniques I describe throughout this book, and almost none refuse to try them out. This is true even of persons I initially suspected would be unusually conventional and resistant to the new and odd-appearing ideas. It simply hasn't worked out that way.

• Many people, and not just my coaching clients, are over-achievers, who have developed skills and are highly motivated to do well. The problem is not that they are not competent or passionate, but rather than they carry old baggage around with them (for example, fears and phobias, the themes of this chapter) that keeps them from acting on and enjoying their skills. The metaphor of the Pikes Peak marathon runner comes to mind again.

• After experiencing rapid change, many people have trouble believing their experience, and may say that while they feel no disturbance, still they do not dare assign a "zero" to their experience.

• Rapid change, initially suspect, comes to be perceived as normal and natural, often something that the client seems to take for granted. JoAnne waited two months to write me. I suspect she waited to see if the positive benefits would indeed hold this time. When she did write, she made her report sound like things were perfectly expected, natural, and normal.

As I wrote in the introduction, JoAnne was a serious student who worked diligently during our session *and* continued to practice the exercises prior to the staff presentation. Had she not continued to practice, the benefit she enjoyed in the session may have waned, she may have concluded that the exercises had no lasting value, and she may have ended failing instead of succeeding in her work. This in turn would likely have further reinforced her self-doubts and eroded her self-esteem – and so the cycle would have continued. Instead, agreeing to practice the simple exercises seems to have helped her stay on her journey to become proficient in how she felt, thought, and acted.

Case example: Fear of flying revisited

A lawyer called for a session to work on his fear of flying. He was missing some chances to do work out of state and seemed motivated to make the necessary efforts to resolve his problem. We worked with various exercises, and he responded well. He said he would follow the instructions for TAT, EFT, and the energy shortcut as necessary. Several weeks later he called to say he had made a successful flight, did not have to take medication, and actually enjoyed part of the trip.

A few weeks after that he called to say that "everything fell apart." In revisiting the issues I asked a few questions about his recent disappointing experience, and discovered that he had taken a heavy dose of prescribed tranquilizers before he could even walk on to the plane. "And where were you headed?" I asked. "My wife and I were going to see her parents," he answered. "That's different from going to work", I said. "Can you tell me more?"

The reader may already have suspected that the issue was no longer simply flying, but rather the destination. What has been called "secondary gain" in medicine" also appears in psychology: a person keeps hold of a symptom because it has a secondary purpose. In this case, the phobia could be his excuse for not making more frequent flights to visit his in-laws. I mentioned in the introduction that I would expect the exercises to be useful in about 75% of the time; this is one instance where they are not sufficient.

The lawyer and I had to meet formally several more times so he could figure out why he so disliked, in this case, his father-in-law. After he had understood this, he worked on some of his unresolved antagonism toward his own father, and then practiced some strategies for not overreacting to his father-in-law's very real tendency to improve on anything anyone else had to say. The lawyer was eventually able to fly without further need for medication.

The exercises

For the purpose of this discussion I will consider that the word fear can take many forms, including anxiety, agitation, phobia, anguish, alarm, consternation, panic, terror, trepidation, cold feet, trembling, and fright. These terms are not equivalent: terror and panic are certainly in a class different from agitation. Yet they share the common purpose of putting us on alert because of a real or perceived expectation of danger or threat. Because of this commonality, you may find that the exercises below will be helpful regardless of the kind of fear you might experience. Because fear can appear in different degrees of intensity, the impact of the exercises will likely vary.

You will find the exercises I introduced in chapter one repeated here, with minor variations. Exercises #2 and #3 are particularly worth learning. Preliminary research offers scientific evidence that both EFT and the tapping shortcut are effective in the treatment of fear, phobia, and other anxieties. This is consistent with the basic assumptions of subtle energy theory: disruptions at an energetic level accompany most of the disturbances we experience in life; and correcting those disruptions can produce balance and health once again. This also has the practical value of simplifying the learning curve, as the same or similar techniques and exercises serve to resolve a wide variety of problems.

Fear reduction exercise #1: Deep breathing

Review pages 25 and 26 for the procedural steps for deep breathing.

It is mostly true that you cannot be fearful and relaxed at the same time, and deep breathing is a powerful tool for creating the relaxation response. Physiologically speaking, breathing puts into operation a nervous system called the "parasympathetic." If you feel at times as if your fear is overpowering you, or getting out of control, the most immediate and natural step might simply be to notice you breathing – you are likely to find that you are breathing shallowly, quickly, and inefficiently – and then simply slow and deepen your inhalations. (If you also could do the TAT pose or tap some key EFT points, you would probably notice your breathing growing even more rhythmic and calming.)

I repeat the graph that some individuals find helpful as they practice deep breathing. The arrows on the left and right sides are longer, showing that the time spent on inhaling or exhaling lasts 2 to 3 seconds. The top and bottom are shorter to indicate that the pauses after inhaling and exhaling is only about one second. Persons who feel nervous when they are asked to pause and hold their breath (either after inhaling or even more likely after exhaling) can notice with this graph that the pause period is relatively brief.

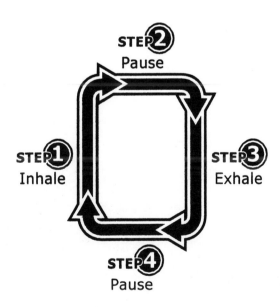

Fear reduction exercise #2: TAT

This is one of the two exercises that proved so powerful for JoAnne, and which has been useful to other persons who had trouble managing their fears and anxieties. Follow the same procedures as outlined on pages 28 through 34. Feel free to photocopy the one-page short form for TAT printed below. Because fear is often a complex emotion, I would encourage you not to be too surprised, and not necessarily to stop the procedure, in the event that you find that working with TAT opens up additional memories of fear. Frequently a person has forgotten the original event, or the worst event that caused and maintains the present day maladaptive fear symptoms. You may also find that you will feel other emotions, such as grief or anger. While you can certainly choose to stop doing TAT and to stop feeling these new emotions, you might also consider this to be fortunate for you as you will be remembering what you had forgotten, and perhaps developing new appreciation for why you first learned to feel the fear that today seems so out of place in your life.

A difference between how this exercise is presented here and how it was described in chapter one is that fears are often about events that have not yet occurred, so you can use TAT while you think ahead and visualize the *next* event that is likely to be overwhelming in its anxiety-provoking powers. Examples might be, the next time I have to make a public presentation, or the next time I have to talk with my boss, or the next time I expect to be in an intimate sexual situation with my partner. If you would like to work on future fears, follow the same TAT steps already described.

Figure 23. **TAT short form for reducing fear**

Fear reduction exercise #3: EFT[2]

The procedural steps for EFT can be found on pages 36 through 43. The one-page short form for EFT, which you may photocopy, is on page 42 and reprinted below. As I mentioned, fear can be a very complex emotion, and sometimes the best approach with EFT is to tap (or touch) all the points while being particularly attentive to any point or points that cause an especially meaningful shift for you. If there are such points, continue on that point longer to add continuing stimulation to your energy system. Memorize the points that are especially useful for you for future use.

I repeat what I just wrote about future fears: EFT seems to work equally well for fears about events that have not yet occurred. While you do the EFT exercise, concentrate on the *next* event that seems likely to provoke an exaggerated fear or phobic response and use EFT as described on pages 36 through 43.

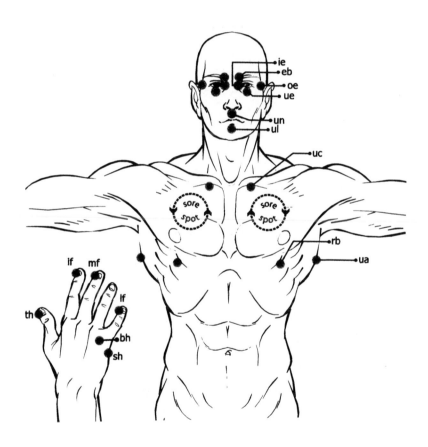

Figure 24. **EFT short form for reducing fear**

Fear reduction exercise #4: Tapping shortcut[3]

If you find some especially powerful points while doing the exercise #3, you may have discovered your own tapping shortcut for fear and anxiety. If not, you might try the next short form that has been reported by many persons to be a powerful tool for them. The figure below shows the specific points for reducing anxiety. I have added several points to the usual sequence as a result of feedback from my clients [the more common algorithm includes only the ue, ua, and uc points]. Use pages 88 and 89 together.

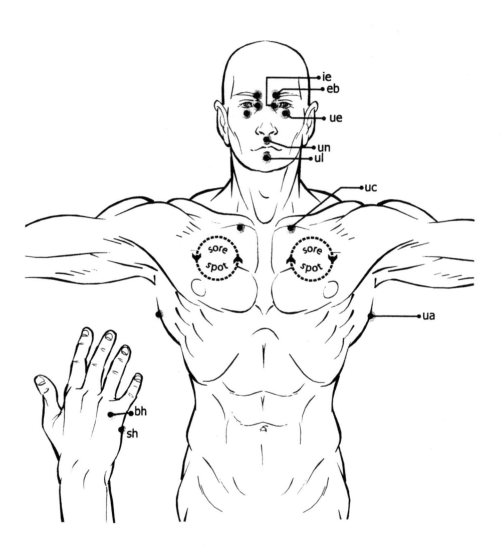

Figure 25. **Tapping shortcut for reducing fear**

• Think about what is causing your fear. Notice where you feel your fear in your body. Calculate the number that represents how fearful you feel, 0 to 10. Ten would be the most fearful you could possibly imagine.

• Then stimulate the points. (For a review of all the abbreviations, see page 39.) Using two fingers of each hand, tap the spots at the beginning of your eyebrows (**eb**), just above the bridge of your nose. Tap 5 or 6 times, firmly but not hard enough to cause pain or bruising. If you prefer to touch, *you can touch* the point at the inner corner of each eye (**ie**). If you do touch and breathe instead of tap, touch for the duration of one breath. This touch option holds true for the rest of this procedure, even though I will write only about "tapping" the points. Recall that **eb** and **ie** are the only interchangeable points.

• Tap about 10 times under the eyes (**ue**) with two fingers. Then tap about 5 to 10 times each on these points: **ua**; **un**; **ul**; again **ue**; **uc**; and **sh**. If you prefer the touch-and-breathe approach, you may touch each of these points and take a slow breath each time.

• While tapping the back of one hand (**bh**), do the 9 brain balancing procedures: close your eyes, open them, look down left, look down right, eyes in a circle, eyes in a circle opposite direction, hum any tune for 3 seconds, count to 5, and hum any tune.

• Tap about 5 to 10 times again on each of the original points: **eb**, **ue**, **ua**, **un**, **ul**, **ue**, **uc**, and **sh** points. The touch-and-breathe method substitutes the point inside the eye for the eye brow point: **ie**, **ue**, **ua**, **un**, **ul**, **ue**, **uc**, and **sh** points.

• Take another measure on the 0 to 10 scale; if there is no change, massage the sore spots (page 38) and then repeat *all of the above* until you are as free of anxiety as you wish. If you do not get to a zero, consider using one of the other exercises that I describe next.

• If after doing the procedures you notice that your anxiety has been reduced but that some still remains (for example, you have gotten to a 2 or 1 on the zero to ten scale), you might be able to lower your anxiety further by doing the eye roll: while tapping the back of one hand (**bh**), very slowly raise your eyes from floor to ceiling, keeping your head level.

As mentioned, you can notice whether one point or another seems particularly calming or meaningful for you, in which case you can continue tapping, or simply holding the point, for as long as you wish. If this does not work, try exercises #1, #2, #3, or #5.

As is the case in using TAT and EFT with future fear, you can also use this shortcut as you think about the *next* event that is likely to trigger a too much fear and anxiety or phobic response.

Fear reduction exercise #5:
Leading with your heart

When we confront a true danger and the choice we have is to flee in order to save ourselves, the heart in a normal body will speed up to send more blood, oxygen, sugars, and fats into the muscles we will need to run away. Blood is borrowed temporarily from places where it would be a luxury, such as the stomach (no need to concentrate on digestion at the moment), skin (which is why anxious people report feeling clammy), and extremities (which is why we say that a fearful person "has cold feet").

After the danger is over, a normal and healthy response would be to return the borrowed blood, and to allow the heart to rest again. A chronically anxious person does not do this, unfortunately. The heart of such a person continues to beat quickly, keeping the person in a state of alert, as if the danger has continued. And in these modern times, it would appear that a number of dangers we believe we are facing are not really matters of life and death.

The exercise I described on pages 48 through 51 will enable you to "entrain" and empower your heart so that it can eliminate unnecessary fear and anxiety. It involves placing your hand over your heart to bring your heart rate into a synchronized and coherent rhythm, and may be one of the most effective exercises for handling anxiety. I suggest you practice the exercise exactly as it is described there.

After you have completed the steps outlined on pages 48 through 51, you can refer to pages 52 and 53 for ideas on how to connect your heart's coherence to some other part of your body that is not yet coherent. Anxiety often produces strong sensation in some special part of our body, such as the neck, shoulders, or face, and for many people the stomach and respiratory areas. This sensation may appear to be residue from longstanding anxiety. If this strong sensation continues even after you notice that your heart rate has already begun to feel more balanced and coherent, you can use the heart's energy to connect with and to soothe the energy frequencies of the remaining sensation of anxiety. Because the heart's energy is stronger than that of other organs or parts of the body, you can expect that your heart coherence will gradually train the rest of the body (in this case, the area where you still notice an anxious sensation) to come into line with more optimal physiological functioning.

To make this connection happen, keep one hand over your heart and place the other heart over the place where anxiety seems to have produced tension, burning, pain, or other unpleasant sensation. Hold both hands in their respective places for several minutes, pay as close attention as you can to the feeling you experience under each hand, and notice any changes that occur. You may feel a slight relaxation in a muscle, or a tingling, or a warming or cooling sensation – all signs of healing of your anxiety. You may also notice that you begin to recall, visually or not, specific scenes from your life, perhaps a time of having forgiven or having been forgiven. And you may also notice that certain thoughts occur to you rather spontaneously, such as "I can appreciate myself", "I can appreciate differences", "I prefer love to anger." If and when these changes occur to you, remain with them for a few minutes more, with your hands in their respective places, until you are ready to face the challenges of life with your renewed spirit. Remember that it is normal to become distracted and to let negative thoughts drift into consciousness. Simply notice when this happens, and intentionally take your attention to memories of gratitude and love.

If you doubt you have the power to effect these changes, check for scientific support for this exercise in the notes[4].

Fear reduction exercise #6: The Butterfly Hug

Begin by reviewing pages 54 and 55 where the Butterfly Hug is described. I recommended caution in chapter 2 when using this exercise for the purpose of reducing anger, and I will repeat those comments here: using the Butterfly Hugh to try to reduce anxiety can sometimes stimulate other related memories that could cause you to feel even more anxious – sometimes a great deal more. This is particularly true for adults who tend to have stored away relatively numerous unresolved memories. Children do not seem so susceptible to this risk, particularly when they use the Butterfly Hug under professional supervision. Since unresolved memories of anxiety may well have had to do experiences where the person truly felt in danger of dying, the anxiety that he or she feels should never be trivialized. Let us look at how to try out this exercise experimentally.

You can begin the Butterfly Hug by noticing your anxiety, rating it on the 0 to 10 scale, then doing only one or two alternating taps to each side of your chest, first one side, then the other, then the first side, then the second, then stop. Check to see if your anxiety has changed, and if it diminished or increased, and how much. If you noticed that your anxiety suddenly surged, perhaps the process of bilateral alternating tapping poses a liability for you. Please keep in mind that perhaps 5% of my clients who use the Butterfly Hug *while thinking forgiving and loving thoughts* report that they begin to feel upset rather than peaceful, particularly when they first begin. If this happens to you, I would suggest using exercises #2 (TAT), #3 (EFT), #4 (Tapping Shortcut), or #5 (Leading with your heart).

If on the other hand the gentle tapping, first on one side and then on the other, *reduces* your feelings of anxiety, fear, anguish – or whatever the form of fear that you feel – you might consider that your anxiety is relatively isolated and is not connecting with other old memories that could exacerbate your anxiety, memories of when you felt threatened or treated in some other way that led to an anxious feeling. In this case, continue gently tapping as above. The advantage of the Butterfly Hug is that it appears to stimulate communication between the two brain hemispheres, which in turn can help you to integrate important experiences that up to that point have been disassociated from one another. In my experience, integration of our various memories and experiences is always preferable to their being disconnected.

Fear reduction exercise #7: physical activity

Physical exercise has been scientifically shown to reduce anxiety and fear[5]. Some would say that the best forms of exercise for a person hoping to reduce anxiety are those that simulate the flight response. You can experiment to see if this is true for you. Activities that look like flight would include running and bicycling. Some activities combine swift movement with pounding of the hands, arms or feet, particularly swimming, tennis, soccer, and raquetball. Experiment for yourself. Some people find a particular sport or activity that initially causes them to feel a certain emotion, and then, after a period of exertion, to experience the emotion much diminished.

Other considerations

The exercises just described are powerful for eliminating negative feelings, thoughts, and images. They are also useful for strengthening positive alternatives. Chapter 8 is dedicated to this concept of "performance enhancement".

Generally speaking, anxious individuals must pay attention to their anxiety long enough to allow the anxiety reduction exercise to do its work. In this sense a period of "exposure" to the anxiety is required as a first step.

The phrase "fear-of-fear" suggests that some people are "afraid to" experience or face their initial fear, and so end up with a double layer of fear, as it were. As another example of this phenomenon, some persons will start to feel anxious for some reason or another; they then notice their body responses, such as stomach tension, dry mouth, and flushing in their cheeks; they respond to these symptoms by inventing conclusions such as "Oh-oh, here we go again" and "It's taking over again"; these words cause even more anxious thoughts and emotions; and they are soon in a vicious cycle.

One traditional solution has been to teach these individuals to detect the earliest signs of their overreactions to their body responses and to use various techniques to stop this nonproductive thinking.

Another solution has been to offer these individuals a modest dose of anxiety-reducing medication, temporarily, to help them to reduce the fear-of-fear and allow them to work on the initial fear itself. Then, as they progress at resolving their basic anxiety, they find that it is no longer so important to use the medication. Instead of medication, some will prefer to drink a soothing tea or other natural substance.

Unfortunately, using thought stopping does not go to the cause of the anxiety, and will likely have limited value for preventing a reoccurrence. And consuming synthetic substances to reduce anxiety can work too well in the short run: by bringing relief its use is reinforced and repeated, quite possibly leading the person to use more and more of the chemical that makes them feel so much better. Persons who use medication (or other chemicals) in this way can eliminate too much of their anxiety, along with their motivation to find the causes of their anxiety. The short-term relief has unfortunate negative consequences.

The exercises in this chapter have the benefit of reducing anxiety almost immediately. The sense of relief becomes reinforced and more likely repeated. And because the person practices the exercise alone, a sense of empowerment and hope will likely follow. The individual learns to depend on his or her own personal resources. There are also no known negative side effects, not the least being economic costs. The techniques are portable, and with time tend to become more powerful, the reverse of what is found when a person comes to depend on an external resource such as a drug.

Other forms[6] of non-addictive anxiety reduction resources are meditation, autogenics, and prayer.

Notes to Chapter Three

1. Fear tends to give rise to the flight side. Selye (1974, 1976) and Everly & Lating (2003) have written about both the adaptive and maladaptive functions of fear and anxiety.

2. There is preliminary evidence for the benefit of EFT (exercise #3) in the treatment of anxiety and phobia. Carrington (2001), for example, has reported on a study that showed EFT helped persons with animal-related phobias.

3. Two doctoral students that I have advised found the tapping shortcut (exercise #4) to be effective in reducing fear and anxiety. Schoninger (2004) used the tapping shortcut to help persons with public speaking anxiety and avoidant behavior. Subjects were exposed to real-life speaking engagements during the study, and various validated instruments were used to measure changes. Compared with a speech-anxious group that did not receive treatment, the persons that were treated with the tapping shortcut reported a significant reduction in shyness, confusion, and the physiological signs of anxiety. They also expressed more interest in giving a speech in the future, and more poise in the present. Schoninger treated each of her patient-subjects for only one hour. Darby (2001) conducted a study of persons who had been unable to receive necessary medical attention because of intense needle phobias. Following treatment, subjects were exposed to a hypodermic needle and syringe and most made comments such as "It doesn't bother me now" and "It's just an instrument now." Benefits held at follow-up a month later. Given that treatment was only for one hour, we might wonder how much more benefit could result if the shortcut were made part of one's daily routine. As a final example, Leonoff (1996) used a tapping shortcut to treat anxious persons who call in for help on a radio program. He reports that virtually all of the callers said they felt better after a brief on-air treatment. We can question whether such informal reports are worthwhile. On the other hand, I applaud Leonoff for his willingness to work so publicly. After all, it might have turned out differently: most of the callers could have announced to thousands of listeners that they did *not* feel any better and that the treatment was a hoax.

4. Consult http://www.heartmath.com Serban-Schreiber (2004) for scientific references.

5. Katula, Blissmer, & McAuley (1999) have studied the effects of exercise intensity in reducing anxiety in older healthy adults.

6. Davis, Eshelman, & McCay (2004) offer ideas reducing anxiety naturally. Farrow & Herbert (1982) and Benson (1996) have written about the value of meditation for reducing anxiety. Studies at the Touch Research Institute have shown that massage therapy reduces anxiety symptoms as well (Field, 1998). Many books are available that show how to employ autogenic techniques to relax oneself naturally. Interested persons can browse through a bookstore and search for a workbook that seems most suitable.

Chapter 4:
Resolving grief and depression;
how to feel more joyful

Depression is complicated. It can be caused by a number of different factors. Let us consider a few of the causes and the different types of depression [1]:

• A chemical imbalance that developed sometime before birth or later in life;

• A temporary hormonal problem, as in post-partum depression;

• The misuse of chemicals such as alcohol or other sedating drugs;

• A recent catastrophic event that would likely affect most people, such as the loss of one or more family members;

• A traumatic loss now long past which continues to be troublesome.

The depression implied in the last example is the focus of this chapter: a sense of sadness and joylessness that endures even though the loss was experienced long ago. In some cases, the second-to-last example can also be treated successfully with the techniques I will be describing. The other types of depression noted above are *not* likely to improve significantly with these techniques.

Even though depression is complex and not always treatable with the exercises I will describe, the vast majority of the depressed people who consult me have reported at least some relief from their problems. This is significant as depression affects so many areas of our lives, and is one of the main causes of absenteeism at the workplace. Even when a depressed person arrives at work, productivity is likely to be compromised, and one's sense of meaning and passion will be severely curtailed.

How do you tell if it is worth trying these techniques to see if the depression you experience is self-treatable? The best answer: try them. In my experience they do not worsen a problem of sadness or depression. They either help or make no difference.

If you have already sought medical assistance and have not found psychotropic medicine to be very useful, or to be somewhat useful but with terrible side effects, clearly it would be recommendable to try out these techniques, as they have, as I said, no known side effects and often will help.

Or if you have tried traditional therapy and found that talking about a troublesome memory brings relief, but only temporarily, you might well find that these techniques will help. It appears that the language area of the brain is very close to a site that produces positive emotions, and it could be that by talking you were activating those positive emotions. Unfortunately, depressing memories can "bounce back" after we stop talking, a too common experience in traditional therapy. The techniques described in this book appear to be able to change brain functioning in ways and with a speed that are not usually reported in traditional talking therapy.

A third indicator is a "negative attitude". If you think of yourself as a "pessimist", if you tend to see the glass as half empty and find (or have been told) that you use negative words and thinking negative thoughts, you might well find that using the techniques will help you to change your way of thinking and talking *by way of* changing the emotions and memories that underlie those feelings and thoughts[2].

A final and very important indicator is if you can find a specific event or events that seem to trigger your depression. For example, if whenever you recall a memory of a particular loss you feel bad and sad about it, I would recommend you use these techniques because they are particularly powerful in resolving specific upsetting memories. The specific memory, by the way, could be of almost any event – it could be the loss of a loved one, or the loss of an important role or career position, or the loss of an opportunity, or the "loss of face" during a moment of shame. It is also usual for such a memory to be recalled with special intensity: we can clearly see the faces of the people involved, or feel the original emotion over and over again, or hear the hurtful words as if they were being repeated. In this sense it can be said that depressed people affected by traumatic memories have *better* memories for those events than do happy and optimistic people. Memories of this sort are particularly responsive to the techniques I discuss below.

Case example: The many sides of sadness

An experience I had taught me about the complexity of sadness.

A number of years ago I was asked to deliver the eulogy for a very dear friend of mine who had died a few days earlier. As I stood at the podium, I realized that the church was filled with what seemed to be most of the residents of the small town where she had spent her last years. I then noticed an old man stumbling in, and recognized him as the woman's estranged spouse who had done much to antagonize and belittle my friend through her life with him.

I began my eulogy, recalling how much the community had meant to her, and reminded them that she felt truly loved in her later years. I noticed that many people were wiping their eyes, and I felt tears welling up in my own, plus a pressure in my head. I stopped to take a break, wondering if I could continue talking. For some reason I then massaged my right temple for a few moments, noticed that my strong emotion subsided, and was able to continue with the eulogy. This happened once more: when I realized that something I had written seemed to affect my audience, I felt strongly affected as well, and again the emotion lessened when I rubbed my temple.

That evening I took a long run alone into a northern Minnesota snowstorm and allowed my tears to flow freely.

Years later when I studied energy psychology, I learned that the temple spot is traditionally associated with rage, and I wondered: was I actually treating my anger towards my friend's estranged husband, instead of my sadness? Is that why a few seconds of massaging alleviated my strong emotion?

I will never know for sure, of course. I offer this personal example, however, because it was so typical of what other people have told me as they worked through their own feelings of sadness and depression: these strong emotions endure because they are not simply signs of loss and grieving, but frequently a mixture of other emotions such as anger, fear, disappointment, rage, and so forth.

In the exercises that follow, I will describe strategies that can resolve many different emotions, and for that reason I believe they are particularly useful for managing emotions that are complex, such as depression.

The exercises

You will find that most of the exercises I introduced in chapter one will be repeated here as strategies for reducing depression and sadness, and for increasing joy, happiness, and optimism. Deep and slow breathing, exercise #1, assists with optimal human functioning for just about every human activity other than a true emergency. Exercises #2 through #5 follow subtle energy theory, which predicts that disruptions at an energetic level accompany most of the disturbances we experience in life (including those produced by depression) and correcting those disruptions helps to produce balance and health once again. Exercise #6, the Butterfly Hug, will be recommended here with reservations because of the risk that it can open up other memories related to loss and depression. Physical exercise, #7, is a marvelous but too often under-appreciated tool for producing the chemicals that simultaneously reduce depression and stimulate joy.

Exercise #1 for reducing depression: Deep breathing

Depressed people often breathe in a choppy and shallow manner. They can also be frequently observed bending forward, which further constricts breathing and limits lung capacity. The combination of shallow breathing and a depressive posture then give powerful instructions to the mind to think in hopeless and helpless ways. The connection between body and mind is quite intimate.

Deep and rhythmic breathing, on the other hand, puts into operation a nervous system called the "parasympathetic". If you feel at times as if your depression is controlling you, the most immediate and natural step might simply be to notice your breathing, and then simply slow and deepen your inhalations. (If you also could do the TAT pose or tap some key EFT points, you would probably notice your breathing growing even more rhythmic and calming.)

Because depressed people rarely breathe in an optimal way, I will mention several options for breathing practice. The goal in each case is to increase the ability to take a deep breath and to feel the intake of air first in the stomach, then the lungs, and finally in the upper chest

Option 1: Begin this option by reviewing pages 25 and 26 for the basic procedural steps, using the oblong box to demonstrate graphically the inhale, pause, exhale, and pause. The top and bottom arrows are shorter, indicating that the pause after inhaling or exhaling lasts only one second. Some people who become nervous when asked to hold their breath may feel relieved to notice that the pause lasts only a second.

Option 2: Begin by inhaling (or ask the other person to inhale) as you slowly count to eight. You can count as follows: one-thousand-one, one-thousand-two, one-thousand-three, and so forth. If your lungs fill before you reach the eight, simply hold your breath for the remainder of the count. Then exhale for another count of eight, again holding the breath if you empty the lungs before arriving at eight. *If eight is too long*, begin with the count of four or five, and gradually increase both numbers up to eight. The practice effect of doing this procedure will most likely reduce the depressed feelings gradually.

Option 3: This procedure is as above except the person gradually increases the time of the exhale until it is *twice as long* as the inhale. This could begin with three counts inhale and six exhale, and gradually be increased. Some people will find it possible with practice to count up to eight (or one-thousand-eight) on the inhale and sixteen (or one-thousand-sixteen on the exhale. Remember that the person always determines the pace, and that counting the final numbers can be done while holding the breath either at the end of the inhale or at the end of the exhale.

Exercise #2 for reducing depression: TAT

Follow the same procedures as outlined on pages 28 through 34. Notice in particular the specific instructions that Tapas has suggested on pages 31 through 33, and see which have particular power for you. The references to "I deserve to live" and "I can accept love" have special importance for many depressed persons.

Depression is often a mixture of (and sometimes a cover-up for) other emotions. I would encourage you not to be too surprised, and not necessarily to stop the TAT procedure, in the event that while you are working with TAT you notice that you recall other memories and feel other emotions. These unpredicted experiences may stimulate feelings such as rage, which may feel unfamiliar and ever frightening. While you can certainly choose to stop doing TAT and to stop feeling, you might also consider this to be fortunate for you as it will be a chance to remember what you had forgotten, and perhaps allow you to develop new insight into why you have been unable to shake your depression.

Figure 26. **TAT short-form for reducing depression**

Exercise #3 for reducing depression: EFT

Depression can be a very complex emotion, and sometimes the best approach using energy treatment is to tap *all* the emotional points on the body, which EFT should cover. Be particularly attentive to any of the EFT points that cause a particularly meaningful shift for you. You might keep tapping on that point longer to add continuing stimulation to your energy system. Remember that you can also simply *touch* each point during the length of one breath, which makes it less obvious to do EFT while in public. Memorize the points that are especially useful for you for future use. You may review the EFT protocol on pages 36 through 43, and then photocopy the one-page short form on page 44, figure 13. With practice, many of my clients prefer to carry with them only the picture of all the points, which they tap or touch during the day as necessary. The picture is reprinted next.

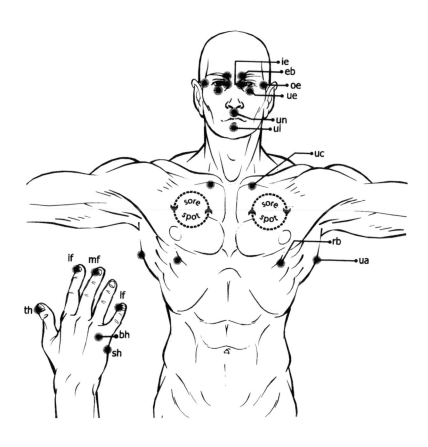

Figure 27. **EFT short form for reducing depression**

Exercise #4 for reducing depression: Tapping shortcut

If while doing exercise #3, EFT, you find certain points to be particularly helpful, you may already have discovered your own tapping shortcut. If not, you might try the next short form that Callahan discovered for depression, one that has been reported by many persons to be a powerful tool for them. The figure below shows the specific points for reducing depression and for increasing joyfulness. Connect the figure below with the instructions on the facing page.

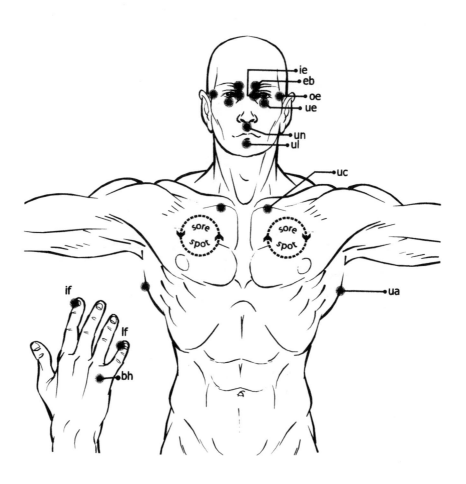

Figure 28. **Tapping shortcut for reducing depression**

• Think about what is causing you to feel depressed. Notice how you feel. Determine a number from 0 to 10 that represents how depressed you feel, 0 to 10, with 10 the worst.

• Using two fingers of each hand, tap the points on page 102: Tap first, about 10 times, at the beginning of your eyebrows (**eb**). If you prefer the "touch and breathe", you can instead touch the point at the inside corner of each eye (**ie**) for the duration of one breath [recall that eb and ie are the two interchangeable points].

• Using two fingers, tap about 10 times (or touch and breathe) on each of the following points: **oe, ue, un, ul, ua, uc, lf, uc, if,** and **uc.** Refer to page 39 if you would like to review what each of these pairs of letters stands for.

• Then tap repeatedly, for approximately 30 to 60 seconds, on the back of the hand point (**bh**) which often will release strong feelings of loss and sadness. If this happens to you, do not be surprised because your response is perfectly normal. It may be that this release is facilitated because the previous meridian point taps resolved some of the other emotions that were interfering with the experience of depression. My example about how sadness can often be an extremely complex emotion may be relevant here.

• While continuing to tap the back of one hand (**bh**), do the 9 brain balancing procedures: close your eyes, open them, look down left, look down right, eyes in a circle, eyes in a circle opposite direction, hum any tune for three seconds, count to five, and hum any tune. The 9 brain balancing procedures are detailed on page 42.

• Repeat the above sequences as long and as often as necessary: **oe, ue, un, ul, ua, uc, lf, uc, if,** and **uc.** Tap again the **bh** point repeatedly if you still notice feelings of sadness.

• Take another measure on the 0 to 10 scale. If you do not notice a continuing and positive change, or if you are unable to eliminate as much of your depression as you would like, massage the sore spots (as described on page 40) and repeat the entire exercise.

• Finish with the eye roll: while tapping the back of one hand (**bh**), very slowly raise your eyes from floor to ceiling, keeping your head level.

As mentioned, you can notice whether one point or another seems particularly calming or meaningful for you, in which case you can continue tapping, or simply holding the point, for as long as you wish. If this TFT shortcut does not work, try exercises #1, #2, #3, or #5.

Exercise #5 for reducing depression: Leading with your heart

So often depression results from loss of a loved one, which can falsely teach us to believe that we are no longer loveable. Prolonged depressive behavior, in turn, can cause others to distance themselves from us or to criticize us, which ends up fulfilling our worst fears and prophecies. Fortunately, it appears more and more that we can choose the direction of this cause-effect relationship. On pages 48 through 51 I described a very simple exercise for "entraining" and empowering your heart. It involves placing your hand over your heart to bring your heart rate into a synchronized and coherent rhythm, and may be one of the most effective exercises for handling depression. I suggest you practice the exercise exactly as it is described there.

After you have completed the steps outlined on pages 48 through 51, you can refer to pages 52 and 53 for ideas on how to connect your heart's coherence to some other part of your body that is not yet coherent. Depression often produces strong sensation in some special part of our body, such as the neck, shoulders, stomach, or face. If this strong sensation continues even after you notice that your heart rate has already begun to feel more steady, you can use the heart's energy to connect with the energy frequencies of the remaining sensation of depression. Because the heart's energy is stronger than that of other parts of the body, you can expect that your heart coherence will gradually train the rest of the body (in this case, the area where you still notice a sense of depression) to come into line with more optimal physiological functioning.

To make this connection happen, keep one hand over your heart and place the other heart over the place where depression seems to have produced tension. Sometimes the feeling will be in the area of your heart, so place both hands there. Hold both hands in their respective places for several minutes, pay as close attention as you can to the feeling you experience under each hand, and notice any changes that occur. You may feel a slight relaxation in a muscle, or a tingling, or a warming or cooling sensation – all signs of healing of your depression. You may also notice that you begin to recall, visually or not, specific scenes from your life, perhaps a time of having loved or having been loved, or the opposite – not loving and not feeling loved. And you may also notice that certain thoughts occur to you rather spontaneously, such as "I can appreciate myself", "I can love myself", "I prefer love to hate." If these changes occur, stay with them for a few minutes, with your hands in their respective places, until you are ready to face the challenges of life with your renewed spirit. Remember that it is normal to become distracted and to let negative thoughts drift into consciousness. Simply notice when this happens, and intentionally take your attention to memories of gratitude and love.

If you doubt you have the power to effect these changes, check for scientific support for this exercise in the notes[3].

Exercise #6 for reducing depression: The Butterfly Hug

Begin by reviewing pages 54 and 55 where the Butterfly Hug is described. Be careful when using this exercise for the purpose of reducing depression, as it can sometimes stimulate other related memories that could cause you to feel even more sad – sometimes a great deal more. This is particularly true for adults who tend to have stored away relatively numerous unresolved memories. Children do not seem so susceptible to this risk, particularly when they use the Butterfly Hug under professional supervision.

You can begin the Butterfly Hug by noticing your depression, rating it on the 0 to 10 scale, then doing only one or two alternating taps to each side of your chest, first one side, then the other, then the first side, then the second, then stop. Check to see if your depression has changed, and if it diminished or increased, and how much. If you noticed that your depression suddenly deepened, perhaps the process of bilateral alternating tapping poses a liability for you. Please keep in mind that perhaps 5% of my clients who use the Butterfly Hug *while thinking forgiving and loving thoughts* report that they begin to feel upset rather than peaceful, particularly when they first begin. If this happens to you, I would suggest using exercises #2 (TAT), #3 (EFT), #4 (Tapping Shortcut), or #5 (Leading with your heart).

If on the other hand the gentle tapping, first on one side and then on the other, *reduces* your feelings of depression – or whatever the form of depression that you feel – you might consider that your depression is relatively isolated and is not connecting with other old memories that could exacerbate the memories of when you felt unloved or unloving. In this case, continue gently tapping as above. The advantage of the Butterfly Hug is that it appears to stimulate communication between the two brain hemispheres, which in turn can help you to integrate important experiences that up to that point have been disassociated from one another. In my experience, integration of our various memories and experiences is always preferable to their being disconnected.

Exercise #7 for reducing depression: Physical activity

The general concepts of physical activity were presented on pages 56 and 57.

Let me summarize a few of the scientific studies that suggest that exercise is a powerful antidote to depression, and why.

• A study by Duke University researchers found that patients with major depression who exercised regularly reported declines in their depression equal to those of a group that took antidepressants. Additionally, the exercisers were less likely that the medication group to relapse six months following treatment. Patients who continued to exercise during follow-up were 50% less likely to become depressed than those who didn't exercise. The exercisers were not marathoners: exercise was defined as brisk walking three times a week[4].

• Exercise seems both to heal depression and to prevent it. A group of persons without diagnosed depression was studied over a period of 25 years. During the course of the study, those persons who were exercising at the beginning of the study were much less likely to experience depression during the next 25 years compared to those who were not exercising[5].

• It may be that exercise reduces depression by producing endorphins, the body's natural morphine. In this regard, exercise may also be a good antidote for persons who use drugs to experience well-being and satisfaction. This is the sense of the term "natural high," or "runners' high" often mentioned by elite athletes[6].

• Finally, there is preliminary evidence that people who exercise regularly show greater cardiac coherence than do people who do not exercise regularly[7]. As I discussed above on pages 48 to 51 in the context of the "leading with your heart" exercise, and on page 104 in this chapter, heart coherence is definitely correlated with physical and psychological health.

Other considerations for reducing depression

The exercises described so far – powerful as they are for eliminating negative feelings, thoughts, and images – are also useful for strengthening and enhancing positive alternatives. Chapter 8 is dedicated to this concept of "performance enhancement".

It may be obvious that using alcohol or other sedating chemicals can exacerbate depression. It is one of those peculiar paradoxes: a person takes a drink to feel better, and in fact may feel better for a period of time. In the long run the good feelings dissipate, and the person is left with one more memory of failure. In this sense, substance abuse support groups designed to help the person forgo a drink or other medicating chemical may be useful.

However, anything designed purely to fight an urge is not something I can recommend, be it a self-support group, "inspirational" reading, or prayer that is designed to pump a person up. The metaphor I mentioned in the introduction about the hiker with the backpack is relevant here. It would be much more efficient for the hiker to remove the useless backpack, and *only then* to practice being more fit. Too many depressed people, in my experience, continue to walk around with their backpacks loaded with memories of loss and failure. They may try desperately to spur themselves into joy or happiness before they remove the causes of their depression. This attitude is also evident in the advice that well-meaning people may give a depressed person: "It's all in your head", or "Mind over matter", or "It must mean you have too little faith." There are also those clever but often unhelpful vignettes some people tell, again often with good intentions: "Two men looked through prison bars; one saw mud, the other stars." Another is: "What doesn't kill you will make you strong." The error is in assuming that *simply thinking* positively is enough to *cause* changes in how a person feels and acts. We now know, however, that the brain of a depressed person will sometimes simply not respond to positive talking and thinking, nor to cajoling, badgering, or shaming! The good news, on the other hand, is that the techniques just described have the power to change the brains of many depressed individuals, so that their attempts to think and talk positively will actually have their intended effect.

Nutrition is being increasingly identified as a treatment for depression. More and more is being written about how depression can be caused or aggravated by imbalances in tryptophan, serotonin, melatonin, phosfolipids, and so forth – and how these elements can be supplemented with dietary change, in turn reducing depressive symptoms. I limit my comments here to one particular dietary factor that seems particularly important, namely omega-3 fatty acids, which appear to prevent and treat depression. Omega-3 fatty acids are found in fish oil, and the algae that fish eat. The most reliable fish sources are mackerel, anchovies (whole, not the salted ones on pizza), sardines, herring, tuna, haddock, and trout[8]. Vegetarian sources are flax seeds and flaxseed oil, canola, and all green leafy vegetables[9].

The reports and books by Dr. Andrew Stoll at Harvard convincingly support the use of omega-3 fish oils in stabilizing mood swings in persons with manic-depression[10]. Apparently, many persons with this disorder respond as well as or better than patients who take psychotropic medications.

These positive comments about omega-3 are somewhat compromised by other factors, for example the rise of toxins in the food chain. Women in countries with the highest consumption of fish and the highest omega-3 levels in their breast milk are much less likely to report post-partum depression or persistent "baby blues"[11]. Unfortunately, certain kinds of fish have become so contaminated with mercury in certain areas of the world that pregnant women and young children are advised to consume them sparingly, or to avoid them altogether[12].

Where omega-3 sources are safe, however, their use is to be recommended, not only as an antidote to depression, but also as a means to promote functioning of the immune and cardiac systems.

Light treatment is a second factor that deserves attention here, as this intervention is also something we can easily control. The observation that certain persons seem to feel normally alert and happy during long summer days, but become depressed during the shorter winter months, led the American Psychiatric Association to construct the diagnosis called Seasonal Affective Disorder, SAD for short. Treatment, in turn, involves exposing oneself to light that can be artificially manufactured but that produces the kind of light units that can mimic natural sunlight and balance circadian rhythms. One company sells not only light boxes, but also an alarm clock that wakens the sleeper to a simulated sunrise, which reportedly helps to start the day in a better mood and feeling more refreshed[13]. My clients who use these devices generally report that they are useful, though not necessarily sufficient, and they supplement their self-treatment by doing the energy methods I have described as exercises 2, 3, and 4 in the previous chapters.

Massage has also been found to reduce depression according to studies conducted at the Touch Research Institute[14]. It is believed that the kind of massage involving deep tissue manipulation stimulates pressure receptors, which in turn release chemicals that combat depression. Benefits, however, appear to be relatively short-lived and ongoing treatment is generally required. Because not everyone can afford regular visits to massage professionals, this approach has relatively less merit than the self-use techniques already discussed (unless you live with a masseur or masseuse).

There is preliminary evidence that **homeopathic** remedies help persons with major depression[15]. In about 80% of the controlled studies on homeopathy, persons with mental or psychological disorders improved. It is noteworthy that these were patients with a history of poor or partial response to conventional therapies[17].

Notes to Chapter Four

1. Cummings (1999) has pointed out that some forms of depression respond better to medications, others to psychotherapy (i.e., the exercises in this book). Even a severely depressed person may require medication but may also benefit from doing the exercises.

2. The underlying principle of cognitive therapy might be called "we are what we think" or "thoughts control emotions". This treatment approach can help a depressed individual examine and modify the negative beliefs that maintain depressive symptoms. Albert Ellis and his colleagues (Ellis, 1975; Ellis, Young, & Lockwood, 1987) and Aaron Beck (1967, 1976) among the pioneers of this type of therapy, and as far as I can tell much of the early writings remain valid and up-to-date. Combining principles of cognitive therapy with the exercises in this book, particularly #2 through #5, can enhance the positive impact of both.

3. See McCraty & Barrios-Choplin (1998) on heart rate variability and emotional experience.

4. Blumenthal and associates (2000) documented the effects of exercise training on persons with major depression.

5. Paffenbarger and associates (1994) have studied the effect of exercise in the prevention of depression later in life.

6. Endorphins, the natural morphine-like chemical in our bodies, can be released through vigorous exercise. As has been noted many times in this book, endorphins can also be released through stimulation of the subtle energy circuits in our bodies. See appendix A for further information on acupuncture.

7. Furlan and associates (1993) have studied the effects of exercise and athletic training on neural mechanisms controlling heart rate.

8. See *The Omega-3 Connection*, (Stoll, 2001).

9. Flaxseed oil can become toxic (and bitter) unless refrigerated and protected from light. Freshly pressed oil that is protected from heat and light is recommended.

10. For information on the power of omega-3 fatty acids in reducing symptoms of depression, see Stoll (2001) and Zanarini & Frankenburg (2003).

11. The importance of fatty acid consumption during pregnancy to prevent the baby blues following birth has been studied by and Hibbeln (1998) and Hornstra et al. (2000)

12. The FDA Consumer Advisory publishes mercury warnings: [http://www.cfsan.fda.gov/~dms/admehg.html].

13. Just as diminished daytime light can cause certain people to feel depressed, so can light management during the winter reduce depression. In addition, the timing of light can affect mood, as is evident in jet lag. See Haggerty and colleagues (2001) for information on seasonal affective disorder (SAD). Avery et al., (2001) and Levitt et al. (1991) have studied how light treatment can improve the symptoms of SAD.

14. Field (1998) has reported that children traumatized by natural disasters were able to reduce their symptoms of depression when treated with massage therapy.

15. See articles in *The Lancet* by Linde, Clausius, & Ramirez (1997) and Reilly et al., (1994) for information about the homeopathic treatment of depression.

16. See Bassman & Uellendahl (2003). Information about competent homeopathic practitioners can be found on the website for the National Center for Homeopathy: [http://www.homeopathic.org/find.htm].

Chapter 5:
Trauma: When memories continue to trouble us

Background

There is overlap between this chapter and the previous ones; frequently persons who report problems with stress, anger, and phobias will also be able to identify early memories that continue to haunt them and that seem to explain why they feel stressed, angry, and anxious in the present. I use the word "trauma" to mean "an experience that was so upsetting that it continues to trouble us." Such experiences remain in our memories even though some of the time we do not think about them. However, from time to time something happens that reminds us of what we experienced, or that "triggers" the memory. This tendency to be affected in the present by an earlier event that is still "hot" also makes it difficult to focus on the future. Let me comment on each of these components in detail: past, present, and future.

The past refers to an incident that in some way was troubling and continues to be troubling. Most of the time, and for most people, difficult events get worked through naturally and spontaneously: we think about them, talk about them, wait for time to heal, sometimes pray over them – and eventually put them in their place in the past. However, for reasons still not well understood, sometimes a difficult event will stay with us and continue to generate the same feelings and thoughts and images that we originally experienced. A frightening event that is still unprocessed, for example, might keep us in a state of alert long after the true danger has passed. This is the notion of a traumatic memory. We do know that the emotional or limbic part of the brain is involved here, but cannot say for certain why it sometimes functions well and sometimes gets frozen, as it were. When a natural disaster occurs, for example, we do know that some people will be made stronger by it, and others will be weakened, but we cannot accurately predict which person will respond in which way.

Sometimes an apparently innocuous event will continue to be more troubling than a life-threatening event, and it is also difficult to explain this phenomenon. For example, a person might survive a war, be strengthened by a near drowning, even seek out high-risk sports for adventure – and then be "devastated" by a social rejection or a failure to be promoted. In other cases, a person may have no conscious memory of a traumatic event, yet be plagued by physical reminders of that event, as if it were a purely "body memory."

What we have learned is to listen to a traumatized person's story, and to allow that much more can be understood if we allow that perception is all-important, and that trauma is largely a subjective (though very real) experience[1].

The present is affected in two main ways. First, the traumatized person will report having symptoms that the unfinished memory maintains, such as sleep disturbance, worry, weight changes, distractibility, anxiety, depression, and irritability. Additionally, life feels hard. Many traumatized persons (most of those I just described) can still be successful in may ways, though they tend to report that life is not very joyful, nor natural, nor energizing, and even when life goes well, the person may fear that "this cannot last." Those who suffer severe traumas often will take self-destructive steps to forget or avoid the memories; many people, for example, use chemicals, or work, or even shopping to distract themselves from remembering. Some of these persons can be said to be suffering from post-traumatic stress disorder or PTSD[2]. Whatever the level of symptoms, they generally are maintained by the emotional brain and cannot be willed or reasoned away – nor can they be easily talked away. For these reasons, it is not helpful to tell a traumatized person to "get over it" because "it's all in your head", nor is it always useful to remind them that "It's not the event itself, but what you think about it that's hurting you". On the contrary, such comments often worsen matters, as the person now has to manage the sense of shame and inadequacy at being unable to heal the memory.

Secondly, any number of stimuli in the present that *should not be particularly bothersome* nonetheless have the power to *trigger* various and inappropriate reactions, such as hypersensitivity, panic, a heightened startle response, and so forth. War veterans will often report being easily startled or angered by sounds, such as the backfiring of a car, that are themselves neutral. A person still affected by a failure may be hyper-reactive to the slightest criticism. And someone still processing a loss may cry through soap operas.

The future may be difficult to imagine, plan for, or wonder about, as the person seems so stuck in the past and present. Sometimes a procrastinator deep inside fears failure, and puts things off in a superstitious way, as if getting one's hopes up can change the future. Or a person may wait for things to happen rather than be proactive because of an old belief about not being worthy.

Let me give a few examples from my clients about how the past, present, and future can become compromised:

• A community leader appears to observers to be a self-confident and successful man. They do not know that he feels guilty every time he smiles, as it reminds him of the time he witnessed a fatal accident and found himself spontaneously laughing; he knows now it was in response to his panic, but his logic does not help him.

• A nun has insomnia because, she says, nighttime reminds her of the time she was unkind to a childhood friend, and a teacher had wondered aloud, "I don't know how your conscience can let you sleep".

• A successful executive actively avoids another promotion because she fears repeating a time she was unceremoniously demoted, a memory that still can cause her to blush with shame.

• A war veteran volunteers at the local VA, though does not look for competitive employment. He says that if his life got any better he would feel disloyal to his buddies who died in battle.

• A bright university instructor has reached a professional plateau. The professor is seen by colleagues as quite defensive; little do they know that she is actually terrified by criticism, which is a reminder of past memories of living in a home with cold parents and cruel siblings.

• A person begins to feel butterflies in his stomach every time he is in a group of competent peers or bosses, then pays more and more attention to the butterflies until he is in the midst of a full-blown panic attack.

In each of these scenarios there is a stimulus that *should be* fairly neutral but that, instead, triggers a stronger negative feeling. Respectively, the triggers are *a smile, nighttime, the very thought of a promotion, the very thought of success, criticism,* and *an internal sensation.* Each trigger has power because it is fueled by one or more memories of trauma that still affect the person, which is to say that the memories were never processed. As a result, the individual suffers a limited life (don't smile, don't feel, don't be successful) and a curtailed view of the future.

The good news in this chapter is that consistent practice with the exercises I will describe can heal the emotional sting of traumatic memories, reduce the power of triggers, and allow greater freedom to dream about the future. With continued practice, many persons will be able to neutralize entirely the emotional part of the memory. That is, they may continue to be able to recall what happened, but the event will no longer trouble them.

There are now several powerful psychotherapy methods that help such a person to get updated and to leave the past in the past. One of these is called EMDR (for Eye Movement Desensitization and Reprocessing, (in Appendix A you can find information on EMDR and on how to contact EMDR practitioners). The science supporting EMDR has convinced the American Psychological Association to recommend EMDR for treatment of traumatic memories. However, EMDR should be experienced only under the guidance of a trained and experienced professional therapist, usually in individual treatment. And not everyone is ready to enter professional treatment.

There is further good news. Techniques in addition to EMDR are now available that can be practiced without professional help. I refer, of course, to those I have described already in earlier chapters. These same techniques can be helpful to persons who would like to treat themselves to see if they can lessen the power of their troublesome memories all by themselves. In the remainder of this chapter I will describe them again, now within the context of trauma.

First, let us look at a list of some of the more common symptoms that my clients have reported as being caused and maintained by troublesome memories of past traumatic events, and which often can be treated effectively with the techniques.

- Depression (or loss, grief, sadness)
- Lack of joy (which is qualitatively different from depression) and motivation
- Lack of concentration and distractability
- The stress reactions I discussed in chapter 1
- Irritability, impatience, and general grumpiness, moodiness, hyper-sensitivity
- The kinds of anxiety and fear that I already discussed in chapter 3.
- Physical pain, including chronic pain
- Allergies and asthma
- Addictive urges

If you use the exercises to treat yourself for any of these symptoms, and find that you are successful, you can continue what you started. If you are partially or not at all successful, I will refer you to one of the practitioners in appendix A for personal assistance. The exercises can be especially powerful when taught be professional coaches or therapists. Trauma treated with one of the techniques in this book generally report partial or complete healing of their traumatic memories, and generally after a relatively short period of time of treatment.

What is it like to be burdened by a memory? I close this background section with a quote from a successful corporate manager for employee health and safety. His commentary on how the past can intrude into the present is one of the most articulate I have read.

Adjusting my rear view mirror

Experiencing the past as if it is still going on in the present reminds me of a car analogy. The car isn't broken, but there are things in the past that, at times, have varying levels of distraction. The rear view mirror allows me to look at those things in the past but keep them in perspective. Occasionally, the past may be more intense (like someone behind me with their bright lights on at night), and the distraction becomes overwhelming and impedes my ability to focus forward. It's those times that I need to adjust my rear view mirror (such as flipping the lever on the mirror). The past is still visible, as it needs to be, but is manageable and allows me to focus on where I'm going. The goal is to figure out how and when to flip that lever.

David Gillespie, 2003[3]

As I think of David's analogy, I am reminded of hundreds of people with whom I have worked who might have said something similar: "My 'car' is tuned (i.e., I have good skills, I work hard, treat others well as I promote my own success) but there are things that seem out of my control that don't allow me to take full advantage of all of my hard work. The energy exercises help to adjust the mirror so that when I see the past, I recall that it is just a memory. Sometimes I wish that what happened had not happened, but it did. I can still recall it. But now it is faded, and does not interfere with who I am and what I do today." Others might add, "My mirror is now permanently flipped to fade mode."

Let me introduce the exercises with stories of how two high achievers "flipped the mirror" on their memories of failure, put the past behind them, and freed up their energies for the present and future.

Case example:
The executive-in-training pursued by a failure

I was asked to coach a manager who had until recently been on track to become a vice president of his software company. Several months before our first contact, he had been told to attend a week-long "executive training" experience. He arrived at the training site to find that 15 other men and women from other company branches had also been invited. None of the 16 had been warned that they were to be tested in a sort of "survival of the fittest" experience, to include academic and outdoor competition with one another. They were told that they were the best and brightest the company had. They were then informed that there were only four VP positions available: 12 could not be promoted in the foreseeable future. This challenging setting was described as a "real life" experience. They were assured that they could leave at any point and continue in their present careers with the company; that the trainers would write reports only on the four strongest candidates; and that the performance results of the other 12, including information on whether they completed the course or not, would be kept confidential. Not surprisingly, all stayed.

My coaching client began the course as an average performer, which meant that he was immediately behind the four front runners. Instead of using his slow start to strategize a more effective approach to the unfamiliar challenges, he became more and more nervous, began to hear old messages about being "not good enough", and slept poorly. He also said that he thought he began to make self-fulfilling prophecies, such as "I'm going to screw up", and in an orienteering experience he read his compass backwards. He left after day three. The training team never reported his early departure to his company, but my client took a deep sense of failure back with him that eroded his confidence and lowered his productivity.

He returned to work fairly despondent. His supervisor told him to ignore the gossip that had already reached the company corridors and to focus on his strengths. The supervisor was actually fairly sympathetic, and called the training program a farce. But as so often happens in these cases, the memory of failure had already become embedded in my client's nervous system, and at that stage words have limited power.

In our first two-hour coaching session he immediately told me about this experience that, in his mind, was about to derail him. We agreed that we would need to deal with this truly traumatic memory before he could even attend to other issues, and I taught him TAT to use while we planned for a second meeting the following month. We would stay in touch by email in the meantime.

He practiced the TAT several times a day for about 20 minutes, and emailed me about his improving condition. By the time I saw him again a month later, he had difficulty recounting the experience that had been so vivid and emotionally disturbing barely 30 days earlier. At one point we laughed about his "memory loss", and he agreed to have me read my previous notes to him. He nodded as I read, and said he recalled the story but it was almost as if I was reading an account of some third party. For the rest of that coaching session he told me about how his life had changed for the better.

Case example: the imperfect piano player

I was contracted to do a site visit in Singapore to coach a banker on her career plans, and during our first meeting we talked about how she could delegate certain tasks so as to free herself up to meet with her direct reports in different cities. At the end of that meeting we had a few minutes to talk about life balance. Still single, she spoke of how she took time to remain physically fit, about her dedication to her parents and extended family, and how important it was to her to find time to develop her spiritual life. Almost in passing she said she also played the piano – very well, she said, but only when she was absolutely alone in her apartment.

At the second meeting a few days later we spoke only about her piano playing. She said she was terrified of making a mistake on the keyboard, and that simply hearing sounds from neighboring apartments was enough to cause her to freeze up, which inevitably caused her to make a mistake and end her playing. It was natural enough for us to connect her piano playing to the rest of her life, and she immediately realized that her difficulties in delegating tasks to others was another example of fear of failure: she doubted they would perform the tasks as well as she did, that their mistakes would reflect poorly on her, and that she would not be able to tolerate the shame of failure. Eventually people would realize she was a fraud and her carefully laid plans to become a successful manager or executive would collapse around her. I asked where she had learned that she had to be perfect, and she answered, "It would be more economical were I to tell you where I did *not* learn that message."

116

I reminded her that I was a clinical as well as an organizational psychologist, and asked if she would like to learn some simple exercises that might be helpful. We had an extended session so that I could teach her several techniques from energy psychology. She laughed and said it was most paradoxical that I should travel to Singapore to teach her about Asian acupuncture concepts. On the other hand, we had immediate rapport on a topic that not infrequently raises eyebrows elsewhere in the world.

While she imagined playing the piano, I taught her to tap the EFT points. Over the course of an hour, she remembered past moments from her music lessons, cried as she revisited memories of error and shame, and slowly began to feel better and better as she imagined playing in public. When we completed our session she said she felt no anxiety anymore when she thought of her piano. "At least for the time being", she said. I told her that we would never know until she actually put it into practice – just as she would not know if she could delegate until she actually assigned a task to her direct reports, left them alone, and found she no longer felt anxious about it. She then gave herself a dare. "I know you will be meeting with the rest of my group for dinner this evening. There's a piano in the nearby bar. Maybe it's time for me to face this. Maybe it's time to play in public."

A long story made short: she did, indeed, play the hotel piano in front of a small group of trusted friends that evening, the first public event in 25 years, she told me later. She began by asking them if she they would help her in an "experiment", and explained the EFT exercises and her piano-playing phobia. One of her friends shared that he had once thought to become an acupuncturist, but it seemed so "stereotypical" so he turned to accounting. Someone else noted how strange it was for them to be learning an Asian healing method from a North American – and we had a good laugh about that. My client then asked if she could make one more request: would they all join her while she did one more EFT routine? Someone said it would be good to return to their "roots" for a change. More laughter. I led them all in the energy exercises for a few minutes before she began to play. She made her first mistake within the first minute, and stopped playing. I intervened and said it was such a great opportunity for her to practice making mistakes and living with the fact that she is human. "What do you think?" I asked her friends. They responded with cheers and support. My client cried just a little, and returned to playing. Within another minute she made another mistake, but this time continued to play. Her friends gathered a bit closer, encouraging her to continue, telling her it was beautiful, saying her mistakes were nothing. With a few more mistakes she completed a beautiful classical piece. She was bathed in applause and amidst many tears of joy. A month later, after I had returned to my home, I received an email. Among other comments was this: "I haven't given any formal recitals, but I find that I can play in front of my friends in my home, something I could never imagine doing before. I also finally went to the dentist. I used those energy exercises that I learned to manage my perfectionism and found they worked equally well with dental phobia! My dentist has been trying for several years to get me to visit him. Of course I had to tell him all about the exercises. He also had a good laugh about our having to learn Asian healing from a non-Asian."

117

The exercises

My traumatized clients report that their memories cause them to feel fear, so the exercises I describe will be similar to the ones you encountered in the previous chapter. Emotions other than fear can also appear, and I encourage you to be open to all possibilities. I will introduce the exercises as tools for "trauma reduction", though you can think of them as ways to "reduce fear of failure" or to "resolve traumatic memories" or something similar, depending on the memory you wish to heal and the future plans that you want to enhance.

A cautionary note: The exercises have proven generally helpful in resolving mild to moderately troubling traumatic memories. Think of the two cases as guidelines. People report that the problem gets better or does not change, but does not generally worsen to the point where it is intolerable. The vast majority of persons I have worked with have not reported risks, so I conclude that the exercises are not inherently dangerous.

However, some traumatic memories are so powerful that it is not likely for a person working alone with these exercises – and without professional guidance – to have much chance of resolving them. Additionally, there is a slight chance that using some of the exercises could cause the person to feel somewhat worse as a result, rather than better.

One way to begin this chapter is to reduce the possibility of risk to yourself by first listening to guided imagery tapes or CDs on your own. As an example of how to proceed, I offer the following scenario using CDs produced by Belleruth Naparstek and available from www.healthjourneys.com.

First, begin with a tape designed to build inner resources, one that focuses only on the positive. One of Belleruth's tapes for this purpose is called "A meditation to help you improve self-confidence." I find the positive content combined with her soothing voice and background music to be powerful and positive. Listen to this (or a similar tape or CD) repeatedly until you feel powerful enough to confront your traumatic memories. Only you can be the judge of when you feel prepared.

Then listen to her CD designed to help you confront trauma (called "A guided meditation for healing trauma – PTSD"). The first six minutes or so continue the theme of building inner resources. Then comes her invitation to the listener to enter which she calls the "deep pockets of sorrow" around the heart. At this point follow her (and my) recommendations to *continue only as long as you feel comfortable.* This tape has been carefully researched and proven to help in the healing of trauma, but it can also test a person's ability to manage the feelings and memories that can arise. *Whether you are listening to her tape or proceeding with this chapter, please trust yourself to know when to take a break from your processing.*

118

Trauma reduction exercise #1: Deep breathing

Deep breathing is a powerful tool for creating the relaxation response. Physiologically speaking, breathing puts into operation a nervous system called the "parasympathetic." If you feel at times as if the recall of a memory, or the thought of a possible future event, is overpowering you, the most immediate and natural step might simply be to notice your breathing – you are likely to find that you are breathing shallowly, quickly, and inefficiently. What you can choose to do then is simply slow and deepen your inhalations. (If you also could do the TAT pose or tap some key EFT points, you would probably notice your breathing growing even more rhythmic and calming.)

In chapter one I noted that deep breathing, quite paradoxically, will at times produce even greater upset in a person. This is a possibility when one works with traumatic memories. If deep breathing makes you feel even more troubled, return to what is normal breathing for you. This could signal that the memory is too strong for you to work on alone, and that you might be advised to seek a professional to assist you.

Because people rarely breathe in an optimal way when recalling unresolved traumatic memories, I will mention several options for breathing practice. The goal in each case is to increase the ability to take a deep breath and to feel the intake of air first in the stomach, then the lungs, and finally in the upper chest.

Option 1: Begin this option by reviewing pages 25 and 26 for the basic procedural steps, using the oblong box to demonstrate graphically the inhale, pause, exhale, and pause. The top and bottom arrows are shorter, indicating that the pause after inhaling or exhaling lasts only one second. Some people who become nervous when asked to hold their breath may feel relieved to notice that the pause lasts only a second.

Option 2: Begin by inhaling (or ask the other person to inhale) as you slowly count to eight. You can count as follows: one-thousand-one, one-thousand-two, one-thousand-three, and so forth. If your lungs fill before you reach the eight, simply hold your breath for the remainder of the count. Then exhale for another count of eight, again holding the breath if you empty the lungs before arriving at eight. *If eight is too long*, begin with the count of four or five, and gradually increase both numbers up to eight. The practice effect of doing this procedure will most likely reduce the depressed feelings gradually.

Option 3: This procedure is as above except the person gradually increases the time of the exhale until it is *twice as long* as the inhale. This could begin with three counts inhale and six exhale, and gradually be increased. Some people will find it possible with practice to count up to eight (or one-thousand-eight) on the inhale and sixteen (or one-thousand-sixteen on the exhale. Remember that the person always determines the pace, and that counting the final numbers can be done while holding the breath either at the end of the inhale or at the end of the exhale.

Trauma reduction exercise #2: TAT

This is one of the two exercises that proved so powerful for JoAnne, the executive-in-training I described in the first case example, and which has been so useful to other persons who had trouble managing their impulsive anger. Follow the same procedures as outlined on pages 26 through 32. Or use this TAT short form:

First hold the TAT pose while saying or thinking, "I deserve to live and I can accept love, help, and healing." Continue holding for a minute or two, or until you feel a shift. Drop your hands and write down your experience. Secondly, hold the TAT pose again, this time thinking about your traumatic memory. After a minute or two drop your hands and notice your experience. Thirdly, hold the TAT pose, this time saying something opposite, such as "It's over" or "I'm OK now and I can relax." At this point you can either hold the pose while noticing what else comes up for you, or refer to pages 26 through 32 for additional steps having to do with healing the origins of your trauma, "secondary gain," forgiving, and asking for forgiveness.

Figure 29. **TAT short form for healing traumatic memories**

I have already mentioned how complex a traumatic memory can be. Equally, fear of the future can represent a myriad of thoughts, emotions, and sensations thoughts: we probably all have experienced the worry and anxiety that can arise when we think ahead to *events that have not happened* yet but which we dread nonetheless. In my clinical and personal experience, these strong negative feelings about the future almost always have root in past traumatic memories that we have not yet resolved. For this reason I encourage you not to be too surprised – and not necessarily to stop the TAT procedure – in the event that your working with TAT opens up additional memories of fear, as often a person has forgotten the original event, or the worst event, that caused and maintains the present day maladaptive fear symptoms. You may also find other emotions, such as grief or anger. While you certainly can choose to stop doing TAT and to control the unpleasant feelings, you might also consider yourself fortunate to be remembering what you had forgotten, and perhaps developing new appreciation for why you first learned to feel the fear that today seems so out of place in your life.

As I mentioned in the last chapter, fears are often about events that have not yet occurred, so you can use TAT while you think ahead and visualize the *next* event that is likely to be overwhelming in its anxiety-provoking powers. Imagine it not as it happened but *as you think it might happen*. Otherwise, follow the same TAT steps. I have never found the use of TAT for trauma work to pose a risk to my client. That does not mean a risk could never occur, particularly if you take on too traumatic a memory. It could also be upsetting if you were to recall only *a part of* the memory that you have chosen to target. In this case, using the TAT could begin to loosen the boundaries that you have established between the memory and consciousness, with the result that you could begin to remember parts of the memory, or even other memories, that had been hidden or dissociated or in some other way stored away from awareness. This new awareness can, indeed, be upsetting and even frightening. If you find that using the TAT pose causes you to feel too upset, stop the pose and consider using exercise #5, leading with your heart, instead.

On the other hand, notice how each person in the case examples worked on some fairly significant memories without negative consequences. I believe it is important, in this context, both to appreciate the power of the TAT exercise, and to respect the choice of the user.

Trauma reduction exercise #3: EFT

The "imperfect piano player" described above found EFT especially helpful. The steps for EFT are detailed on pages 34 through 41. Traumatic memories can be complex, so EFT is particularly valuable because it involves the stimulation of all of the key meridian points.

The EFT map is below. While you tap (or touch and breathe) the EFT points, give particular attention to any sensations, emotions, images or memories that come to you, and notice the point you were stimulating that seemed to trigger that special experience. Then refer to the two lists on page 123. One list shows the negative emotions for each EFT meridian point; the other shows the associated positive emotions and thoughts. Identify the emotion and thought related to the meridian point you were stimulating. Does the list help you understand your trauma better? Continue to tap or touch any point that feels especially meaningful until you move through the issue.

There is preliminary scientific evidence that EFT reduces symptoms of posttraumatic stress[4]. However, when you first begin to use EFT, you might feel worse for a while. It appears that such initially negative experiences are quite rare[5] but this does not mean it could not happen to you. If you do notice EFT increases your trauma symptoms, you can choose to stop and instead use exercise #2 or one of the other basic exercises. You can also refer to Appendix A for information on how to consult with a professional.

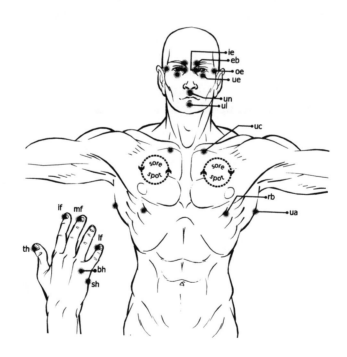

Figure 30. **EFT points for healing traumatic memories**

EFT Point	Associated negative emotion	Associated positive emotion and thought
(1) **ie,** or **eb**	trauma, frustration	acceptance: "I am in peace and harmony"; "every issue in me has been resolved"
(2) **oe**	rage, wrath	forgiveness: "I extend myself with forgiveness and love"
(3) **ue**	anxiety, fear	tranquility: "I am content, I am tranquil, I am satisfied"
(4) **un**	hopelessness, powerlessness, embarrassment	hopefulness: "I am hopeful, I can"
(5) **ul**	shame, worthlessness	worthiness: "I am deserving, I am worthwhile"
(6) **uc**	lack of possibilities, sexual/creative indecision	security: "My sexual and creative energies are balanced, I have possibilities"
(6) **ua**	future anxiety, addictive urges, worry	faith: "I am confident in the future, I feel secure"
(7) **rb**	lack of joy, anger, resentment	joy: "I have humor, I have a positive attitude"
(8) **th**	intolerance, disdain scorn, prejudice	tolerance: "I am modest, I have humility, I am tolerant"
(9) **if**	guilt, self-punitive, negative attitude	forgiving of one self: "I am pure, good; I am deserving of unconditional love"
(10) **mf**	jealousy, regret	generosity: "I am relaxed and free of the past"
(11) **lf**	anger (usually towards a specific person)	love, forgiveness: "I forgive you [here you can name a specific person]"
(12) **sh**	sorrow, vulnerability, sadness	happiness: "I am full of happiness"
(13) **bh**	depression, loneliness, despair	lightness: "I am light and buoyant, I feel encouraged and hopeful"

When doing EFT, it is usual for a person to notice that one or more points will stimulate a special feeling or sensation, or stir an image or memory. You may consult this list to identify a possible emotion or thought that is associated with a point. There are several ways to proceed: continue tapping or touching the point until the sensation resolves itself; stimulate the point while repeating the negative emotion; or say the positive emotion and statement while you stimulate. Different procedures seem to work better for different persons.

Figure 31. **List of emotions associated with the EFT acupuncture points**[6]

Trauma reduction exercise #4: Tapping shortcut

If you do find certain points from the EFT exercise to be especially powerful, you may use them repeatedly. The short list below is another useful option for many people.

I have found this tapping shortcut to be safe for my traumatized clients. Nonetheless, it is possible that new emotions could arise when one works on unresolved memories of trauma. Always respect your own experience rather than a book or advisor. If using the following sequence of points causes you to become more upset, you have at least three options. First, you could stop the procedure. Second, you could continue working with the attitude of "Isn't that interesting" or "Now I understand why I feel the way I do." And finally, you could stop for a while and continue later on your journey with a professional who practices energy psychology or EMDR (see Appendix A).

If you refer to the list of the emotions on page 123 you will notice that the tapping shortcut I describe next may involve treating the emotions of trauma, anxiety, depression, anger, and guilt. My goal in offering this information is to help the reader to normalize any unusual emotional experiences that could appear while using the Tapping sequence.

Refer to the figure below while following the instructions on page 125.

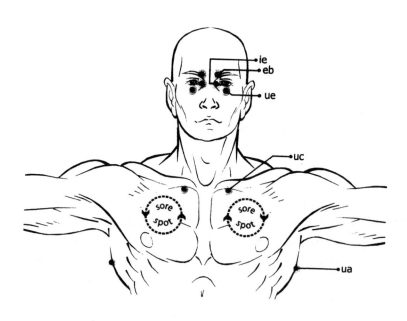

Figure 32. **Tapping shortcut for healing traumatic memories**

Refer to figure 32 as you follow these steps:

• Allow yourself to experience your thoughts, emotions, and any images that appear to you. If you are targeting the past, see if you can identify a time and place for the event. If you are targeting a future event, notice how you imagine it to be.

• Rate your feeling with the number that represents how upset you feel, 0 to 10. Ten would be the most upset you could possibly imagine.

• Using two fingers of each hand, tap the spots at the beginning of your eyebrows (**eb**), just above the bridge of your nose. Tap 5 or 6 times, firmly but not hard enough to cause pain or bruising. (If you *touch*, begin with **ie**, and hold your fingers on that point for the duration of one breath. Recall that eb and ie are interchangeable.)

• Tap (or touch) under the eyes with two fingers. This is the **ue** point in figure 32. Tap about 10 times, or hold the point for the duration of one breath.

• Then tap/touch the points under the arms on the sides of your body, 4 inches under the armpits (**ua**, figure 32).

• Tap/touch the collarbone points about 5 times (the **uc** point in figure 32).

• Take another measure on the 0 to 10 scale; if there is no change, do the sore spot massage on page 40, and repeat the tapping above, i.e. **eb/ie**, **ue**, **ua**, **uc**.

• Do the 9 brain balancing procedures on page 42.

• Tap about five times again on the **eb/ie**, **ue**, **ua**, and **uc** points.

• Take another 0 to 10. If the number is not where you would like it to be, repeat the above exercise (**eb/ie**, **ue**, **ua**, **uc**; the 9 brain balancing procedures; **eb/ie**, **ue**, **ua**, **uc**).

• Finish with the eye roll (page 43).

If this shortcut does not work, try exercises #1, #2, or #3. You can also refer to the EFT list on page 123 to see what emotion is involved when one or another of these points seems particularly calming or meaningful for you. Notice the emotion involved and continue tapping or holding the point until the emotion is resolved.

As is the case in using TAT and EFT with future fear, you can also use TFT as you think about the *next* event that is likely to trigger a strong fear of failure.

Trauma reduction exercise #5: Leading with your heart

On pages 45 to 50 I described a very simple exercise for "entraining" and empowering your heart. It involves placing your hand over your heart to bring your heart rate into a synchronized and coherent rhythm, and may be one of the most effective exercises for handling trauma. I suggest you practice the exercise exactly as it is described there.

After you have completed the steps outlined on pages 45 through 48, you can refer to page 49 for ideas on how to connect your heart's coherence to some other part of your body that is not yet coherent. Trauma can produce strong sensation in any part of our body: neck, shoulders, stomach, face, other organs and muscle groups. It is believed now that trauma can even initiate allergic responses. After doing the cardiac coherence exercise, and after you notice that your heart rate has already begun to feel more balanced and coherent, you can use the heart's energy to connect with and to soothe other places in your body where you feel a disturbing emotion or sensation. Because the heart's energy is stronger than that of other organs or parts of the body, you can expect that your heart coherence will gradually train the rest of the body (in this case, the area where you still notice a negative sensation) to come into line with more optimal physiological functioning, more the way you want to feel.

To make this connection happen, keep one hand over your heart and place the other hand over the place where you feel tension, pain, or other unpleasant emotion or sensation. Hold both hands in their respective places for several minutes, paying as close attention as you can to the feeling you experience under each hand. Continue to pay attention to the positive thoughts you chose initially (from page 50): an experience of gratitude and love, a moment of personal excellence, a sunset, a sea shore, mountain mist, desert cactus in bloom … Notice any changes that occur within you. You may feel a slight relaxation in a muscle, or a tingling, or a warming or cooling sensation – all signs of healing. You may also notice that you begin to recall, visually or not, specific scenes from your life, such as a time of having forgiven or having been forgiven. And you may also notice that certain thoughts occur to you rather spontaneously, such as "I can appreciate myself," "I can appreciate differences," "I prefer love to anger." If and when these changes occur to you, remain with them for a few minutes more, with your hands in their respective places, until you are ready to face the challenges of life with your renewed spirit.

Remember that it is normal to become distracted and to find negative thoughts drifting into consciousness, such as memories of disappointment, or memories of having been hurt or having hurt someone else. Simply notice when this happens, and intentionally take your attention to memories of gratitude and love, personal excellence, truth, or beauty.

If you doubt you have the power to effect these changes, check for scientific support for this exercise in the notes[7].

Trauma reduction exercise #6: The Butterfly Hug

Begin by reviewing pages 51 and 52 where the Butterfly Hug is described. Be careful when using this exercise for the purpose of reducing anger, as it can sometimes stimulate related memories that could cause you to feel even more angry – sometimes a great deal more. This is particularly true for adults who tend to have stored away relatively numerous unresolved memories. Children do not seem so susceptible to this risk, particularly when they use the Butterfly Hug under professional supervision.

You can begin the Butterfly Hug by noticing your anger, rating it on the 0 to 10 scale, then doing only one or two alternating taps to each side of your chest, first one side, then the other, then the first side, then the second, then stop. Check to see if your anger has changed, and if it diminished or increased, and how much. If you noticed that your anger suddenly surged, perhaps the process of bilateral alternating tapping poses a liability for you. Please keep in mind that perhaps 5% of my clients who use the Butterfly Hug *while thinking forgiving and loving thoughts* report that they begin to feel upset rather than peaceful, particularly when they first begin. If this happens to you, I would suggest using exercises #2 (TAT), #3 (EFT), #4 (Tapping Shortcut), or #5 (Leading with your heart).

If on the other hand the gentle tapping, first on one side and then on the other, *reduces* your feelings of rage, upset, irritability – or whatever the form of anger that you feel – you might consider that your anger is relatively isolated and is not connecting with other old memories that could exacerbate your anger, memories of when you felt threatened or treated in some other way that led to an angry feeling. In this case, continue gently tapping as above. The advantage of the Butterfly Hug is that it appears to stimulate communication between the two brain hemispheres, which in turn can help you to integrate important experiences that up to that point have been disassociated from one another. Integration of our various memories and experiences is always preferable to their being disconnected.

Trauma reduction exercise #7: physical activity

In chapters one through four I summarized some of the evidence that physical activity can help reduce symptoms of stress, anger, fear, and depression. As it turns out, these four problem areas are largely the result of traumatic memories that have not been resolved. In a related way, much of what we mean by "posttraumatic stress" is related not just to stress, but also anger, anxiety, and depression. For these reasons, the comments in the earlier four chapters are also relevant here.

While I do not know which sports or physical activities are best to reduce trauma in general, those who subscribe to the sociobiological theory of sports would say that a person hoping to reduce anger resulting from a trauma should engage in activities that simulate the fight response (i.e. striking something), while anxiety reactions would be better managed with activities mimicking flight (i.e., bicycling or running). You can experiment. Some activities combine swift movement (flight) with pounding of the hands, arms or feet (fight), particularly swimming, tennis, soccer, and raquetball. Some people find a particular sport or activity that initially causes them to feel a certain emotion, and then, after a period of exertion, to lose the emotion.

If engaging in certain sports exacerbates rather than calms your negative emotions, consider doing your physical activities in conjunction with the other exercises.

Other possibilities for managing trauma

For years the fact of psychological trauma was ignored, then it was recognized but largely medicated, then it became viewed as a correctable problem but one that only a professional psychotherapist or physician could treat. More recently we have seen models that involve both an optimistic prognosis for improvement and greater appreciation of the ability of trauma victims to be advance their own healing.

As an example, an Internet-based self-help intervention has been reported as an efficient intervention with persons with PTSD. A Web site is described that allows therapists to provide assistance by phone. The person receiving help does daily homework, mostly directed towards changing negative belief patterns[8]. My experience suggests that the exercises in this book would increase the positive impact of a phone- and Web-based intervention.

Finally, there is preliminary evidence to suggest that the use of homeopathic remedies can relieve symptoms of trauma[9].

Notes to Chapter Five

1. It appears that a person who has experienced early and repeated trauma will be more likely to be negatively affected by later critical events. Differences in the emotional (limbic) brain have been noted in persons with early histories of traumatic experiences, compared with persons who do not report such experiences. It is not unexpected, then, that when two persons experience a natural disaster or a war, one could become traumatized and the other not. The difference has nothing to do with character or will power, but rather seems to be largely related to structural and functional differences in the brain. In a way it seems to be a matter of luck: the non-traumatized person is likely to have had a more privileged childhood, either because the person was protected from undue harm, or because there were nurturing adults on hand to help the child to view the event in the most benevolent way possible. On the other hand, the person who responds to the crisis by developing posttraumatic stress disorder (PTSD) is likely to have had a difficult personal history.

Trauma memories, then, are the result of experience, and here we have the good news. Negative experiences can be unlearned, and positive experiences once forgotten can be recovered. The exercises in the book are based on these premises. Additionally, I recommend the reader to the section on EMDR in Appendix A. EMDR has been carefully studied and is now recognized by mental health associations in many countries as a preferred treatment for PTSD.

2. As I write in early 2005, news of troops returning from wars indicate that many of those who experienced combat arrive at their homes traumatized, often with PTSD. PTSD is a relatively new psychiatric diagnosis that was denied in earlier wars; symptoms were called "shell shock" and often attributed to an individual's weakness. Some say this was because those responsible for veterans' care had neither the funds nor the methods to treat PTSD, so it was easier to deny the existence of PTSD.

It is also likely that victims of the December, 2004, tsunami will be reporting increasing symptoms of trauma, now that the immediate shock of survival has lightened somewhat. It is fairly typical for victims of traumatic events to experience delayed symptoms.

Fortunately, we now know how to treat and heal PTSD, both combat related and that resulting from natural disaster. At this time there are many projects being planned to treat returning veterans and others who have developed symptoms of psychological trauma. The best treatment projects, in my view at least, involve one or more variations of the exercises in this book.

3. I thank David Gillespie for giving his permission to be quoted.

4. Swingle, Pulos, & Swingle (2002) reported on a study of persons involved in motor vehicle accidents who reported traumatic stress associated with the accident. Eight males and two females each received two sessions of EFT. All ten clients reported improvement as measured by the zero to ten scale and by questionnaires assessing anxiety, depression, and avoidance of driving or riding in motor vehicles. Of special interest were brainwave changes detected by quantitative electroencephalographic measures, and commentary on how psychoneurophysiological research can provide important data for increasing understanding of the processes involved in subtle healing.

5. Gary Craig's report on the rarity of negative side effects using EFT is found in Carrington & Craig (2000).

6. The list of the emotions associated with the various meridians varies somewhat from practitioner to practitioner, just as the significance of specific meridian lines is debated by acupuncturists. The list I offer is consistent with those of others I have seen, and has been of practical use for clients.

7. Cardiac coherence is correlated with reductions in depression and anxiety. Because these two emotions are frequently maintained by unresolved traumatic memories, emotional healing can be expected to be accompanied by healing of other symptoms of trauma, such as eating and sleeping disturbances, avoidance behavior, intrusive thoughts, and addictive impulses.

8. A therapist-assisted Internet self-help program for traumatic stress was reported by a group of psychologists and psychiatrists: Litz, Williams, Wang, Bryant, & Engel (2004). Their focus was on helping their PTSD clients to manage anxiety, develop new skills, and reframe their ways of thinking. Williams & Poijula (2003) have written a workbook on "simple effective techniques for overcoming traumatic stress symptoms."

9. See Bassman and Uellendahl (2003) for information about complementary and alternative approaches to medicine and psychology.

Chapter 6:
Solutions for sleep problems
And jet lag

This chapter begins with a general section on sleep and sleep problems, with suggestions for resolving those problems. In the subsequent section I comment on jet lag.

Sleep and sleep problems

Despite spending nearly a third of our lives doing it, we know little about sleep and what happens during it. It is clear that this seemingly passive state is tied to the rhythms of the body and the wanderings of the mind, and is vital to the restoration and well being of the whole person. Regrettably, about half of us report sleep problems of some sort.

Forgetfulness, inattentiveness, and poor performance in school or the workplace are a few of the problems that result from poor sleep patterns. Medical problems include high blood pressure, heart disease, and reduced resistance to viruses. Many people with sleep disturbance will report depression, which generally causes us to seek even more sleep – quite a paradox since the sleep we do already get is so inefficient in resolving depression.

Just what are "normal" sleep patterns, and what causes sleep problems? Each night the body completes four or five cycles of sleep. Each cycle lasts about 90 minutes, and each contains five stages.

We are generally in stages 1 and 2 for the first hour. Stage 1 sleep is light and characterized by slow eye movement and slow muscle activity. This stage lasts about 10 minutes. In stage 2, lasting about 50 minutes, eye movements cease and brain waves mostly slow down.

Stages 3 and 4 are deep sleep. We do not awaken easily during these periods. There is no eye movement or muscle activity and very slow brain waves that are interspersed with smaller, faster waves. Each of these stages lasts 7 to 8 minutes.

During the last 15 minutes or so of a sleep cycle, stage five, we are in REM (rapid eye movement) sleep, characterized by increased breathing, eye movement and heart rate. Dreams occur here. To keep us from acting out those dreams, the brain tells the spinal cord to inhibit limb movement.

The implication of the 90-minute, 5-stage sleep cycle is that we need to complete all five stages to awake feeling refreshed. A person who sleeps four complete cycles (6 hours) will feel more rested than will someone who has slept 8 or even 10 hours, but who has not been able to complete any cycle because of being awakened before a cycle was completed. Any disruption, particularly during REM sleep, can cause us to feel drowsy the next day[1]. There are exceptions as some individuals will have a cycle that is as short as an hour or as long as two hours.

In any case, the implication is that we want to be able to fall asleep and remain sleeping through each of the cycles. Being awakened is not so disruptive, provided it is between cycles. Hence, a person may be awakened between cycles by a full bladder, or by a minor stimulus, and will still experience restful sleep provided it is easy to fall asleep once again. Apparently, a person who is getting sufficient sleep is also easier to waken between cycles. This can also explain why experts recommend 20- to 25-minute naps.

The suggestions I mention next are designed to allow us to fall and to remain asleep during sleep cycles. I have mentioned the eye movements involved during different stages because one of the exercises I will suggest involves eye movements, and the exercise may in fact be effective because it mimics the eye movements of sleep.

Three recommendations for correcting sleep disturbance

Recommendation #1: Check your diet, exercise routine, and life style

Late night eating can cause indigestion, trips to the bathroom, and other disruptions. I wonder if it is coincidental that dinners are taken very late in Spain, and that Spaniards are also reported to sleep the least of all Europeans.

Many people will find that a glass of warm milk can have a sleep-inducing effect.

Most people should not consume foods and drinks containing caffeine in late afternoons and evenings. Popular culprits are coffee, colas, and chocolate. On the other hand, some people I know (from Turkey, Brazil, and Israel) drink coffee late at night and report sleeping restfully.

Exercise also seems to affect people differently. It seems to make some people more alert, while causing others to feel drowsy. Experiment to find what the best time of day is for you to exercise. Some people will find that they should stop all aerobic exercise several hours before going to bed. Insomniacs are encouraged to exercise in the morning.

Recommendation #2: Consider a medical check-up and/or use a device conducive to undisturbed sleep

After examining our life style, the next best thing we can do in my opinion is to consider a medical examination to rule out physical causes of sleep disturbance. For example, about 10% of us experience sleep apnea, which is a kind of "forgetting to breathe". Apnea is a physical condition involving structures in the back of the oral cavity that serve to block the airway during the relaxed state of sleep. Apnea is made worse by obesity. Snoring, frequent awakenings, difficulty falling asleep, and excessive daytime drowsiness are among the symptoms of apnea ("sleep apnea-hypopnea syndrome" or SAHS).

Apnea can be diagnosed in a sleep lab; many people are diagnosed more informally by their bedmates. For those who experience apnea, devices are on the market that can help to ensure a constant passage of air into the lungs, a sort of reminder to the body to continue breathing[2]. Others may benefit from the application of positive airway pressure (PAP) therapy, or by surgery. Though apnea sufferers have an organic condition, it is not recommended that such persons take the antidepressants and sleeping pills that are so often prescribed. Some persons who use the exercises described below will find that they can sleep without having to take any kind of medication.

Recommendation #3: Practice this four-step sleep-inducing exercise

• Step One: Set up your optimal sleeping conditions

Optimal sleeping conditions are highly personal. I have met a number of couples where one person feels lonely, hence sleeps poorly when sleeping alone, but the other person sleeps poorly in a communal bed because of being easily awakened by having someone else in the same bed! Resolving such a dilemma will require more assistance than is available in this chapter. Each of us may have peculiar definitions of what it means to live under "conditions conducive to restful sleep." One man I know moved from New York City to a rural community and claimed he had to move into a house next to the freeway before he could sleep well. There are other conditions that will be positive for one person, negative for another, such as late-night exercise or caffeine consumption.

Some people find it useful to dedicate their bed solely to sleep-inducing activities. Some activities to avoid in bed, then, might be reading reports that require concentration and attention, or having eye-opening arguments.

Folklore tells those of us who are worriers to have a pad and pen nearby so we can jot down tasks requiring our attention. This may allow us to feel comfort in knowing that we *can* put something off until tomorrow. This habit is also useful as we practice step 3 of this exercise.

• Step Two: Eye movement exercises

This activity has for many decades been a recommended practice in the Buddhist and energy medicine traditions. It is also consistent with the mechanisms of the more recent discovery of the psychotherapy method called Eye Movement Desensitization and Reprocessing. While this exercise is not for everyone, my clients with sleep problems who try this exercise have reported benefit more often than not. I personally use this exercise to fall asleep or to return to sleep that has been disrupted (I am one of those with sleep apnea).

I have not heard of any negative side effects from those who use this exercise. From time to time someone may report that the eye movements seem to stimulate additional disturbance and hence more sleep disruption, but these reports are very rare, and in any case the person will likely stop the eye movements spontaneously when disturbing thoughts or feelings are elicited.

The procedure may work because of the way it mimics the natural eye movement activity that occurs during the various sleep stages, as I suggested above. The procedure is quite simple. It consists of moving the eyes back and forth, *about ten times* in each of the following ways:
◆ from side to side
◆ diagonally (for example, from lower left to upper right)
◆ diagonally in the opposite direction (for example, from lower right to upper left)
◆ vertically (up and down)
◆ in a circle (10 circles)
◆ in circles in the opposite direction

Pay attention to whether your eyes begin to feel sore. The above sequence would require that you move your eyes about 60 times, something we would rarely do during a normal day. Do not continue if you feel any pain or strain.

This procedure can be varied. If you find one direction to be especially powerful, you may repeat it. When first beginning the exercise, you may wait several minutes after completing a round of eye movements and see if you fall asleep. If not, repeat the exercise as necessary. Some people find a figure eight movement to be better (for example, first make a circle to the left ending in the middle, then continue to make a circle to the right to complete a figure of a eight on its side.

After practicing this exercise, you may find that it becomes more and more effective. I personally find it to be virtually 100% effective for me, and can often fall asleep after making less than the first 10 horizontal movements.

CAUTION: Do not do eye movements if you experience any eye pain or strain!

A variation that is helpful for some people, especially for those who should not do eye movements, is to gently tap your opposite shoulders, or two opposing sides of your chest, with your hands. It may be that the important factor is not the eye movement but rather the bilateral effect (of eye movement or tapping) as registered in the brain.

• Step three: Awareness of your body

This exercise allows us to take our attention away from disturbing thoughts, which often are the reason for our lying awake at night.

Some people will begin this procedure by writing thoughts in a journal or notebook kept at bedside. This seems to tell the brain that the thoughts are being safely stored and can be retrieved the following morning, and that it is OK to stop attending to those thoughts which often seem so much more important at night. (Some writers advise that when negative thoughts occur, they too should be written down. I *do not* recommend this activity. Instead, use this awareness of your body procedure to gently take your attention to other and more sleep-inducing considerations.)

The awareness exercises consist simply of noticing different body parts in a way that takes attention from thinking and which *does not* cause further distraction. Neutral body parts are any that allow you to experience a sensation without causing distress. For example, you might slowly put your attention to how your feet or legs can feel the sheets, or how you notice the pressure of a blanket. As you attend to these sensations, your attention will drift away from the thoughts that had been disturbing you (and which are now stored in your notebook). Continue the eye movements or bilateral tapping from time to time, and then return again to bodily sensations.

You can also refer to the deep breathing exercise explained in the chapter on stress reduction. When you breathe deeply and intentionally, you can use the sensations produced as another focus of attention. Notice how the air enters your stomach and lungs, and how it slowly releases when you exhale. Move your eyes from side to side a few times, or tap from side to side, and put your attention again on your bodily sensations.

If it helps first to tense certain muscles and then to release, you may also use this practice to increase body awareness. This is particularly helpful for persons who are not able to notice body sensations, or for those who are more aware of what they think than of how they feel. Begin this procedure by choosing a set of muscles that seem to feel tense, for example the shoulders, face, stomach, or legs. If your face feels tense, you could purse your lips and wrinkle your forehead for about 3 seconds, and then release the tension. If you prefer to work the muscles of your legs, first push your toes down as if you were standing on your tiptoes, hold that for about 3 seconds, then release. You could then lift your toes, hold briefly, and release. Continue this process, depending on the muscle group you choose. Whatever muscles you tense and release, notice the difference between tension and relaxation (in your face, legs, stomach, etc.) and *continue deepening your awareness of this difference*, perhaps adding that "I am releasing tension, I am relaxing these muscles, I am aware of my ability to dissolve tension and to deepen my sense of calm and tranquility." You can also add other comments that directly put your parasympathetic nervous system into motion: "My forehead is cooling; my hands are warming; my feet are warming." This exercise has two purposes: one is to increase the sense of physical relaxation that is conducive to sleep, and the other is to help you further your awareness of your body and to use your heightened consciousness of your body to take your attention more and more away from the thoughts that interfere with your sleeping.

• Step four: Experiment with the other exercises

If these steps are not sufficient, use any of the exercises already described in previous chapters. Some persons tell me that they can fall asleep more easily after using the TAT exercise and noticing their stress melt away. A similar experience may result from doing EFT exercises for a few minutes.

If you have identified stress and stressful thoughts as significant sleep disruptions, consider using any or all of the other exercises explained in chapter one. Use the exercises you find most powerful prior to going to bed for the night.

A variation of the TFT exercises, one recommended by some for sleep, is to hold the fingers of one hand on the inside of the wrist (the same side as the palm) of the other hand until you begin to feel drowsy. There are several important acupuncture points on the insides of each wrist. Others may find that tapping that area of the wrist will work better than simply touching it. The figure below shows key acupuncture points on the insides of the wrists.

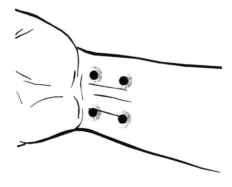

Figure 33. **Acupuncture points for sleep problems**

Jet lag

Map of the time zones

Times of the day and night beginning with one o'clock in the morning:

1 2 3 4 5 6 7 8 9 10 11 12 13 14 15 16 17 18 19 20 21 22 23 24

1 West Europe time
2 Mid-Europe time
3 East Europe time

1 Indian time
2 China time
3 Japan time
4 New Zealand

1 Yukon time
2 Pacific time
3 Mountain time
4 Central time
5 Eastern time
6 Atlantic time

World time zones

Background

If we look at a common globe of the world (or the map on the top of this page) we can
see lines of longitude running from pole to pole. There is a theory that twelve of these
lines equidistant from each other coincide with 12 energy meridians that also run along
the earth. According to this hypothesis, the energetic power of each meridian is said to
vary, depending on whether that part of the earth is in sunlight or in the sun's shadow.
That is, at a given period of time one of the meridians will be in its so-called power
phase; other meridians in turn have their power phases.

Through the course of evolution the human body has learned to coordinate waking
activities with light, and sleep with darkness. The meridians of the body also became
associated with periods of light and darkness.

Another premise of this theory now there is an intimate relationship between the
meridians of the earth and those of the human body, and that light and darkness are
implicated.

The human body, then, is ready for sleep in part because of the darkness, perhaps because the body's meridians are synchronized with those of the earth. The ideal situation is for the body to follow the routine of light/darkness, *and* the routine of the earth's rotation. Sleep disruption occurs when either routine is disturbed.

When people used to sleeping at night are asked to work the night shift, they experience sleep disruption; it may require many days to adjust to the change, and even then some people never seem to adjust completely.

Jet lag refers to the speed of travel made possible by jet planes. We can now move so rapidly across the earth's meridians that our bodies are unable to adjust to the meridian energy at the new destination. The light-darkness routine may not have changed; the traveler may have planned activities during the day when the locals are wide-awake. What has changed with jet lag is that the body of the traveler is at the new *destination*, but the meridians of the body are still synchronized with the meridians of the earth at the place of *departure*. With time, both sets of meridians will become coordinated, and the body will become synchronized with the meridians of the destination site, but in the meantime many of us suffer until the body has completed its readjustment. This experience can also be described as a disruption of our built-in circadian rhythms.

NASA (the US space agency) calculates that on average we need one day for every one-hour time zone crossed to regain normal rhythm and energy levels. (I do not know if this is true for all of us, but their formula does reflect the adjustment difficulties most east-west travellers seem to experience.) While adjusting, people with jet lag report being tired and disoriented, feeling unmotivated, and having difficulty concentrating. These symptoms in particular interfere with activities that require effort and skill, such as teaching, discussing a business deal, reading, and driving. However, jet lag can even tax our capacity to enjoy tourist activities.

Case example: Sleeping on the job

For years I suffered from chronic jet lag. After long flights I would find myself drowsy during the day and wide-awake at night. If I made it to an appointment at all I worried if I might doze off, or at best find myself in a kind of "brain fog.". Once while traveling among the islands in the Indonesia archipelago, I boarded a plane for a midday flight. I recognized the attendant from a previous flight. She welcomed me aboard with a smile and asked if I needed a pillow so that I could sleep through this flight *too*! My physical and mental well-being suffered severely. It also took a number of days for me to return to any sense of normalcy after arriving at my distant destination.

After learning the energy exercises I describe below, I now experience about five percent or less of my previous discomfort. I have since flown many times on flights that lasted 20+ hours and took me half way around the globe. The exercises have helped me every time.

The purpose of the exercises is to accelerate the process of re-synchronization so that when the traveler completes the last leg of the flight, the meridians of the traveler's body will have adjusted to the meridians of the earth at the destination site.

Exercises for preventing jet lag

On pages 140 and 141 you will find photographs of key energy points; each point is used to stimulate a specific meridian during a prescribed two-hour period of time throughout the day and night. On page 142 are the instructions[3]. Essentially, what you will be doing is tapping several meridian points for a few minutes, beginning with the time of your departure. One pair of meridian points will be related to the time of day at the place of departure, and the other pair will be related to the time of day at the place of arrival. Two hours later you will tap two different pairs for a couple of minutes. This will continue throughout your trip, up to the time of your arrival at final destination. Following these procedures will enable your body to adjust itself energetically throughout the flight, so that by arrival the meridians of the body will be in sync with the meridians of the earth at the destination site.

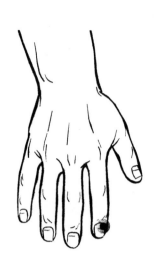

5 a.m. - 7 a.m.

Curve of index fingernail,
on the side closest to thumb

7 a.m. - 9 a.m.

Under knee cap,
slightly towards outside

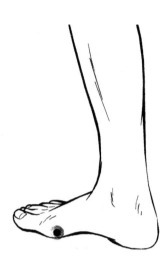

9 a.m. - 11 a.m.

Inside edge of foot,
just behind ball of foot

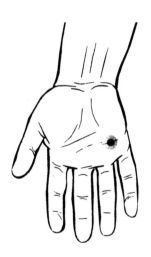

11 a.m. - 1 p.m.

Palm of hand, along the
valley between the
4th and 5th fingers

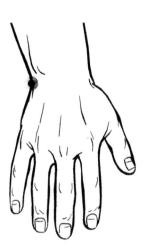

1 p.m. - 3 p.m.

Side of wrist, where the hand
swivels or hinges on the wrist

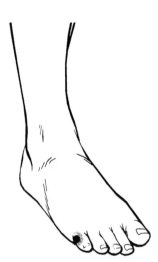

3 p.m. - 5 p.m.

Outside of foot, second (most
obvious) joint of the little toe

Figure 34a. **Jet lag energy points**

140

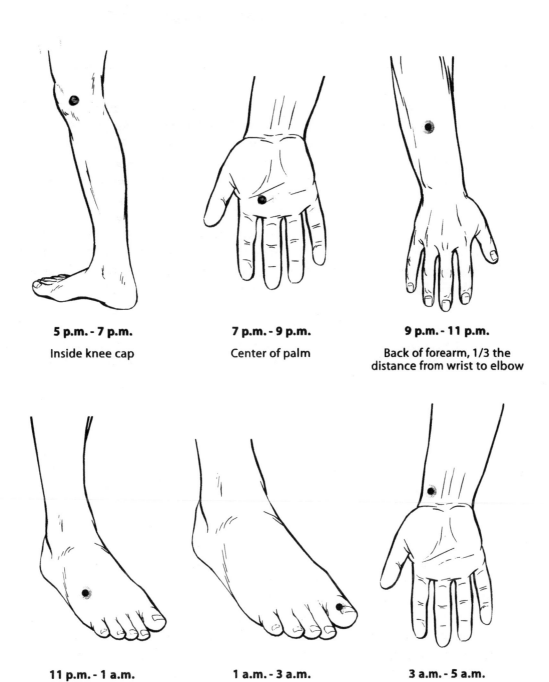

5 p.m. - 7 p.m.
Inside knee cap

7 p.m. - 9 p.m.
Center of palm

9 p.m. - 11 p.m.
Back of forearm, 1/3 the
distance from wrist to elbow

11 p.m. - 1 a.m.
Outside foot, just up and over
the outside edge, 1/3 the
distance from toe to heel

1 a.m. - 3 a.m.
Big toe, on the inside curve
of toenail

3 a.m. - 5 a.m.
Inside wrist (thumb side)
where watchband would be
located

Figure 34b. **Jet Lag Energy Points**

141

Instructions for preventing jet lag

1. Before leaving for the airport, photocopy pages 140 - 142 and take them with you.

2. Once you have taken your seat on the plane, notice the *current* time where you are at that moment. Then consult a time zone map to calculate the *current* time at your final destination. Find these two times on pages 140 and 141, and notice the associated energy points on your body. I will refer to these as "departure points" and "destination points." You will be tapping these points while you are waiting for your plane to depart. Note this information on your photocopies.

3. First tap one side of the body, then the other side. If you can tap the departure point simultaneously with the destination point, do so. If not, tap first the departure point, then the destination point, first on one side of the body, then the other. Tap each point for about a minute, fairly vigorously. At maximum, this will take 4 minutes.

For example, if you depart at 8 a.m. your time, and it is presently 8 p.m. where you plan to arrive for your final destination, you would first tap under the knee cap and on the center of your palm on one side of your body, then the same points on the other side.

4. Every 2 hours you will move to the next set of points and tap as instructed above. Check off each set of points as you tap them.

5. If you sleep through any of the times, simply refer to the notes you made on the photocopies so that you know where you last tapped. Begin with where you left off and tap in sequence until you are caught up to the present times at the places of departure and destination.

6. If your flight is longer than eight hours, add this procedure to what you are already doing: for the last four hours of your flight, find the point associated with the time you expect to arrive at your destination and tap this point for a minute every hour. If you can, tap both sides simultaneously. For example, if you plan to arrive at 8 am, find the 8 am energy point (which is under the knee cap). If you are awake at 4 am (4 hours before your expected arrival time), tap the points under both knees simultaneously for a minute. If you are not awake at that hour, don't worry: tap the points when you wake up. From the time you awake, tap those same points every hour or so until you arrive.

7. When you arrive at your destination, you should notice that the "destination points" coincide with the current time at your destination.

Recommendations for long-distance travelers

The above exercises will be more effective if used within a broader strategy. The longer the trip, the more useful they will likely appear.

• Prior to a trip

It may help to supplement your photocopy of pages 140 – 142 by making a graph that lists all of the points you will be tapping at given hours while on your flights, and check them off as you complete each series. Some travelers find it helpful to wear earphones that produce a white noise to cancel out sounds from within the plane. Ditto for eye covers. You can also find recommendations for special diets. One example is [www.antijetlagdiet.com][4]. You can also access on this website information about homeopathic remedies for preventing jetlag.

• During a trip

Practice the exercises on pages 140 through 142. When you are awake, take time to walk and stretch on the plane. I carry a clock and a watch so that I can double check the times for departure and destination. If you prepared a chart that lists all of the points you will be tapping at given hours on your flight, check off the points as you tap them. (I find that after napping I will have forgotten how far I had gotten on my list, and sometimes will have to repeat unless I keep notes.) If you are sensitive to diet, also practice special dietary habits while on the flight and at stopovers.

• After arrival

The jet lag exercises may need to be supplemented with the following.

1. Get into a routine that matches the locals', meaning that you sleep when it is dark and are awake in the light.
2. If you find it difficult to fall asleep even though it is dark, or if you wake up at night and find it difficult to return to sleep, use the various exercises described above on pages 142 through 145. Additionally, you can tap the key meridian points on pages 148 and 149 that match the local time, that is, the clock hour at the place where you are sleeping. For example, if you find yourself awake at 3 a.m., tap the point for 3 a.m. to see if you can train your body to become synchronized with the darkness at your destination. The theory is that the darkness-related meridian point will induce sleep (at least it does for me).
3. Likewise, if you find yourself dozing when you should be awake, tap the relevant key meridian point on pages 148 and 149. The theory is, again, that a lightness-related meridian will energize you.
4. Even though it may be difficult, do what you can to maintain the routine that you have found to be suitable for your health and welfare, which can include exercise, solitude, moderation in drink and food, and scheduling.

5. Whether or not you have the custom of napping, you might consider taking 20- to 25-minute naps while you are residing at your travel destination. Jet lag often involves both loss of requisite sleep and disruption of adequate meridian synchrony, and it is best to attend to both of these issues.

Benefits

Sleep researchers claim that good sleep may be the best single predictor of life span and quality of life[5]. Trauma researchers find that those who suffer from continuing trauma (see the previous chapter) require additional deep sleep to resolve disturbing memories naturally. Paradoxically and unfortunately, trauma victims experience nightmares and other sleep disturbance, and actually report sleeping less than non-traumatized persons.

The sleep disturbance associated with jet lag is but one form of sleep disturbance. To the degree that we can prevent and resolve jet lag, we can expect to increase our quality of life.

I have found that an investment of relatively few minutes of time before, during, and after a long-distance flight saves me hours or days of recuperation time, and immediately improves alertness and efficiency. I can now begin training or teaching a class immediately upon arriving at a new site in the early morning hours. The recommendations I listed are sufficient for my use, and I have found no further need to change dietary, light, exercise, nutritional, or other habits.

However, the varieties of sleep disturbance, and sleep aids, comprise a subject much more complex than this chapter might suggest. While my recommendations are sufficient for me and will help some readers, they will not be suitable or sufficient for everyone. Some people experience sleep disturbance that precedes and exacerbates their jet lag, and would be wise to consult a sleep lab or sleep specialist. For these reasons I refer the reader to other sources of information[6].

Notes to Chapter Six

1. For more information on sleep, refer to chapter 7 in Howard (2000), and the National Sleep Foundation website [hhtp://www.sleepfoundation.org].

2. The Respironics website [hhtp://www.respironics.com] is one source for devices designed to facilitate breathing.

3. The instructions are largely based on the book by Donna Eden and David Feinstein (1998), and included here with permission. I have made slight modifications to their protocols.

4. The following quote is taken from the website of the University of Chicago's Argonne National laboratory [http://www.antijetlagdiet.com] which is the only website licensed to provide information about this diet:

"The Anti-Jet-Lag Diet can reduce or prevent jet lag for anyone traveling east or west across three or more time zones. Developed by Argonne biologists studying the body's inner clocks, the Anti-Jet-Lag Diet uses nature's time cues to help your body adjust quickly to a new time zone."

5. As an example of conferences that feature leading experts in sleep research, see the article by Greer (2004).

6. The book by Pressman & Orr (2004) paints the bigger picture of sleep disorders.

Part Two: Accentuating the positive

The first part of the book was a focus on eliminating negative ways of thinking, feeling, and acting. In this second section we will look at some of the innovative methods that help us to replace the negative with positive substitutes.

We begin part two with strategies for balancing energy, and for increasing positive energy (chapter seven). In chapter eight I how to use the exercises from part one to emphasize the positive, something you were introduced to in the earlier chapters. In chapter nine I suggest some ways to make the exercises part of your daily life and routine.

Chapter 7: Our subtle energy

A. Rebalancing your Energy

Background; energy testing

An assumption of subtle energy theory is that the energy systems in our bodies interact with our emotions, thoughts, actions, health, and so forth. We are one system, body-mind, or bodymind. This assumption can be easily checked out with a simple muscle test[1]. The figure below shows a person being tested and a person doing the muscle testing.

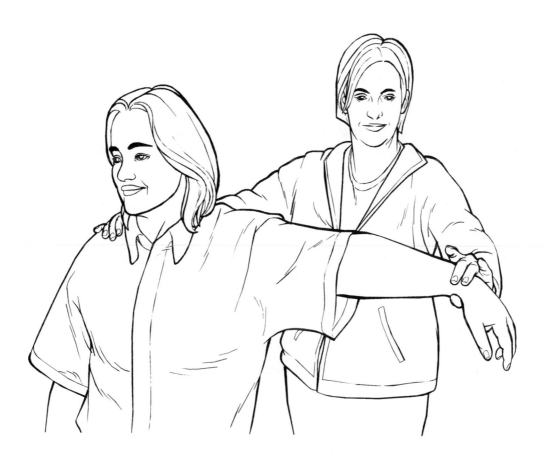

Figure 35. **Muscle testing positions for person tested and person testing**

The reader may already be familiar with chiropractic uses of muscle testing. I first experienced this in the mid-70s. A chiropractor asked me to hold a nutritional supplement in my hand while he pressed on my extended arm to see if the supplement would weaken or strengthen me. A weakening was taken as a sign that I was deficient on that supplement. In recent years muscle testing has been used more and more for psychological issues.

The most usual way to do a muscle test is to have one person extend an arm away from the body, parallel with the floor, while another personal *gently and briefly* applies pressure downwards on the extended arm – as you can see on page 147. Meanwhile, the person being tested thinks or says different things to see if the muscle strength of the extended arm varies. The different thoughts should produce different results. If you wish to try this out, do so with a trusted partner by taking the positions on page 147 and following the next steps.

Procedural steps for muscle testing:

1. The person being tested first needs to decide which muscle will be used for the test. Usually the extended arm is used, with the person testing standing behind the other person. Check first to be sure that the arm and shoulder being used are not injured or fragile in any way. We do *not* want to cause damage or pain. Options are to have the person relax the arm down the side of the body and to resist while the person testing gently tries to pull the arm away from the body. A third option is to have the person being tested bend the arm at the elbow and extend the forearm to the front, away from the body and parallel with the floor; the test is done by gently pressing the hand downward while the person being tested resists.

2. We then want to test the muscle "in the clear," that is, while the person tested maintains a clear or neutral mind (because thinking can affect the testing, as we shall see). The person being tested stands with feet about a foot apart and toes turned slightly out. A suggestion is that both persons take deep breaths, say "my mind is in the clear," and on the exhale the test is conducted. I repeat: use very slight pressure. Use only one finger to push if necessary to ensure that you are using a gentle pressure. Repeat this to make sure you know more or less how strong the muscle is under these neutral conditions.

3. The person being tested then says something *true* or *pleasant.* The usual suggestion is for the person tested to say his or her true name, as in "My name is _____." The person testing then says something like, "Hold your arm now" and then applies the same slight pressure again. Some suggest that a better statement is, "Resist my pressure as I push on your arm." If the person tested has balanced and flowing energy, the response will be strong, perhaps even stronger than under the initial neutral condition. An option is for the person being tested to think of something pleasant. Another option is to say something true such as "One plus one equals two.")

148

4. The person tested then says or thinks *the opposite*. If the first statement was the true name, then the person says a false name, such as "My name is George Washington", or "My name is Benito Juarez". If the statement was one plus one equals two, this time it might be "1+1=27." If the person had a pleasant thought, this time it should be unpleasant. Repeat the muscle testing exactly as described in step 3. Under this condition the person testing should notice that the muscle is significantly weaker.

There are other ways to do muscle testing. A common one is to have the person tested put his or her hand above the head, palm down, an inch above the head. The opposite and extended arm is used for the testing. This should produce a strong response. The hand is then reversed with palm up, again an inch above the head. This should produce a weak response.

Whatever procedure used, the first test should produce a *strong* response, the second a *weak* one so that the next step is interpretable.

5. As just indicated, the person being tested "should" have produced a strong response first, and then a weak response. These responses would indicate a balanced and flowing energy system. The notion is that when we are healthy the truth (or the pleasant) will strengthen us, and the false (or the unpleasant) will weaken us. However, the person being tested may or may not be balanced, so the expected two responses (first strong, then weak) may not appear. Actually, there are four possible responses to the testing procedure that begins with a statement that should prove strong, and follows with a statement that should prove weak:

• Strong-weak   • Weak-strong   • Strong-strong   • Weak-weak

If strong-weak: As mentioned, this first option is what we hope for. "The truth makes us strong" and "the false weakens us." The person who tests strong-strong has an energy system that is ready for healing and that will likely respond optimally to the exercises you have already learned, in particular those called TAT, EFT, and the tapping shortcut.

If weak-strong: The second possibility is the exact opposite of the expected. If you find this, simply turn to page 150 and have both persons do the correction exercise, and re-do the muscle test.

If strong-strong: This probably indicates that the person being tested has an overabundance of the energy being evaluated. Turn to pages 153 and 154 and try one of the two options for correcting the condition called "neurological disorganization" or "energy overcharge." Redo the testing.

If weak-weak: Weakness under both conditions can usually be corrected by having both persons drink a glass of water each. The assumption is that the energy conductivity is inadequate, and hydration will correct this. Re-test.

Some implications: It is assumed that a person who responds strong-weak will then be reliable for testing his or her sensitivity to a variety of environmental and other substances. For example, you can then have the person hold in the other hand a food or drink or medication that is suspect as a possible allergen. If while holding the substance, the muscle-testing arm of that person grows weak, it is assumed that there is something in the energetic connection between the person and the substance that is not beneficial for the person. An allergic reaction is a likely explanation. The options are to avoid the substance, put up with the side effects, or – and here is more good news – be treated energetically for the problem. (For information on available treatments, see the "allergy treatment" section in Appendix A.)

Correction for Reversals (weak-strong response)[2]

A person who responds weak-strong is said to have a psychological reversal or energy reversal, because the responses are exactly opposite from what is expected. If you have read Part One, you are already acquainted with the correction. You also know now why it was suggested there: to correct reversals in the energy system prior to treating that system with the exercises. The correction involves the use of the sore spot, which is a point the lymph system drains. Recall that the heart pumps blood to keep it circulating. The lymph system has no equivalent pump, and the lymph fluid needs to be pushed around in other ways to keep it flowing, and to help keep the immune system healthy. We will be pushing lymph fluid, and stimulating the energy system that accompanies it.

Using the figure on page 151, locate the sore spots. Start by crossing your right hand over to touch your left shoulder, then press down and walk your fingers towards your right elbow until you find a sore spot between your arm and chest. This sore spot is the location of a lymph drainage area, called the "neurolymphatic reflex." Once you have located it, follow the arrows on the figure and make a clockwise circular movement while pushing down on the sore spot. Do the same with the left hand over the right side of the chest, but do a circle in the opposite direction. Follow the arrows. You may feel pain when you do these movements, which is a sign that you are on the spot and that your lymph system may be in need of massaging.

As you make firm circular movements, say the following statement three times:

"I accept myself deeply and completely with all my problems and limitations."

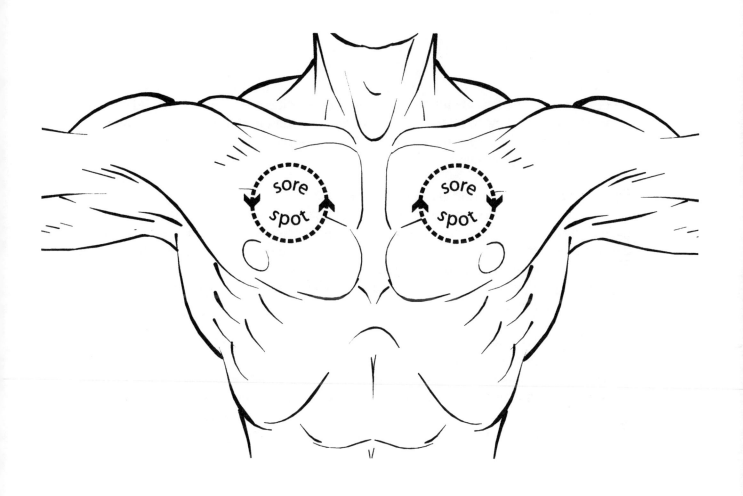

Figure 36. **Neurolymphatic reflex points ("sore spots") and
direction of massage for correcting energy reversals**

It is not necessary to use muscle testing. Many people simply practice the sore spot
correction from time to time during the day. It takes less than a minute to do.

Benefits

Benefits reported as a result of using this correction include increased alertness and concentration. Some of my clients with addictions, particularly those who use this regularly, report that their urge to use a cigarette or other substance diminishes. I have also noticed that some persons will be able to reduce physical pain after doing the exercise. I learned this during the energy courses I conduct.

For example, I was once teaching in a high mountain area in Latin America. As is usual, I first asked participants to list the problems they would like to be treated for during the course. I then took a few minutes to teach the sore spot technique simply to prepare their energy systems for subsequent treatment. Two participants had mentioned that they had arrived with headaches, so I asked if they would be willing to start the course by allowing me to treat them publicly for their pain. By then, however, both said that their headaches had vanished during the energy balancing.

Energy balancing is traditionally thought of not as a treatment per se but only a preparation of the energy system for subsequent treatment (which would involve one of the techniques described in chapters 1 through 5). Nonetheless, sometimes just balancing the energy system will feel like a treatment. If you notice something similar – that is, that some of your symptoms vanish during the balancing procedures – consider yourself in special company. If your symptoms remain, especially those of pain, consider using the TAT or EFT techniques already described.

I have been told of studies in which healthy individuals will exhibit balanced energy systems when muscle tested, while another group of individuals, with diseases such as cancer but comparable in other demographic ways, will exhibit energy reversals[3]. We do not know if the imbalance was in place before the cancer and may have made cancer more likely to develop, or if the illness caused the energy imbalances. Nonetheless the findings are consistent with the assumption that energy disruptions are associated with physical illness.

Two corrections for neurological disorganization (strong-strong response)

A few people who response strong-strong simply have so much muscle strength that the person testing cannot move the arm. Generally, however, the strong-strong response indicates an overabundance of the *subtle* energy that can be corrected with one of the following corrections. Refer to the figures as you follow the instructions:

Correction #1[4]

- Place left ankle over right.
- Extend arms, palms touching, and cross right hand over left, backs of hands touching.
- Turn hands, clasp fingers, fold arms to rest on chest. Do not touch hands to chin.
- When breathing in (through nose), place tongue on hard palate behind top teeth without touching teeth with tongue.
- When breathing out (through mouth), place tongue against lower palate below teeth, without touching teeth with tongue.
- Continue for two to three minutes.
- Repeat the above, with right ankle over left, left hand over right.

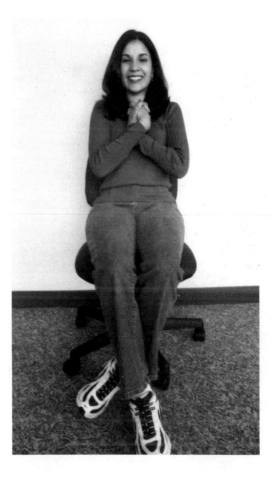

Figure 37. **Correction #1 for neurological disorganization**

153

Correction #2[5]

If muscle testing still shows a strong-strong response, try this next exercise.

- While seated, place your left foot on top your right knee.
- Grasp left ankle with right hand.
- With your left hand grasp the bottom of left foot. The palm of that hand covers the ball of foot, and the fingers wrap around the bottom of the foot. Notice how your hands are crossed.
- Breathe deeply: on the inhale pull up your foot up with both hands, and on the exhale lower your foot to a resting position again. Do this routine six times.
- Change this position to the other side: right foot over left knee, left hand grasping right ankle, right hand covering the bottom of the right foot. As indicated, lift your foot on the inhale and lower it to a resting position on the exhale. Do six times.
- Repeat all of the above one more time.

Figure 38. **Correction #2 for neurological disorganization**

It is also unnecessary to do muscle testing to see if one of the above two corrections will be of use to you; some people simply practice these corrections as part of their daily routine. Each one takes about a minute or two to do.

Benefits

Benefits reported are an enhanced sense of mental and physical balance, increased coordination, and alertness. These two techniques have been reported as useful to many students who have trouble concentrating and learning. The belief is that with some children with learning disabilities there is a failure in the communication between brain hemispheres, and the cross-over aspect of both of these corrections helps the brain to more properly store and access information. Readers who have studied applied kinesiology[6] may be reminded of techniques such as the cross crawl that are used in various school systems with reportedly positive benefit for these children. I was once conducting a course on the theory and basic exercises in the book, and when I got to this section on energy corrections a trainee told me she recalled being in a school with a group of rowdy kids and their music director. The director began the class by simply saying, "Hook-up!" The children immediately did one of the exercises in figures 37 and 38, and settled down for the rest of the class. The trainee had not understood the theory behind those effective procedures, only that the children were clearly happy to do the exercises, which immediately changed the entire atmosphere in the class.

Some people who feel particularly fatigued after physical exercise report that doing one or the other of these two corrections *prior to exercising* helps them to feel energized later. If you believe you are one of thee persons, you can do muscle testing as follows. First have a partner muscle test you under neutral conditions as described on pages 147 - 149. Then walk *forward* for about ten steps and repeat the muscle testing. If walking forward weakens you, you may have an energy system called "homolateral"[7], which means that your energy currents are working in isolation instead of together. To double-check this, walk *backwards* and repeat the muscle testing. If you are now strong, this is more evidence. What is more interesting is that if you do one or both of the corrections for neurological disorganization, you will probably find that you become strong and weak, respectively, when you repeat the muscle testing following walking forward and walking backwards – which is the way we are meant to function.

In this example you can also rely on your own perception. If after doing the corrections you find that you feel more energized following exercises such as walking, you can consider making these corrections part of your daily routine.

B. Increasing Positive Energy

Background

After doing one or another of the above corrections for energy balancing, you can then practice the 6 exercises from this section for increasing the positive subtle energy in your "bodymind". The first exercise is intentional breathing. In the second example I suggest doing the energy corrections described above on pages 150-154, prior to engaging in physical exercise, in order to feel more energetic during a workout. Exercises #3 through #6 are taught by Donna Eden, a splendid energy healer whose book *Energy Medicine* (1998) is highly recommended. Even more highly recommended are her courses on energy healing, mentioned in appendix A.

The assumption underlying TAT, EFT, and the tapping shortcuts is that we can use our fingers to generate electromagnetic impulses within our bodies, stimulating the brain and releasing neurotransmitters. This stimulation, in turn, reactivates the natural healing systems in our bodies that can be shut down during times of stress or physical inactivity.

Virtually every relaxation and energy balancing exercises begins with the person focusing on breathing naturally, deeply, and rhythmically.

Exercise #1: Deep breathing

Breathing has been discussed in chapters one through five as the first of the basic seven exercises. Some energy practitioners teach breathing exclusively on the belief that proper breathing is all we need to do to produce optimal mental, physical, and emotional functioning. I do not disagree with this, but also have found that focusing only on breathing takes a much longer time than is required if one combines breathing with other exercises (which I discuss next). Additionally, I have observed that persons in exclusive breathing courses can initially become frustrated with the breathing exercises, because noticeable benefits do not appear until after one has practiced breathing routines for a long period of time, and has developed a proper breathing habit.

In conjunction with the other exercises, however, I find that breathing a good beginning point. In this sense I view breathing as a *desirable but not sufficient* activity for most people.

You might also experiment with inhaling and exhaling for longer periods of time, as this chapter is focused on the positive and you are presumably already in a fairly relaxed state. You might try counting for as long as eight seconds while you inhale, and even longer than eight seconds when you exhale. If on the inhale you fill your lungs before you reach eight, try holding your breath while you finish your count. And if on the exhale you have completely emptied your lungs before you finish counting, you might try to maintain your lungs empty for a few seconds longer before inhaling again. Always trust yourself to know when to take a break from this routine as deep breathing sometimes will produce anxiety – which is *not* the goal of this chapter.

Exercise #2: Physical activity with energy corrections

I have already commented on physical activity in chapters one through five. As a means of producing positive energy, it seems that at least for some people it is important to correct the flow of subtle energy prior to exercise. I commented earlier on how some people can be shown through energy testing to be neurologically disorganized, and how they may report that activities such as walking seem to fatigue them rather then energize them. Also on those pages you learned some simple techniques for correcting what is known as "neurological disorganization".

Instead of doing energy testing, an alternative experiment would be to engage in some routine physical activity (swimming, walking, running, bicycling) without doing any energy corrections beforehand, and to rate your energy level after you have completed your exercise, using a subjective measure such as the zero to ten scale. On another occasion you could do the corrections on pages 150-154 prior to exercising, then do your exercise routine as usual, and afterwards rate yourself again. If after several of these experiments you notice a pattern that suggests an energy correction before physical activity makes that activity more invigorating for you, you could make the corrections part of your routine.

When we run or walk naturally we produce both a bilateral alternating stimulation (first one foot forward, then the other one, for example) and a cross-over effect (the left arm is forward as the right leg is back, and vice versa). This alternating and cross-over effect also occurs between the brain hemispheres which mediate the physical movements. This inter-hemispheric activity can cause certain memories to connect, which can produce an unexpected experience of anxiety or other strong emotion. If and when this occurs you can continue exercising to see if you can continue moving through the experience. Another option is to take a brief break from exercising while you perform one or another of the techniques (I recommend particularly TAT or EFT from chapter one). Once you experience an improvement in how you feel, you can resume your physical activity.

Exercises #3 through #5 are what Donna Eden (1998) calls the three thumps. The instructions for these exercises begin on page 159 and are done in conjunction with the figure on page 158. I find these very valuable and do them as part of my own fitness routine.

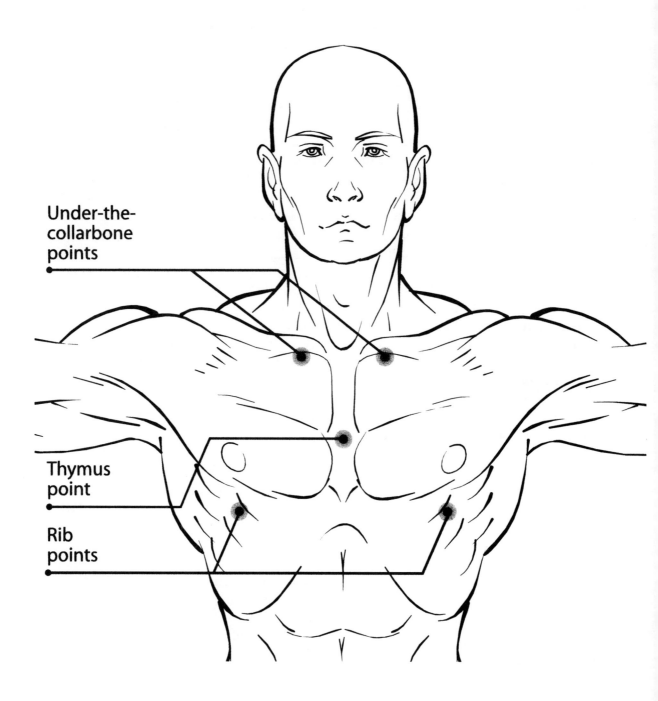

Under-the-
collarbone
points

Thymus
point

Rib
points

Figure 39. **Locations of energy points for the three thumps, exercises #3, #4, & #5**

158

Exercise #3: Tapping under the collarbones

Locate these first points on figure 39, page 158. They are acupuncture locations that you will be tapping instead of stimulating with needles. People report that this exercise is particularly helpful when feeling drowsy or having difficulty concentrating. There are two steps involved.

1. Place the index and middle fingers of both hands on your collarbones. Now slide your fingers towards each other and find the notch in the center of your collarbones. Then go down an inch and out an inch and you will find an indentation in your chest; you are now just below the collarbones and just to the outside of the sternum (breastbone) – that is, you are on a muscle indentation, *not* on any bone. These are the points you will be stimulating.
2. Cross your hands over (taking the place of each other) and tap vigorously on these points for about 20 or 30 seconds, several taps per second. Breathe deeply, inhaling through your nose and exhaling through your mouth. As you exhale act as if you are blowing out a candle, with lips pursed. If you cannot use both hands at once, use the thumb and middle fingers of one hand and tap both points simultaneously.

You can practice this during a boring meeting or conference by massaging the points firmly instead of tapping – as tapping publicly, according to one of my clients, might have people thinking you are a "mental case."

Benefits include a cross-over function which can help with learning while energizing.

Exercise #4: Tapping the thymus

Locate the thymus on figure 39, page 158. This is a single point in the center of the chest and a couple of inches below the collarbone points. To teach the location of the point in a course, I will ask a participant to do an experiment with me. "Jaime, I will call your name, and you will say, 'Who? Me'? and touch yourself with an index finger." Invariably the person will touch the thymus point, no matter the country or cultural context where I happen to be teaching.

The thymus in energy theory is the surveillance system of the body. The thymus is considered an important part of the immune system that requires manual stimulation from time to time because the immune system does not enjoy a built-in pump such as is the case with the heart in the circulatory system. Many would agree that the most effective of massages would involve stimulation of the lymph nodes, including the thymus, to increase immune system functioning.

Follow these 2 procedural two steps.

1. Find the point.
2. Tap vigorously with all the points of the fingers of one hand for about 20 or 30 seconds, one tap or more per second. Breathe deeply inhaling through your nose and exhaling through your mouth.

Benefits from vigorous tapping of the thymus usually include a sense of invigoration. Eden speaks of the importance of the thymus in immune functioning, and concludes that stimulating the thymus will strengthen the body's natural defenses.

Exercise #5: Tapping the rib points

Locate these points on figure 39, page 158. Stimulating these neurolymphatic energy points can increase your energy, balance your blood chemistry, and strengthen your immune system. Follow these steps.

1. Find the points as indicated on the figure on the previous page. They can be found immediately below the breasts. You will be sure to stimulate them if you place four fingertips (index through pinky) vertically directly below the breasts, and tap on the ribs.
2. Tap firmly for about 15 to 30 seconds, breathing through your nose and out through your mouth.

Benefits reported include increasing a sense of joy and enthusiasm.

Exercise #6: Crown pull

If you feel tired upon waking, doing this next exercise will help you to feel fresh and invigorated. It is said to increase lymphatic flow so can also energize your immune system[9]. Refer to figure 40 on the facing page. Here are the steps:

1. With your thumbs on your temples on the sides of your head, curl the other fingers and rest them just above your eyebrows, as in the figure below.
2. Slowly, and with pressure on your forehead, pull your fingers apart, stretching the skin of the forehead.
3. Move your fingers up an inch and repeat the stretching movement, with pressure.
4. Move your fingers up an inch again. Your fingers will be at your hairline. Repeat the stretching.
5. Repeat the stretching, each time moving your fingers slightly higher. Continue over the top of your head, stretching at each position, and continue down the back of your head for as far as you can reach.
6. Repeat the entire procedure as you wish.

Figure 40. **Crown pull**

161

Notes for Chapter Seven

1. Muscle testing is used to determine how well nerve impulses are transmitted. Studies have examined interexaminer reliability of the manual muscle-testing procedure (Lawson & Calderon, 1997; Leisman, Ferentz, Zenhausern, Tefera, & Zemcov, 1995; and Monti, Sinnott, Marchese, Kunkel, & Greeson, 1999) and the neurophysiological basis of the action of applied kinesiology (Leisman, Shambaugh, & Ferentz, 1989). Also consult the Web site for the International College of Applied Kinesiology [http://www.icakusa.com].

2. The corrections for psychological reversals can also be found in Gallo (2005) and Lambrou & Pratt (2000), and in many other energy psychology sources.

3. Langman (1972), following earlier studies by Burr (1972), studied the cervical electrical charges of 241 women, about half of them with benign, half with malignant gynecological conditions. Over 90% in the first group were found to have normal electrical charges as measured by a Hewlett-Packard direct current vacuum tube voltmeter. Over 90% in the malignant group evidenced an energy reversal. Langman concluded that malignancy operates electrically, and that energy reversals can indicate failure of normal physiological functioning. This information is anecdotal only and does not imply cause and effect relationships. It is interesting to me that smokers will generally be psychologically reversed with muscle testing, suggesting that tobacco reverses most people energetically. The Langman study suggests that cancer victims are often reversed, and smokers suffer high rates of cancer.

4. The first correction is generally called Cook's Hook-up and attributed to Wayne Cook, an applied kinesiologist.

5. The second procedure is also attributed to Wayne Cook, though commonly known as the Overenergy Correction (Gallo, 2005).

6. Further information on applied kinesiology see http://www.icakusa.com

7. Homolateral means that energy flows run up and down along one side of the body or another without crossing over to the other side. The cross-over of energy is thought to be important for learning and many cross-over techniques are recommended for children with certain learning disabilities. A simple one is to walk in place, raising your knees high, and touching an elbow to the *opposite* raised knee in alternating fashion. Another exercise is to crawl on hands and knees. Muscle testing before and after these simple procedures will show a change in muscle strength for persons with homolateral conditions.

8. The 3 thumps procedure is from Eden (1998).

9. The crown pull is from Eden (1998).

Chapter 8:
Performance enhancement: visualizing, thinking, feeling, and acting positively, and making a habit of it

A. Positive visualizing, thinking, feeling, acting

Background

During my 15 years as an executive coach, I have noticed that high achievers and their bosses seem to be slowly but definitely shifting from fear-based motivation to a focus on the positive side of achievement. I have coached men and women from some 40 countries, and while I cannot claim that this trend is being endorsed in all sites and cultures, it does seem that more and more clients see coaching as an opportunity and as a reward for doing a good job, rather than as a sign that they are in trouble and need "fixing." As a consequence, my work as a coach has become more enjoyable.

The term "performance enhancement" also grows in popularity, as more and more people are seeking to be coached toward higher levels of development. Both the word coaching and the concept of performance enhancement took root in athletic and sports applications, and today we are well familiar with Olympic competitors who routinely use visualization, positive self-talk, and performance rehearsal to prepare themselves for an event.

Olympic athletes and corporate officers are being joined by many others interested in enhancing their performance. Any one of us can contract with a workout coach at the gym, hire a life coach to help us to "get better at what I want to do," or join a group dedicated to public speaking excellence. Personally, I applaud all of these applications.

I describe a model that I have found useful with many people in addition to athletes and executives. It is based on the assumption that excellence in performance is largely the result of earlier practice in positive (1) visualizing, (2) thinking, and (3) feeling. These three factors can be further strengthened through the use of certain of the exercises.

I begin with the story of an athlete, though I have seen similar results with many other people: a college student who wanted to feel excited rather than fearful as an actor, an abuse victim who wanted to treat both parents with dignity at an upcoming family reunion, a manager who wanted to feel joyful with the decision to have breakfast with his children rather than to run off to work early, and a spouse wishing to have a happier home.

Case example: The competitive cyclist

Andrea[1] was a professional cyclist. She was rarely more graceful than when she was soaring down a mountain pass on her 12-speed. Along with her team, she sometimes lost a race, sometimes won. She experienced more fear than joy, but was generally able to take both wins and losses in stride – except in one particular event. For eight years she had trailed the leaders in an annual road race through the mountains surrounding her birthplace. Not once had she come in first in this event that was largely unknown except to the locals, but of such personal importance to her. She called me for a consult the day before she would enter the race for the ninth time. I was surprised at how nervous this expert cyclist was. I was also surprised at how much she seemed to be motivated more by her fear of failure than by the excitement of a potential success. We had a half-hour meeting, which included this paraphrased dialogue:

Andrea: I know you do this thing called energy work, and that you work with executives. I wonder if you have had any experience with people in other fields. Like mine.

JH: Some. In any case, it probably wouldn't hurt to try.

Andrea: I would just love to win the race this year. It would be really important to my family. And to me, of course. I have this positive reputation in other countries but in my own home they seem to doubt me. Eight years are shaping up to be a pattern.

JH: I might be willing to work with you. We don't have much time, and you seem to be asking for a lot, but I also have a lot of confidence in what I do. But first let me ask about your competitive spirit. I know that's necessary, but I have also seen people fail almost as a result of being too competitive. It might sound kind of paradoxical, but I think it's true, at least some of the time.

Andrea: You know, the same thing has crossed my mind. There are times I get so worked up and then seem to choke because of my nervousness. I wonder if my wanting to win so badly has actually worked against me.

JH: I've got an idea. What if you talked to yourself in certain friendly ways while I taught you to do some of the energy exercises. Then you can imagine yourself acting in those certain friendly ways, and we'll do more exercises.

Andrea: OK. Let's do it.

164

JH: Let's start by you rubbing a sore spot near your heart. Put your right hand over your left shoulder to start, and now slowly move your hand down towards your right elbow, pushing hard to find a sore spot. Did you find it? Good. Now rub that spot, with some pressure, in a clockwise direction – like this. [I demonstrate on myself.] *That's good. Keep rubbing and repeat after me, "I love and accept myself even though I have this competitive spirit."*

Andrea: What do you mean. That's good, isn't it? I mean, to feel competitive. Oh, I get it, too competitive. Paradox. Getting in my way.

JH: That's the idea. It might sound illogical, and this may seem different from the way you usually prepare for an event. Just try saying that. Good. And now keep massaging that sore spot and say, "I deeply and completely accept myself with all my problems, especially the ones that may be getting in the way of my being at my optimal self."

Andrea: OK. [Repeats the affirmations.]

JH: Now here is a really odd one. Say this, "Even if I don't win tomorrow, I deeply and completely love and accept myself."

Andrea: Wow, that's really odd. But here goes. [Repeats statement.]

JH: Good work. Now let's try some alternatives. First, visualize yourself being at your best. Not beating out the competition, not winning, not being better than everyone else, simply being you at your best. Good. And now rub that spot again, and say this after me: 'I am resilient. I am strong. I recover from my pain.' Try those ideas out and add some you would like. [Andrea repeats affirmations and makes up her own.]

Andrea: Interesting. I saw myself speeding along. No one else was there. I was alone. And I saw myself with this great big smile!

JH: I like your scene. Keep that scene, and keep saying your positive ideas, and now tap some points on your body as I show you by tapping on myself. Let's begin with your eyebrows. [I demonstrate EFT, repeating the entire process 3 times.]

Andrea: This feels very interesting. Freeing. 'I am resilient. I am strong. I recover from my own pain. I am prepared. I deserve to feel this good for a change. I deserve to win this race after . . .'

JH: [I interrupt]. Hold that just for a second. What did you say? It's starting to sound competitive again, like 'I'm better than they are.'

Andrea: Wow. And it's so automatic. That's usually the way I do things. Beat out the competition. Be not only better than I've been but better than they are.

165

JH: No problem. And by the way, that's a good insight. Just gently take yourself back to where you were. You are not competing with them. You are not even competing with yourself. You are simply approaching your optimal level of excellence. You can see yourself, you can think about yourself, and you can feel it. Notice, by the way, where you feel all of this in your body. And keep tapping for a bit longer. [Andrea returns to non-competitive affirmations, tapping throughout.]

Andrea: Yeah. That's a new way of looking at it. OK. 'I am strong'. I tap the eyebrow. 'I am resilient'. Outside the eye, 'I have trained and I am a serious bike rider, and I recover from my pain'. Under the eye. That feels good. [She continues in this way for several more minutes.]

Our brief session ended. I asked her to repeat the exercises before the race, and to continue to use the visualizing and self-talk while in the race. I was reluctant to make too much of our brief work, and when she won the race I avoided talking about our session. She volunteered that she had practiced the positive visualizing and self-talk during much of the race, and as she headed toward the finish line in second place she noticed herself saying, "I am strong, I am resilient, I recover from my pain." A rush of energy came over her as she found herself adding that "My pain makes me strong." And then she said to me, "I found myself flying past the finish, and I had none of those usual thoughts about 'I've got to beat this person', just feeling good about myself, and powerful."

As I have mentioned, I have heard similar reports from other clients who found it sufficient to rehearse themselves positively in visual, verbal, and emotional ways while practicing an energy technique. I have also thought about the alternative, that is, rehearsing competitive thoughts, and it has occurred to me how odd this would be if all ten coaches of ten competitors followed the same competitive pattern. What if all ten thought that "I will win this race"? What do we say subsequently to the nine who failed to meet this self-imposed goal? In any case, in the words of Andrea, is it possible that wanting to win so badly can actually work against us.

I have followed up with Andrea. I worked with her for several more sessions and in 2000 she tried out for her country's Olympic team. She did not make the 4-person team, and was very disappointed. We continued to work for several more sessions, she seemed to begin to believe more firmly in the energy concepts, and began to practice on her own. In 2001 she set three records for her country, and in 2002 another one. Had she been at that level of physical, mental, and emotional excellence in 2000, she would easily have gone to the Olympic games.

I cannot, of course, know how much of her improvement can be attributed to her energy work. She told me it was significant, and noted that she had always trained hard even before the energy practice but without such high performance. Someday someone will carry out carefully controlled experiments to isolate the contribution of the exercises. Until then, I will continue to promote their use because of what my clients tell me.

166

The model: visualizing, thinking, feeling – in conjunction with energy exercises

There are five components to the model: the client *visualizes* a positive future scene, *thinks* positively, *feels* appropriately, and does the *exercises* simultaneously to strengthen or "lock in" the positive visual, verbal, and emotional factors. It goes without saying (but I will say it) that it is also necessary to practice, practice, and practice the *skills and behaviors* required for performance success.

Some coaches promote one or more of these ingredients. For example, many athletes are taught to visualize a skill and then to practice it. The other factors are overlooked.

Others focus on the power of language and thinking alone. Many years ago in the U.S. Norman Vincent Peale popularized the notion of the power of positive thinking in his book by the same title. Variations on the theme of "we are what we think" now fill the self-help section of bookstores and libraries around the world. The psychological approach called "cognitive" or "cognitive-behavioral" follows the concept of positive thinking, and is supported by hundreds of scientific studies that prove that the way we think (and speak) can change how we feel and act. While this is true, I have found that the use of language and thinking is quite limited. I was what is called a "cognitive therapist" for years before learning energy methods. My clients would grow tired of having to rehearse positive thoughts several hundred times before they had any impact. I also noticed that many positive results of this treatment were too often short-lived.

Other coaches may concentrate on the feeling factor, and focus on bodywork approaches. Some persons will have their musculature reshaped through painfully intense massages, and for a brief period of time they do indeed seem to move and perform differently. With time, however, they may drift back to their earlier rigid or contorted posture.

While each of these approaches has value, their positive impact can be greatly increased when they are used in conjunction with the methods I have been describing. I believe that professional coaches (and psychotherapists) who add these techniques to their verbal, body-oriented, or other methods will find that their work is more robust and produces more lasting benefit to clients.

Depending on the kind of learner you are, you may prefer to use the following exercises while you visualize, think, or feel in specific positive ways. A visual person, for example, may choose to image a scene that he or she would like to enact in the future. One of my clients saw herself taking a professional exam while repeating an energy technique.

On the other hand, a person who prefers language may wish to practice certain positive words or phrases while doing energy exercises. This approach is in line with the self-help books that teach you to think differently and to talk differently to yourself.

A more somatic or kinesthetic person, that is one who prefers to begin with the body as the source of change, may choose to experience first a positive emotion or sensation, and then to do an energy exercise.

I will comment on these and other modalities within the context of the exercises.

It is not sufficient simply to visualize, feel, and think/talk positively, nor simply to add the energy exercises while doing so; we must also practice the necessary skills and behaviors if we wish to be accomplished and successful in a given area of expertise. This may be obvious to the reader. On the other hand, several years ago it was reported that the school children in a particular country were feeling more positively about their math proficiency than had been the case in earlier years. Unfortunately, another report released about the same time indicated that the scores on math proficiency had dropped compared to earlier measures. Columnists had a field day ridiculing unearned self-esteem, and the tendency in that country's school system to avoid giving low grades lest the student feel discouraged. In my experience as a psychologist, professionals in psychotherapy tend to under-appreciate the value of behavior and tend not to encourage their clients to practice hard skills. Professional coaches, on the other hand, overemphasize skill development and tend to ignore the emotional, trauma-based, and thinking patterns that interfere with performance. I hope the reader will approach a balance between the two dimensions.

Procedural steps in the model

If you have already read chapter one you will be familiar with the procedures I now describe. You can begin by practicing the steps as described, then modify and abbreviate them according to preference.

Because the focus in this chapter is on the positive, I begin the procedural steps by asking a client first to concentrate exclusively on an experience that produces a sense of calm, well-being, gratitude, or love.

Step 1. Write down your goals

What do you wish to gain or achieve from doing the exercise? While you can be specific or general, I recommend you come up with some way of determining if the exercises work for you or not, and if you need to change your goals or your approach. One way is to state a goal in such a way that you can measure changes in you. Let us first look at some statements not clearly related to the person who wrote them, and written in such a way that it would be difficult to determine if the person is getting closer to his/her goal.

"I'd sure like to feel better."
"I just can't get going."
"How I'd love to be like him/her."
"Why am I so gloomy?"
"Things just aren't fair."
"Why does life have to be so hard?"
"Lucky them!"
"I'll let my intuition guide me and just go with the flow."
"I'm going to trust my feelings about that."
"Boy but I wish I could do this math!"
"Everybody loves me!"

Notice how the following are more clear, tangible, personalized, and measurable:

"I will have rehearsed my speech three times before I give it, will breathe the way I have
         been practicing, and will enjoy the experience because I will be ready for it.
"I am going to bicycle 100 miles in one day next summer while feeling physically and
         mentally joyful."
"By tonight I will have completed 12 of the 114 chores that have been awaiting my
         attention."
"Today I'm going to be looking for ways where I can be a good Samaritan, and whenever
         I have the chance, I will help out in some way."

Here are two examples of goals that most of us would probably endorse, while not
requiring that they be strictly measured:

"Every day I have more courage to change what I can, more serenity to accept what I
         cannot change, and more wisdom to tell the difference."

"In the words of the Dalai Lama, I grow 'with those qualities of the human spirit – such
as love and compassion, patience, tolerance, forgiveness, contentment, a sense of
responsibility, a sense of harmony – which bring happiness to both self and others', and
throughout the day I increase my awareness of these values."

Step 2. Find your preferred mode

"Mode" refers to whether you think of yourself as having primarily a visual, verbal, or
emotional/body preference or learning style.

If you are a **visual person**, imagine a positive scene[2]. Take some time to add colors,
pictures, people, and texture so that you feel comfortable, light, and soothed. If negative
pictures enter your scene, gently substitute positives. Your scene can be general or
specific. If general, you might imagine yourself in a forest, on a mountaintop, on a beach,
or some other location that feels good. (If you wish a more specific scene, bring up one

that is relevant to a goal you have set for yourself, such as the one of taking an exam that I mentioned above.)

You will be using neural connections in your body to increase communication among the brain, muscles, and other parts of the body. Experiments suggest that the same neural connections used in an actual performance are employed during visualization of those performances. Whether you imagine yourself giving a public address, having a difficult conversation, doing a long jump, or meeting your prospective in-laws, visualizing beforehand will make you more proficient later. And adding the energy exercises will make you even more proficient.

Set up the scene so that it generates only a positive experience for you. If you need to fabricate the scene so that it is unrealistic but positive, do so. Later you bring it more into reality and re-do the exercise with more realistic mental scenes. For now, the only important thing is that it produce in you a positive sense of being.

Some of my clients will prefer to use a visual aid, such as a photograph to help them visualize. Others prefer to draw or sketch out a scene. In some cases, I will draw while the client talks, and then show my sketch to see if it is what the client intended. Use your own ideas to make your mental picture produce a stronger emotion.

If you are a verbal or rational person who prefers the use of language, you can begin with any word or phrase that sounds good[3]. Some of my clients prefer to invent their own statements. For those who would like help, I offer the following list of starter ideas that I have heard from previous clients. You can find more from any of the self-help books available these days.

I am at peace.
I feel loved.
I am loving.
I look for ways to love better and better.
I forgive myself.
I forgive others.
I seek forgiveness.
I enjoy the good fortune of others.
I deserve to be successful.
I am free of the past.
I welcome challenges as opportunities.
I give thanks for this opportunity to learn.
I am tolerant and accepting.
I see the possibility of a better future.

Figure 41a. **List of affirmations**

I welcome my sexual energies.
I welcome my creative energies.
I am creative.
I am intelligent.
I am wise.
The world is a friendly place.
I distinguish between those who have earned my trust and those that have not.
I deserve to be happy. I am joyful.
There is abundance in the world and around me.
I accept my blessings and share freely.

Some people find the body-focused affirmations to be more helpful:

My forehead is cooling.
My hands are warming.
Me feet are warming.

These are but a few ideas. Some of my clients report that repeating someone else's affirmation is not motivating, and prefer to write their own. I encourage this.

Some people find these statements to be exaggerated, or unrealistic, and prefer to begin with more tentative statements, which can then be made more and more definite.

For example:

I *would like to* feel at peace, or *I am working on* being at peace.
I *would like to* feel loved.
I *prefer to feel* loving.
I *want to* forgive, or I *am learning to* forgive.
I *want to* forgive myself, or I *am learning to* forgive myself.

Some people prefer simply to state certain positive words while doing the exercises, such as:

Acceptance … forgiveness … freedom … hope … abundance … kindness … tolerance … love … justice.

Figure 41b. **List of affirmations (continued)**

A more somatic or kinesthetic person may prefer to begin with a positive emotion or sensation[4]. The best way I know to produce such an experience is to begin with deep breathing (see page 162 and the sections on breathing in chapters 1 - 6). Others will prefer to meditate or do yoga. Some people find it helpful to take a walk through a pleasant wooded park or to sit quietly by running water. If you can afford it, a massage can help you put your body in a positive state through activation of your parasympathetic nervous system. A massage that involves specific stimulation of the lymph nodes will also strengthen your immune functioning.

During a coaching session, helpful questions include these:

"What do you call that emotion?" (For persons who have difficulty identifying or naming emotions, a coach may use a list of emotions to which the client can refer to stimulate these important abilities.)

"Where do you feel that positive sensation in your body?" (I will often ask a client to place a hand over the site of the sensation in order better to appreciate this ability they have to manage and produce their desired emotions and sensations.)

An option for those who still have difficulty is to ask, "Where would that sensation likely be if it had a special place in your body?" Then they can be encouraged to place their hand over that site.

At any point during any exercises designed to produce a positive state, the coach can remind the client of the value of breathing properly:

"Now, just notice your breath as you take it in. Breathe in through your nose. Let it fill your stomach, now your lungs, and hold your breath just for a second, and now exhale, and let the air be released through your mouth, and hold for just a second, and inhale again. And this time as you inhale in through your nose, let the air also fill the place in your body where you have your hand, and now let your stomach, and your lungs, and that special place in your body be filled with air and energy. . ." (and complete as above).

Breathing remains a most portable, reliable, and repeatable resource, and deserves mention from time to time. Persons who have trouble with performance excellence will also be found to breathe inefficiently much of the time.

Step 3. While in your preferred mode and in a positive state, do one or more of the next four exercises

Performance enhancement exercise #1: Deep breathing

Review pages 25 and 26 for the procedural steps for deep breathing.

While you keep yourself in your positive state – with all of the visual, verbal, and emotional components possible – experience your breathing as it puts into operation your nervous system called the "parasympathetic". Slow and deepen your inhalations. (If you also could do the TAT pose or tap the key EFT points, you would probably notice your breathing growing even more rhythmic and calming.)

Performance enhancement exercise #2: TAT

Many people report that doing this simple exercise is sufficient to produce and deepen their positive state[5]. You have the option of follow the procedures on pages 28 through 34, or to hold the pose indicated below while keeping yourself in your positive visual, verbal, and emotional experience. Sometimes negative feelings arise to protest, as it were, our wish to do better at something. You can continue with TAT or switch to breathing, EFT, the Butterfly Hug, or the Leading with your heart exercise (pages 48-53).

Figure 42. **TAT short-form to strengthen the positive**

173

Performance enhancement exercise #3: EFT

One good approach to strengthening a positive state is to tap *all* the key EFT energy points on the body[6]. Keep yourself in your positive visual, verbal, and emotional state and go through the points, beginning with your head and ending with the points on the hand. It is not necessary to follow any particular sequence as long as you tap all the points. You can also review the procedure in detail on pages 40 through 43.

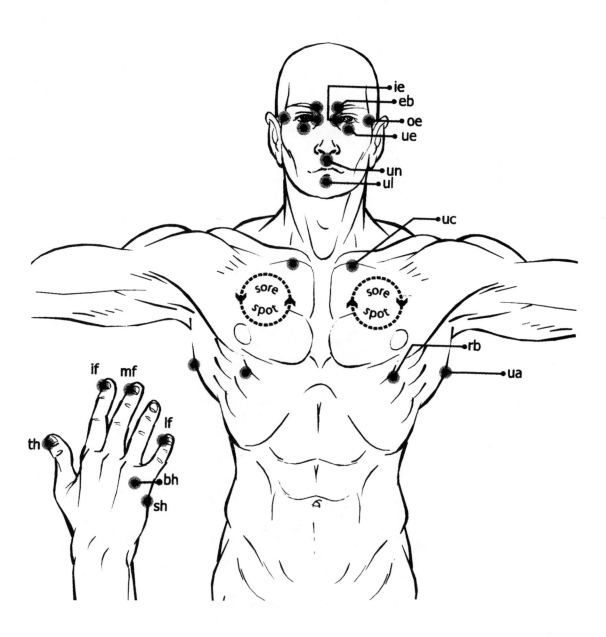

Figure 43. **EFT short form to strengthen the positive**

Some people find that EFT is more powerful if they repeat certain phrases while tapping or touching a given point. The phrases I list below are those traditionally associated with each point (which in turn represents a particular meridian line and body organ). Be attentive to any of the EFT points that cause a particularly meaningful shift for you. You might keep tapping on that point longer to add continuing stimulation to your energy system. Remember the points that are especially meaningfulful for you for future reference.

Example: While *tapping* the eyebrow (**eb**) point 7 or 8 times, or *touching* the inside the eye (**ie**) points while taking one complete breath, you will say, "I am in peace and harmony, every issue has been resolved." You might also invent your own phrase, such as "I seek to be at peace with the world, to share generously, and to allow myself joy at the good fortune of others."

EFT Point	Associated positive emotion and thought
(1) **ie,** or **eb**	**acceptance**: "I am in peace and harmony"; "every issue in me has been resolved"
(2) **oe**	**forgiveness**: "I extend myself with forgiveness and love"
(3) **ue**	**tranquility**: "I am content, I am tranquil, I am satisfied"
(4) **un**	**hopefulness**: "I am hopeful, I can"
(5) **ul**	**worthiness**: "I am deserving, I am worthwhile"
(6) **uc**	**security**: "My sexual and creative energies are balanced, I have possibilities"
(6) **ua**	**faith**: "I am confident in the future, I feel secure"
(7) **rb**	**joy**: "I have humor, I have a positive attitude"
(8) **th**	**tolerance**: "I am modest, I have humility, I am tolerant"
(9) **if**	**forgiving of oneself**: "I am pure, good; I am deserving of unconditional love"
(10) **m**	**generosity**: "I am relaxed and free of jealousy"
(11) **lf**	**love, forgiveness**: "I forgive you [here you can name a specific person]
(12) **sh**	**happiness**: "I am full of happiness"
(13) **bh**	**lightness**: "I am light and buoyant, I feel encouraged and hopeful"

Figure 44. **List of emotions associated with the EFT acupuncture points**

When doing EFT, it is not unusual for a person to notice that one or more points will stimulate a special feeling or sensation, or stir an image or memory. You may consult this list to see if you can figure out which emotion is being stirred up in you. Keep tapping or touching any points that trigger sensations or emotions in you until you feel they are resolved.

175

Performance enhancement exercise #4: The Butterfly Hug

The figure below shows the two points under the collarbones that you tap when doing this exercise. Cross your hands, with the right hand tapping the point on the left side, and the left hand tapping the point on the right side. Tap first one side, then the other side, then the first side, and so forth. Do not tap both sides simultaneously as the purpose here is to produce bilateral and alternating stimulation of the brain. While the exact neurophysiological mechanism involved is not yet known, there are many case studies that suggest the technique is a powerful and safe way to enhance performance[7].

First place yourself in a positive state, *then* do the butterfly hug. This exercise also may also stimulate other experiences that feel negative, so please continue to monitor its impact on you. If the tapping produces a sense of negative feeling or sensation, you can either stop and use one of the above exercises (which usually do not produce this kind of negative side effect) or continue with this strategy to see if it will take you through the negative and into a positive state again. I notice that approximately 5% of my clients who begin focusing on the positive will quickly become distracted by negative memories while they are doing this exercise. If you do this exercise alone, you may not want to risk a deepening negative experience, so consider delaying further work until you have a coach or therapist nearby. Generally, adults run this risk more often than do children, probably because adults have more negative memories stored away that can be triggered.

By furthering communication between the two brain hemispheres, the Butterfly Hug can help you to integrate important experiences that up to that point have been disassociated from one another. In my experience, integration of our various memories and experiences is always preferable to their being disconnected.

Figure 45. **The collarbone points stimulated with the Butterfly Hug**

176

Step 4. Measure the results

You can monitor the changes you experience while doing the exercises, and immediately thereafter, either informally or formally. If informally, you will need to be aware of your body's sensations and emotions, and observe subtle changes. You can also look for changes in the clarity or intensity of your visualizations, and in how you can elaborate your imagination to include sounds, smells, and movement. If you prefer to observe changes in your self-talk and thinking, you can compare the words with which you begin, to those with which you end after doing an exercise. Some of my clients, for example, might begin with something tentative such as "I would like to be successful and generous" and end with "I *will* be."

More formal measures are also popular with many clients. You can invent your own. Begin with a range of numbers that allows you to discriminate among different degrees of positive experience that you would like to have. The three examples[8] that follow would be used to rate "visualization", "positive emotion", and "positive thinking". The zero to four scale I use could be changed to any series of numbers you choose.

I cannot visualize at all   0   1   2   3   4   I can visualize easily

**I do not feel this positive   0   1   2   3   4   I feel this positive
emotion at all   emotion completely**

**I do not believe this positive   0   1   2   3   4   I believe this positive
statement at all   statement completely
(or: This positive thought   (or: This positive thought
feels completely false)   feels completely true)**

Figure 46: **Examples of rating scales for positive experiences**

The objective would be to raise the numbers representing one's experience during the course of doing the exercises. Most of my clients will not choose the highest number until they have actually gone out and done what they have been imagining and thinking about. For example, someone visualizing and feeling confident about giving a speech in public (or riding in a bike race), and saying "I deserve to be at my best", may want to actually perform the skill before allowing themselves to feel totally positive. I concur with this attitude.

The final measure, then, will take place in the future. All of the measures can be kept in a log so that progress can be compared over time, and the differential value of the exercises can be noted.

B. Energy routines and prevention: making a habit out of it

Background

Just as we take vitamins each morning, exercise regularly, and perhaps pray with some consistency, it is recommended that we have a regular energy routine, whether we think we need it or not. John Thie, developer of Touch for Health, paraphrases the well-known axiom: "An ounce of health enhancement is worth a pound of cure" (Thie, 1994, p. 124).

Some energy practitioners prescribe specific programs designed to prevent future psychological and physical problems. For example, Lambrou and Pratt (2000) dedicate 13 pages in their book to EFT strategies for "maintaining emotional fitness." Generally, however, there is no consensus as to the ideal prevention program.

The following few recommendations are intended to prevent energy disruptions, and to supplement our energy reserves before we need them. If you have tried out the exercises in Part One, feel good mentally and physically, and would like to maintain your present state, you may find useful the suggestions that follow. They are meant to be adapted to the needs of the user. Some persons may prefer a regular and daily routine, while others will adapt their schedule depending on the stress in their lives, their exposure to toxic substances, travel demands, and other variations.

If you feel negative emotions, refer to chapters 2 through 5 to review ways to use the exercises to eliminate feelings and thoughts that interfere with the way you would like to be. Then consider using the same exercises for preventive purposes.

The three basic activities can be done in less than 10 minutes. You can also do them while walking or stretching, or in combination with other activities.

The prevention routine involves 3 basic activities

1. **Begin with energy balancing.** Suggestions in this book include the reversal correction (page 150) and two ways for correcting neurological disorganization (pages 152 and 153). These take only a few minutes. Some years ago I underwent meridian testing with a computer-monitored diagnostics procedure which showed that all of my subtle energy lines were over-charged. I did the balancing techniques for five minutes, redid the diagnostics, and was told that all my energy measures were in the normal range. Any doubts I might have had before about the validity of these techniques were forever dispelled. I now do these balancing procedures regularly.

2. **Stimulate your neurolymphatic system and your immunological defenses.** Vigorous tapping on your thymus, under the collarbone, and on the ribs defines the procedure called the three thumps (pages 157-161). The reversal correction mentioned above also activates immune system defenses.

3. **Do a brief energy routine based on key meridian points, with a positive focus.** In my experience, TAT (pages 28-35) and EFT (pages 36-44) are of superior value in terms of efficacy, efficiency, and safety. Some persons may prefer to use cardiac coherence procedures along with related software to provide biofeedback (pages 48-53) or the Butterfly Hug (pages 54-55). How to use these powerful techniques with a positive focus was just described.

Whatever else you add depends on your time and inclination

A physical fitness routine. I have commented in chapters 1 through 5 on the benefits of fitness for psychological as well as physical health. It is worth mentioning that keeping fit by doing something enjoyable can help to maintain a routine.

Your physical environment. Toxic substances in the air, soil, the water we drink, and the food we eat, and chemicals in our own bodies, can cause psychological and physical illness. While it might be desirable for all of us to live in a naturally healthful place, this is not realistic. To some degree we can challenge the impact of a toxic environment. My wife, Nikki, and I once joined with Sandi and Bob Radomski for an allergy treatment training in Mexico City. This city is relatively polluted, yet we were able to help every participant in the program to reduce their allergy symptoms through the use of TAT, EFT, and similar treatments. This is not to say that we should not work to improve our physical environments, only that there is temporary help available while we await more enlightened stewardship of our physical world. The work of Sandi and Bob and others is highlighted in appendix A.

Diet. I have commented on omega-3 and other foods as examples of how the food we ingest can affect our emotions and thinking. Food allergies can also be treated in the way described in the previous paragraph.

This short list is a beginning. Others might add social environment, work, spirituality, community service. If you practice the exercises as described in chapters 1 through 5 for resolving problems, you will learn about your vulnerabilities and liabilities and can add in prevention routines that strengthen the opposing and positive condition. For a modern-day example: I bicycle city streets in different countries and frequently feel intolerant of the way people drive their vehicles (imagine!). Holding my index fingers over the thumbnail points while saying "my intolerance" is a guaranteed way for me to release negative emotions, smile, and enjoy the route (see pages 174-175).

Notes to Chapter Eight

1. I told the story of Andrea elsewhere (Hartung & Galvin, 2003).

2. Visualizing ourselves in a future performance is a powerful way to rehearse neural connections that we will actually use in the future – a principle that Olympic athletes have followed for years. Some people find it difficult to visualize. For these, the verbal and kinesthetic modes are excellent substitute tools. Some persons also find that they are better able to visualize after doing the EFT exercises for a period of time.

3. "A phrase that sounds good" is one way to understand the theory that "we are what we think." The "power of positive thinking," "cognitive therapy," and "phenomenology" are synonyms. This is also the philosophy for many self-help books that teach how to change "self talk". While I do not find cognitive approaches to be particularly potent by themselves, in conjunction with the energy exercises they can have great impact.

4. Synonyms for this section are kinesthetic, body, somatic, emotion, sensation, and physical. Physical movement or focus is the key. In meditation, a kinesthetic person might find yoga to be preferred to a visually mediated practice (for example, where the person meditating visualizes an imaginary candle flame), or one that involves repetition of a vocal stimulus (such as a mantra).

5. Using the TAT pose while focusing on positive thoughts and experiences will often be sufficient to resolve mild traumatic memories as well.

6. Gary Craig, the developer of EFT for solving problems, has more recently focused on positive uses of EFT. His nearly 100-page book titled *The Palace of Possibilities* can be downloaded from Craig, 1999: [file://D|EFT Ideas\palaceof1.htm].

7. If you use the Butterfly Hug to strengthen positive thoughts, images, and emotions, be aware that it will sometimes trigger traumatic memories that are related to the positive aspects you are hoping to strengthen. This is rare, but if it does occur it is prudent to recall that you have two options: continue with the alternating taps to see if you can resolve trauma, or stop and do another exercise. You can also consult a professional who practices EMDR, from which the Butterfly Hug was derived. See Appendix A.

8. You can invent your own scales. I once treated a child who could not imagine the scale, so I showed him a box of polished stones and carved figures that I had in my office. I asked him to choose one that looked happiest to him (which we called "0") and one that looked terrible (which we called "10"). He then picked 9 more to complete a 0 to 10 scale, and lined them up. Then he moved the one that looked like how he felt at that moment. During treatment he moved other stones and figures as his feelings and thoughts changed. Since then I have used this with adults as well as children, and find the symbolic value to be a benefit in addition to the measurement purpose.

Part Three:

Different ways to introduce and use the exercises

In Part One the focus was on eliminating negative ways of thinking, feeling, and acting.

In Part Two we visited some of the innovative methods that help us to replace the negative with positive substitutes.

Part Three begins with chapter nine for persons who want to teach the exercises to others, namely psychotherapists, medical personnel, and coaches.

Chapter ten includes some ideas for introducing the rather unusual ideas and exercises I have described, depending on the perspective and questions of the client.

Chapter 9:
Professional use by therapists, medical personnel, and coaches

I wrote this book in part for persons seeking a self-contained resource. I wanted it to contain a series of instructions sufficiently clear that readers would be able to treat themselves for a wide range of problems without needing additional professional assistance. For those able to use this book all by yourselves, I congratulate you.

I am also aware that even the most clearly written self-help handbooks are often filed away unread. Apparently many of us prefer to rely on another person to guide us initially, and to motivate us until we make the procedures our own. This chapter is written for those guides, specifically those who treat others through therapy and who train therapists; those who teach and practice medicine; and executive coaches, life coaches, and learning coaches. While I limit my comments to these three groups, I hope these suggestions are also relevant to teachers, day-care workers, hospice staff, and others in the helping professions.

Caution:

First let me warn providers about the power you will have using these new treatment methods. It seems clear by now from thousands of clinical reports that the exercises in this book produce significant and permanent change for most people, a claim that has not always been justified in the field. The implication is that those who use the methods need to be informed about the consequences of healing. Some people may allow themselves to be persuaded by providers to use the exercises before they are informed of their power. Whether we are psychologists, physicians, or coaches, we need to assure that we have given our clients all of this information before proceeding with treatment. To clarify this point, I mention two examples.

In one study, EMDR (the basis for the Butterfly Hug) was used to treat law enforcement personnel for stress[1]. Overall benefits were positive. However, two detectives, subjects in the study, said afterwards that they felt they had lost their "edge" because they were no longer able to easily shut out extraneous thoughts and feelings. The term "secondary gain" may need to be reconsidered: some people may in fact be unprepared to resolve all of the problems that trouble them because of real benefits that the problems may afford.

As a second example, I am involved with several groups training mental health staff on military bases where we are acutely aware that treating a *retired* solider for posttraumatic stress disorder (PTSD) is much less complicated than treating PTSD in persons planning to return to a war zone. In the latter case the soldier may depend on certain trauma symptoms, such as hyper-alertness, to increase the chances of survival. Similar cautions need to be considered whenever we treat persons who live in situations of continuing danger, such as a home where domestic violence or suspected child abuse continue.

Psychotherapists

While there remain psychotherapists who choose to work long-term with their patients on the premise that behavior change requires much effort, time, and expense, more and more of the people who work in clinical psychology and psychotherapy are following a brief therapy model. And while some psychotherapists insist that change can only occur through extensive talking and a long-term relationship between the helper and person being helped, others are taking a more direct approach and focusing on immediate relief for their clients.

Psychotherapists and other helpers around the world now use only the exercises in this book to treat their patients for a wide range of presenting problems. Thousands of individuals have been trained in TAT, EFT, and the tapping shortcuts from TFT, for example, and many of these consider themselves exclusive practitioners of one or another of these techniques. Many other psychotherapists (myself included) use the exercises within a broader treatment protocol. We still use the verbal therapies at times, employ other treatment approaches in an eclectic way, and teach specific skills in communications and problem solving as needed.

Some members of the academic and professional community criticize the exercises in the book on the basis that most of these have not been scientifically tested and supported. This is in line with a push for "evidence based" treatment[2]. Those of us who use the new (and scientifically untested) approaches make the following observations:

• "Evidence" usually refers to results of laboratory studies. It is not clear how closely laboratories parallel real life, however. For example, laboratory researchers typically study only clearly defined and highly specific problems. Real-life patients who come to a clinic seeking treatment for complex problems in living would be excluded from the study. By the time all of the exclusions are considered, only about 15% of real-life patients will be shown to have benefited, and yet the treatment will be judged to have been "empirically supported." Such a conclusion is not very relevant to the work of a practicing clinician.

• Simply knowing what the average benefit is from a given treatment tells little about what a patient can expect from a specific therapist using that specific treatment. I have suggested that clients would be better informed if we published our personal histories of success and failure treating persons with specific problems (Hartung & Galvin, 2003). That way a patient seeking help for a phobia, for example, would have some idea of the likely time and expense involved, and the likelihood of benefit, while working with a particular therapist using a particular treatment method.

• Traditional institutions of higher education tend to study traditional therapies. There is relatively little financial or scientific support for the study of alternative psychology (though the situation is improving). As a result, those who find that the new approaches benefit their patients, but who have only case studies to defend their position, are more open to criticism from the scientific community. In chapter three I mentioned a study of the successful treatment of persons with public speaking anxiety using the tapping shortcut (Schoninger, 2004). The study author, who conducted research related to her psychology doctorate, had to fund the costs of the study herself; she could find none of the research grants that are readily available for traditional graduate school research.

• Much of the psychotherapy empirical literature is directed towards professionals. It is not likely that professionals will ever reach more than a tiny percentage of those who suffer, however, and too often those not reached are persons marginalized by poverty and lack of access to services. The new therapies can be taught to non-professionals, are easily converted for self-use, are efficient and cost-effective, can be conducted in groups, are safely used in situations of disaster and crisis where more traditional approaches would be inappropriate, and do not require verbal insight – in short, they have much to justify their use and proliferation.

Medical personnel

I will describe three experiences I have had to exemplify how the exercises I have been describing can be used in medical settings.

I was once called to a hospital to work with a woman who had arrived for pelvic surgery but had become so agitated that her planned operation could not be initiated. A brief consult with the medical staff told me that the patient had become extremely upset when the male surgeon had begun to touch her. The touching had triggered a memory of when she had been raped as a child. The presence of female staff was not sufficient for the patient to feel protected. When I arrived she was speaking as if she were still the seven-year-old child in danger of further abuse. I continued to consult with the staff to educate the patient about the medical procedure, and she eventually agreed to let me teach her some brief exercises to help her feel safe. After an hour the patient had resolved her fear of the surgery, and was able to stay in the present as a grown woman with resources and up-to-
date knowledge. She underwent her surgery later that morning and reported weeks later that it had been a positive experience.

That is an extremely brief summary of all we did together. In essence, I used the exercises in this book to help the patient to get free of the childhood memory of having been sexually assaulted, a memory that had been triggered by the surgeon's touch, and which caused the patient to regress to a very early age. Any attending medical staff person could learn in a weekend the basics of what I had done to help the patient.

On a second occasion I taught TAT and EFT to a group of ER physicians enrolled in a program on alternative medicine. The program took place in a country said to be the one of the most dangerous in the world at the time, which meant that many ER patients arrived with both physical trauma and emotional distress – as a result of a terrorist attack, street violence, or domestic abuse. The ER physicians had gotten frustrated with seeing patients who sought medicine but who clearly would benefit more from help with their psychological traumas. I was to open the program with three days of trauma theory and practice in specific techniques. Subsequent to my course they would study acupuncture, homeopathy, and naturopathy. By the third day they were treating their patients while I watched and supervised. My point is that the exercises I have described can be learned and used with efficiency and safety and that they are splendid bridges for those who accept the mind-body premise. The sponsor of the program, by the way, eventually stopped doing surgery and is presently seeking funds to measure the effectiveness of TAT with traumatized peace officers in his country.

My final comment has to do with those many cases where a client came with a psychological problem and left reporting both psychological and physical-medical benefits. One patient came for anger management and left so relieved of his intestinal distress that his surgeon had to cancel a planned operation: there were no detectable physical symptoms remaining. Not being medically trained, I had not said, "I might be able to help you with your physical pain." Nonetheless, it is not unusual for clients to find simultaneous physical and psychological relief with the new therapies. In another case a person with chronic pain from fibromyalgia was able to eliminate 90% of her pain during a one-hour demonstration in a course I was giving; a year later when I checked in she said she still was well. Another person, blind from age eight, came to resolve deep depression and suicidal ideas. In the process of resolving the awful memory that caused her to become psychosomatically blinded 25 years earlier she began to recover her eyesight, much to the surprise of her ophthalmologist. Again, I certainly would not offer to help a blind person to see, but for those of us who work in trauma it makes sense that if a person can resolve the traumatic cause of this or other psychosomatic symptoms, then the physical symptom might also remit.

I end this section with a quote from an ER physician: "How can we justify giving medicine to those patients that we suspect to be suffering from memories of terrible abuse suffered, when we know of interventions that can help to heal the past in an efficient and safe way, and when we also know that our medicine – with all of its side effects and dependency complications – is at best a short-term fix?" In the appendix I will refer to some resources for medical providers. There appears to be more funding for research into complementary and alternative medicine (than there is for psychology). In the US government, for example, there is a department with this specific focus[3].

Coaches[4]

When I teach the exercises to coaches, I discuss them within a broader coaching model. This section begins with definitions of coaching and ends with the model.

A definition of coaching

Coaching can be thought of as a collaborative relationship between two persons, composed primarily of one-on-one interactions, where the person contracting for services identifies learning goals and the coach uses clearly stated approaches and measures designed for goal achievement. This definition is accurate though neither specific nor very useful, and in trainings I spend some time helping participants to define their own definitions. In one memorable training program a participant described the work of a midwife as a coach, thereby helping the other attendees to get much clearer ideas of their unique goals as coaches-in-training. Through the process they also were able to understand that the operational definition of coaching changes with the needs of the person seeking the coach's services. This will become clearer in the context of the model I present below.

Types of coaching

While there are general skills that overlap from one definition of coaching to another, there are also profound differences among the different fields of coaching. A person competent in one form of coaching will not necessarily be competent in another. As of this writing there were no legal requirements for any type of coaching, so essentially anyone who wishes can market services as a "coach."

Four common types of coaching are development planning with a focus on individual feedback, coaching for specific content, career coaching, and personal or life coaching.

(1) Development planning for an individual usually is sponsored by the person's organization that has a specific interest in seeing the person improve in some area important to the organization. Often 360-degree feedback is used as part of the coaching process. The term "360-degree" means that information about the client is gathered from persons who surround the individual and have varying authority relationships with the individual: a boss or superior, peers, persons who report to the individuals, and the individual him- or herself. Data from different sources are compared, and strengths and weakness are noted.

While there are some constraints on the sense of trust, given that the organizational interests are obvious, I generally find few intrinsic obstacles in this kind of contract. It is essential that confidentiality be established: that none of the information I receive will be shared with anyone other than the client. Once this level of privacy is established, clients will speak openly about their personal goals and developmental needs.

Earlier in the book I described a client who seemed to others to be chronically angry, and other clients who were burdened by memories of failure. All benefited from learning about the techniques in this book even though the coaching contract was brief and occurred over very few sessions, typically one to three. As the reader may recall, in each of the cases described, I had been initially asked to coach an individual on a specific organizational or work-related issue. During that brief period the client then asked me if I might be able to suggest a strategy for reducing anxiety, putting the past in the past, or managing angry emotions. At such times it is particularly important for me to have several efficient and effective techniques that I can teach in a short period of time, without interrupting the original purpose of the coaching contract.

(2) Coaching for content focuses on learning and practicing specific knowledge and skills. Examples include computer literacy, financial expertise, time management, presentation skills, management of the media, and writing skills. The person having difficulty learning a skill is likely to arrive with some sort of fear: performance anxiety, memory of failure, or fear of success. Others have already learned the technical part of the skill, but cannot perform it because of the emotional interference.

I recall a manager (who grew up using paper and pencils) who would break into a sweat every time he sat in front of his computer, and who became even more nervous when he felt observed. I had to meet with him at his office where he would practice anxiety-reduction techniques (from chapter 3) while looking at his computer. He was unable to become friends with his machine until he practiced the techniques in real life.

(3) Career coaching typically consists of a limited number of sessions focused on a client's career aspirations and plans. Career coaches provide expert feedback, advice, and guidance on career and work-life decisions, career transitions, and related activities.

A coach working in this area might listen especially for attitudes and emotions that keep the client from planning wisely, taking calculated risks, or visualizing success. These clients may need to change habits that interfered with success in the past and could limit their reach in the future. To the degree that fears about future success or risk-taking are based on unresolved early memories, the exercises can be quite helpful in helping the client to put the past to rest and to focus more clearly on the prevent and future.

(4) Personal or life coaching has become popular in recent years as an alternative to traditional counseling and psychotherapy. The focus tends to be on client strengths and goals for self-improvement, instead of on pathology.

This may be the most obvious format for using the material in this book. There are fewer obstacles to confidentiality as the individual usually contracts services privately, and conversations are more easily directed towards private (versus organizational) goals. Managing emotions, thinking more positively, or setting personal development goals can take the place of the more business-related objectives that one encounters, for example, in executive coaching. In this role, I find that what I do and say closely parallels my work in clinical psychology.

Personal or life coaching requires many of the skills and attitudes of an effective psychotherapist, but of course the coach must know have more specialized coaching skills. On the other hand, this may be the area where it is easiest for a professional psychotherapist to transition into the coaching profession.

e.m.p.o.w.e.r.m.e.n.t.
A model for coaching and coach training

While putting some final touches to a coaching curriculum I was preparing, I noticed that the abbreviations for the various concepts I was planning to teach spelled out the word "empowerment". I now use this acronym as the basis for my courses on coaching. Beginning coaches can also use the model as a checklist or inventory. Each letter represents, in my opinion, one of the core attitudes or competencies that characterize the effective coaches I know.

The first *e* refers to **education and experience.** I begin the course by asking participants to work in small groups and simply to "list the competencies and qualities you associate with effective coaching." Few of the groups write about the prior education or experience of the coach, so this leads to fruitful discussions about their reasons for attending the course. One usual conclusion at this point: a good coach is also a good psychologist (whether formally trained or not), and good psychologists can become good coaches (though some adjustment is required). Later in the course I might ask each to draw a time line, with specific dates for when they will have accomplished specific learning objectives, and the date when they expect to offer coaching services (if they have not already begun). Throughout coaching we ask: "What do I need to learn next to be an effective coach in such-and-such a situation?"

The first *m* is about how we **market** ourselves and to others. Marketing to a prospective client is an essential skill that must be included in any coaching training. In order to market to others we must have confidence in *ourselves*. Invariably some participants in a course will admit that that they have doubts about their aptitude to become coaches; this self-doubt can become a target for practicing the exercises, especially within the format described in chapter eight. For example, if a participant asks about how to feel more confident about providing a service in which he or she already has skill and experience, the trainer can demonstrate talking to a potential client, then ask the participant to role play a similar encounter. It is also possible to demonstrate the use of TAT or EFT to teach the participant to rehearse positive thoughts and visualizations. If the trainer is attentive to the individual, allows the person to formulate his or her own positive goal without making it sound magical, and is careful not to exploit the individual in any way (not showing off or becoming too directive), this kind of demonstration will produce many benefits: assist the individual, demystify the notion of personal change, establish a learning environment for the course, and allow the trainer to demonstrate one of the techniques. I have found this to be a very natural medium both for introducing the value of the exercises and practicing them. I introduce this idea by reminding participants of our goals in the course: to leave with greater self-knowledge, not just greater knowledge.

P = **presentation or presence**: physical style, manner, posture, and so forth. This relevant to first impressions, and ongoing demeanor. Some coaching relationships fail because the coach does not appear to be professional, serious, friendly, or interested. This is one of the specific skills that can be practiced with videotaped, debriefed in a small group setting, and re-practiced. The power of videotaping for increasing self-awareness in this kind of learning context cannot be overstated.

O = **ownership**. This refers to how much the client "owns" or feels accountable for the problem to be tackled in coaching. The coach asks how the client defines the problem, and what the client has already done to try to solve it. The coach can then judge how committed the client is before generating new solutions. I notice in my coaching that both coaches and clients are often impatient at this point to get to the next solution opportunity. In the process they can fail to understand the problem, and can overlook the efforts that the client has already made to solve it. This is the moment where the coach questions his or her assumptions, and listens carefully for information about the client's values, history, goals, means, and doubts, and about the resources as well as restraints within the client's cultural context.

W refers to the question, **"What will you do?"** which gives an immediate solution focus to the client's objectives. The previous paragraph has more to do with the past; this one is related to the future. They are quite different issues. Asking about the future opens up the possibility of helping the client to develop problem-solving skills, versus having the coach do this work. Generally the solution to a specific problem is not as important as helping the client to become a more creative problem solver in the future. A beginning coach will often feel anxious at these moments and be tempted to help out. An exercise for reducing this anxiety can be found in this book.

The next *e* refers to **evaluation** processes that assess the present situation and allow for measuring changes later. This can be formal (for example, with 360-degree feedback instruments) or informal.

R = **"relative"** to what? to whom? and to how?. Very little about coaching has meaning in the abstract. The comments about client ownership and the evaluation process need to be interpreted in terms of the client's context: Who wants you to get coaching? What are challenges that you are personally facing at this time? What is the climate and morale in your organization? How are ethics, diversity, and values defined? I recall meeting a single, splendidly ethical and successful financial officer who came to me for career coaching, but who really wanted to talk about how to find a soul mate.

The second *m* relates to the **manner** of the coach, referring to "soft skills" such as attitudes, style, personality, and disposition. This category is consistently over-endorsed during the first exercise in the course where participants write down words they associate with effective coaches: respectful, attentive, energetic, and trustworthy are some that regularly appear. These and other qualities are of course essential, but often a beginning coach (particularly one who comes from the psychotherapy field) will assume that they are also sufficient. On the other hand, beginning coaches who do not have experience in field of psychotherapy may actually underrate these qualities.

The next *e* refers to **expertise**, referring to "hard skills". I ask participants to think of two types of hard skills, the more general (that are useful across different types of coaching), and the more specific (that have to do with the specialty coaching that one chooses to enter). At this point in the workshop I introduce the exercises that I have been describing throughout this book. My assumption, as I have already said, is that every coach can become more effective and resourceful if he or she is able to teach a client how to manage or eliminate emotional and cognitive obstacles to self-development. Here are some common responses from the participants in my courses:

• Participants in my coaching courses widely agree that every coach in at least some coaching situations will probably be able to use and teach the exercises. Whether the coach is called on to help with public speaking anxiety, reducing stress, or jet lag – it seems obvious that the coach who can offer a specific and useful suggestion at that time will be seen as more helpful and skilled.

• Not every client will need this kind of assistance, and it is also important for the coach not to impose recommendations outside of the client's context. Some clients who mention a problem of this type may not yet be ready to want to resolve it, and prior to approaching a solution, the coach needs to ensure that the client sees a real problem. The notion of secondary gain can be useful here: certain problems or symptoms, while causing misery, also produce a desirable benefit that the client is not yet prepared to forego. I recall one client who said he wanted to stop being troubled by the loss of a loved one, then fired me when I suggested this was possible. He later said he though I was trivializing the importance of his loss.

N = **negotiate and renegotiate**. Frequently the person being coached will ask to modify the original contract. Sometimes a client will contract for help on a corporate issue, and then mention that it would be personally more meaningful to resolve a haunting memory or learn to stand up more comfortably in public.

T = **time and timing.** The coach is sensitive to the pacing of the client, and is able to adjust to changing needs. A coach can misjudge by responding too enthusiastically or too casually to a client's request for services.

Miscellaneous learning activities

Participants in coach training are videotaped on at least two occasions so that they can view themselves under pre- and post-conditions. That is, after the first video, we play back the tape with generous time for debriefing in small groups. On a subsequent day they are invited to re-do the exercise they chose to practice. This model allows for practice in the specific exercises in the event that a participant chooses to learn them specifically.

When participants ask for specific training in the self-help exercises we design practice sessions that allow participants to work on something that is personally meaningful while practicing the exercise. Participants may ask to work on self-doubt, public speaking anxiety, fear of failure, or fear of the future. For those who admit to no unfinished problems, we set up a performance enhancement situation as described in chapter eight. I have not yet had a situation where this proposal was rejected. In this latter case participants first imagine positive scenes related to future goals, add in their own affirmations, then work with each other using the exercises (usually TAT or EFT) to strengthen the intensity of the visual scene, the depth of their positive emotion, and the believability of their positive beliefs about themselves and their possibilities.

Psychotherapy "versus" coaching

In virtually every book and seminar on professional coaching, some effort is made to distinguish coaching from psychotherapy. I have had more difficulty with such a distinction since I realized that I could use the innovative exercises both in my psychotherapy work and as an executive coach.

As a psychotherapist, I have found over the years that the average time I spend with a client is being reduced, and at present is about four to five hours. Well over 90% of my clients report satisfaction with the work they do with me within that time frame, so I believe the relatively few hours I spend with them is justified. I attribute this in part to the power of the new approaches to healing that I have learned, and in part to what seems to be more interest in short-term work, be it therapy or coaching.

Other psychotherapists who use these new approaches report similar results, and since 1996 I have become more and more involved in teaching the new approaches to my colleagues. As of this writing I have taught, trained, and supervised in many countries. In some cases the content of a course requires that the student have training and experience in professional psychotherapy. But in many other cases what I teach is a modification of the basic concepts and techniques I have described earlier in the book, which means that nonprofessionals can – and do – attend the courses.

This makes sense to me. If healing were to remain exclusively in the hands of the relatively few professional psychotherapists in the world (psychologists, psychiatrists, social workers, marriage and family counselors) there would be little hope that we would reach more than a small and select sample of those who suffer. The reality is that when people seek out help for their problems, they do not first think of a professional clinician. And in many countries where I have trained, the lack of professional resources requires that one look elsewhere.

I am pleased to report that for the most part, professional psychotherapists and nonprofessionals mingle freely and respectfully in the courses where I teach TAT, EFT, cardiac coherence, or the other exercises I have introduced. I also have difficulty at times predicting which group will learn to use the skills more expertly. As these healing strategies become more widely distributed, more of those potential patients who have gone unnoticed by traditional psychotherapy are being reached. I also find it interesting that psychotherapy is becoming more and more acceptable to both sexes. Fifteen years ago most of my clients were female (as is still the case with traditional therapists); today half or more of my clients are male.

I see something similar occurring in the field of coaching. There are many "traditional" coaches who focus on motivational approaches, talking, encouragement, behavioral rehearsal, feedback instruments, and experiential learning, and as far as these methods go they are positive. Meanwhile there are other coaches discouraged by the rather modest results that accrue from using these resources alone, and who have too often noticed that even when there is reported change, it does not necessarily maintain. Parallel with what has happened in psychotherapy, this group has begun to look for other resources that might help a coaching client "get to the bottom" of what is interfering with excellence. Fortunately there are teachers and mentors who invent and experiment and who are willing to share what they discover. In my own case, when I had what I considered a good collection of new and efficacious resources, I decided it was time to write this book.

I soon found, of course, that I was teaching much the same material to both psychotherapists and coaches. The new approaches to healing, which are changing the notion of psychotherapy, also serve as a bridge to the coaching profession. Even as coaching becomes more standardized and distinctive as a profession, I believe that the new approaches to healing, change, and personal development (the very approaches on which this book's exercises are based) could also cause the distinction between psychotherapy and coaching to blur.

Notes to chapter nine

1. Psychotherapists interested in opposing views on evidence-based practice may consult Beutler & Harwood (2000), Edwards, Dattilio, & Bromley (2004), Fox (2004), Koocher (2004), McCabe (2004), Messer (2004), and Wampold & Bhati (2004).

2. See Wilson, Becker, Tinker, & Logan (2001).

3. US government resources include the National Center for Complementary and Alternative Medicine [http://www.nccam.nih.gov] and the White House Commission on Complementary and Alternative Medicine [http://www.whccamp.hhs.gov/finalreport.html]

4. Books available in 2005 on coaching include those by Auerbach (2001), Busch Lee & Pinney (2002), The Executive Coaching Forum (2001 or latest draft), Fitzgerald & Berger (2000), Goldsmith, Lyons, & Freas (2002), Hargrove (2002), Hays & Brown (2004), Kilburg (2000), Kinlaw (2002, second edition), Leonard (1998), Williams & Davis (2002), and Zaccaro (2001).

See Appendix A for additional information on psychotherapy, medicine, and coaching.

Chapter 10: Some ways to introduce the exercises

I use five strategies to help my clients to understand the exercises, to try them out, and to make them a habit: metaphors, science, reference to esoteric traditions, demonstrations, and practice.

Metaphors

By metaphor I mean that I use something familiar to the person to explain the exercise in an indirect way. Metaphors are especially useful in discussing the mechanism involved with TAT, EFT, and the tapping shortcuts. In an earlier chapter I wrote about the electrician who interrupted my complicated explanation of the body's energy currents; he said it "sounds kind of like the electricity that flows through utility wires, and the step-up transformers sound like those acupuncture points." His comment allowed me to find a way to talk about acupuncture points by drawing a parallel with daily life.

Another way to explain TAT, EFT, and the tapping shortcuts is to begin with the naturally occurring electrical fields in the body. People are already familiar with the biological fields in the heart (measured by the EKG) and the brain (measured by the EEG). They also know that there was a time when these energies were not measurable, but they existed nonetheless. It seems that the three exercises mentioned depend on similar energies, though these are subtle and not easily measured by the devices we have available today. Instead, we look to results, and then we hypothesize as to how what happened might have happened.

I also refer to a device that is used in major hospitals to heal bones. It is known that a healing bone produces a specific vibration – in its cells, molecules, and atoms. Bones that do not heal naturally, on the other hand, produce a different vibratory frequency. A group of researchers was able to build a small direct current generator that produces the vibration frequency required for bone healing. When this device is placed near a bone that has not healed, it seems to recalibrate the vibrations in the bone, so that even patients who have had broken bones for up to 40 years can start their healing[1]. I then suggest to my patients that they may be doing something similar with the TAT, EFT, and tapping shortcut techniques. (Though the bone healing work is scientific, I include the reference as a metaphor because it is only hypothetically related to the exercises mentioned).

Science

There are additional scientific data more directly supportive of most of the exercises. Studies supporting cardiac coherence (exercise #5) and physical activity (#7) were mentioned in chapters 1 through 5.

A recently published book on "attitude breathing" combines a breathing pattern and HeartMath (or cardiac coherence) procedures[2]. HeartMath scientists have researched the physiology of emotion and the mechanisms by which emotions influence thinking, behavior, and health. Studies to date have shown how the process of HeartMath breathing produces a shift in autonomic balance toward increased parasympathetic activity (i.e., relaxation), and how the heart's energy can entrain other body organs. Exciting new research suggests that "positive emotions, such as love and appreciation, [generate] coherence both in the heart field and in social fields", which implies that individuals with love and positive intentions enhance not only their own mental and physical health, but the well-being of those around them[3]. Exercise #5 in chapters 1 through 5 may become more intriguing when these studies are shared with clients.

Exercises #2 (TAT), # 3 (EFT), and #4 (tapping shortcuts) are based largely on meridian theory and acupuncture sites. The World Health Organization, the U.S. National Institutes of Health and many insurance companies recommend acupuncture for various physical problems, and it is a short step to say that the same acupuncture sites are useful for treating psychological problems. One difference is that that needles are not used. Another is that for our purposes only a few of the acupuncture sites need to be stimulated.

Depending on the interest of my client, I may refer to an article that explains how endorphins are produced when needles are inserted into acupuncture points, to studies of the benefits of acupuncture with medical problems, or to articles on the subtle energies[4].

Studies on the therapeutic value of meridian-based treatments are also available. Many case studies reflect the benefits of EFT and the tapping shortcut[5].

The Butterfly Hug is derived from the therapeutic method Eye Movement Desensitization and Reprocessing (EMDR), a powerful treatment for trauma and related anxiety, depression, and anger[6].

A caution: EMDR can be taught to and employed only by professional therapists. The derivative described in this book as the Butterfly Hug is widely recommended for self-use. What is the distinction? EMDR appears to function through a form of alternating bi-lateral stimulation that can be tactile (tapping), or visual-motor (eye movements), or auditory (alternating sounds). Only the bilateral and alternating *tapping* is recommended for self-use. And when one does the Butterfly Hug it is important to do *only tapping* and not to add eye movements or sounds alternating from side to side. The eye movements and alternating sounds have been found to be too powerful and too likely to trigger stronger negative feelings, and are to be avoided unless one works under the direction of a trained and licensed professional psychotherapist. For the same reason, the research on EMDR should be referred to only to support the provision of EMDR by professionally trained clinicians, and not directly to defend the self-use of the Butterfly Hug.

Esoteric traditions

The Asian systems of meridians and acupuncture were already mentioned in the context of TAT, EFT, and tapping shortcuts. The points used for preventing jet lag are also understood within this tradition. For those familiar with acupuncture, the following list[7] indicates which of the meridian points is stimulated in the jet lag figures on pages 140 and 141:

5 am – 7 am = the first point of the large intestine meridian (LI-1)
7 am – 9 am = stomach 36 (St-36)
9 am – 11 am = spleen 3 (Sp-3)
11 am – 1 pm = heart 8 (Ht-8)
1 pm – 3 pm = small intestine 5 (SI-5)
3 pm – 5 pm = bladder 66 (Bl-66)
5 pm – 7 pm = kidney 10 (K-10)
7 pm – 9 pm = circulation-sex 8 (Cx-8)
9 pm – 11 pm = triple warmer 6 (TW-6)
11 pm – 1 am = gall bladder 41 (GB-41)
1 am – 3 am = liver 1 (Liv-1)
3 am – 5 am = lungs 8 (Lu-8)

Figure 46. **Meridian locations of the jet lag energy points**

Many more clients than I would have first expected are not only open to these esoteric theories, but surprisingly many have also received some form of so-called alternative or complementary treatment. It has been interesting both for me and for these clients to note the overlap between western science and eastern tradition. A good example is the relationship between the body's receptor sites and the ancient chakras.

When Dr. Candace Pert[8] of Georgetown University discovered that the concentrations of receptor molecules tended to be found on the sites of the chakras, she also noticed that there was no such overlap with the crown chakra. This was consistent with chakra tradition which held that the 7th chakra actually floated above the head as a connection between the person and the rest of the universe. This information is consistent with the cardiac coherence procedures described in chapter one (pages 48-53) and the practice of Reiki[9]. The figures on the facing page represent my best efforts to show in a graphic way the relationship between these various phenomena.

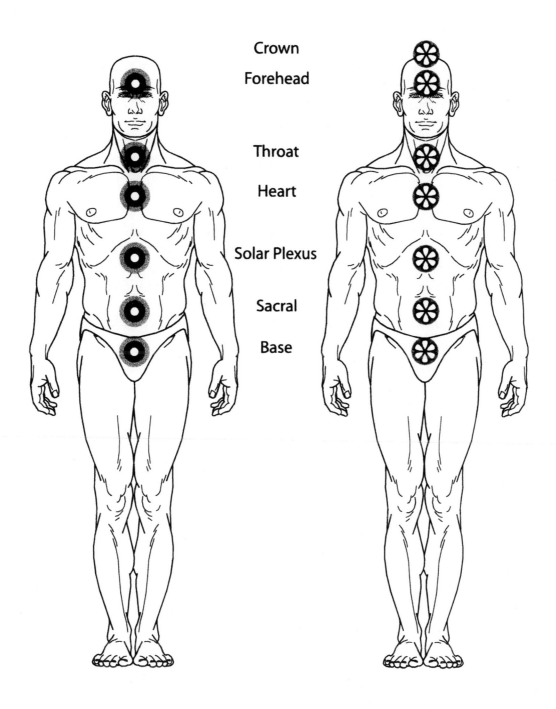

Crown

Forehead

Throat

Heart

Solar Plexus

Sacral

Base

Figure 47. **Receptor site concentrations compared to the chakras**

197

Demonstrations

Most of my clients are quick to request a demonstration of the exercises, which I usually offer during our initial session. Virtually all experience benefit from the treatment, even if we only have a few minutes available to do an exercise at the end of the first hour.

This is contrary to traditional psychotherapy practice where several hours are spent in history taking and relationship building before treatment is even discussed. I have wondered if this could explain why the most usual length of a therapy experience is one hour. But whatever the reason – clients quit therapy early out of frustration at the delays, or we only have one hour with many clients for some other reason – it behooves us to offer some healing resource as quickly and safely as possible. These comments are relevant for all providers – professional psychotherapists, medical staff, coaches, community healers, and so forth.

Muscle testing (chapter 7) usually makes for a convincing demonstration as well. I was part of a clinical group involved in a 3-year study with community-based parolees. To introduce the techniques we would use (which included most of the exercises in the book) we would demonstrate muscle testing in a group of ten clients, inviting one of them to serve as a subject. After the muscle testing demonstration 90% of the men and women in the group volunteered for personal and private treatment. (Obviously, it is particularly important for the treating therapist to be deeply respectful of the person in this group context, and to take pains to avoid any hint of this being a side-show).

Practice

Without practice it is unlikely that initial benefits from using the exercises will endure, any more than a once-a-month workout at the gym will keep us physically fit. I refer the reader to the end of chapter 8 for ideas on how to set up a routine.

There are opportunities for practicing the exercises that we may not notice. A trainer or teacher, for example, could lead a class in one or more exercises from time to time throughout a day. One of my colleagues does this when training high-level leaders. In particular, the exercise forms suggested in chapters 7 and 8 lend themselves to group format, humor, and personalized application. For example, when I teach (whatever the subject) I will take occasional breaks to conduct "an activity designed to increase our energy just in case anyone is drifting off", and will do the three thumps or an EFT exercise. The three thumps can be used to stimulate; EFT can help to sedate or stimulate, depending on the intended need. It is important to *invite* students to join in the exercise and to answer any questions they might have.

As a coach or therapist, I will often ask a client to report back to me any homework they have done between our sessions. I find this helps to motivate clients and to give them an additional opportunity to sample the exercises to see if they will be useful to them. It is often the beginning of a routine.

In summary, we need to respect the needs of our clients for information prior to their trying out what we might want to teach them. The more scientifically oriented will expect that we have some solid empirical defense for what we offer. The skeptical might want to experience the power of an exercise before agreeing to give it a serious try. Those who arrive with urgency and with little apparent interest in understanding the exercises beforehand may require, paradoxically, even more information before your begin to treat them – they should be told of the consequences of healing and of how the exercises often produce permanent resolution of problems. In this regard all providers should be most respectful of informed consent (that is, the client knows what could happen prior to agreeing to let it happen) and prepared to answer any questions that arise.

When these precautions are honored, I have found that persons from all cultures, religious persuasions, educational levels, and geographic regions can benefit from the exercises.

Notes to chapter ten

1. Information about pulsed electromagnetic field therapy can be found in Bassett (1995), Bassett, Mitchell, & Gaston (1982), Bright & colleagues (1981), and Frohlich (1968). John Zimmerman (1990) of the University of Colorado School of Medicine and Seto & colleagues (1992) describe the generator used to stimulate bone healing in non-union fractures.

2. A description of the HeartMath procedures is found in Childre & Rozman (2005).

3. McCraty (2005) is the director of research for the Institute of HeartMath.

4. The best source I know of for scientific information about the subtle energies is Oschman (2000 or latest edition).

5. Examples of clinical case studies on the effectiveness of EFT and the tapping shortcuts are Carbonell (1996), Darby (2001), Johnson, Shala, & colleagues (2001), Sakai & colleagues (2001), and Schoninger (2004).

6. EMDR has been shown to be efficient and effective in the treatment of PTSD and related problems. For examples from the long list of studies supportive of EMDR, see Perkins & Rouanzoin (2002). This meta-analysis will refer you to original scientific studies. The article by Ironson, Freund, Strauss, & Williams (2002) is an example of EMDR compared to other treatment. Levin, Lazrove, & van der Kolk (1999) report on a study of the brain changes produced by EMDR treatment. In this study the SPECT (single photon emission computed tomography) procedure was used to measure changes in the anterior cingulate gyrus and the left frontal lobe. Changes were interpreted by the authors as signs that the EMDR patients learned to distinguish real from imagined threat.

7. The jet lag procedure is from Eden (1998).

8. See the book by Pert (1999). Better still are her audiotapes (2000).

9. A good introduction to the chakras can be found in Eden (1998). Many books are written on the Reiki procedure and are available in most bookstores.

Epilogue and acknowledgements

While in the midst of final editing of this book, I had an experience that reflected what I wanted to write in this epilogue. I was conducting a course on the basic exercises in the book and asked for a volunteer so I could demonstrate the exercises. A young man said he wanted to work on what he described as "a nasty knot in my stomach that I have had for eight years – for which my physician has found no medical explanation." After about twenty minutes of anguish and tears while working with the TAT procedure, the man worked his way through a very painful memory of being a boy witnessing his father's death some thirty years before. As often happens, the origin had been much earlier than, and quite different from, what was first thought. When he finished his work he said the knot was at a "one" on the zero to ten scale. He still noticed it but said that it produced none of the burning and pain he had felt for so many years.

I had been monitoring his heart rhythm throughout the treatment, and though he said he *felt* much better, the computer screen indicated that he was 100% in the "low cardiac coherence" column, not a good sign for his physical or psychological health. I explained what I had been observing and invited him to work further, and he agreed. He worked by himself with both TAT and EFT for a period of time, but his low cardiac coherence scores remained. I turned to the trainees and reminded them that the measurable energy of our patient's heart reached out at least twenty feet and in some way was circulating with their own heart vibrations. I asked our "patient" and the other trainees if they would be willing to do an experiment. They would, they said.

I then invited the two dozen other trainees to do TAT while thinking of our patient, while he would sit quietly with his eyes closed and simply experience what happened. Within two minutes his cardiac coherence score began to register in the *medium* and *high* column on the screen, and then increased (for users of the heartmath software I would note that the percentages in the low-medium-high coherence columns rose from initial measurements of 100-0-0 to 30-25-45). After two more minutes I signaled to the group to change their TAT posture so they would not get fatigued, and at that instant the patient's coherence scores returned to 100% in the *low* column. As soon as the group resumed their new TAT postures, the score in the *high* coherence column again began to register. We saved the data and after the treatment we reviewed this most fascinating phenomenon. I later reflected on the following:

• It appeared that the group was able to help the young man in a way that allowed him to accomplish more than he could all by himself. This causes me to wonder: how much of what we think of as healing depends on the will and effort of the individual, and how much may involve the good will, effort, and "intentionality" of the community? A variation of this question might be: how much do our positive and negative thoughts affect one another, and in what ways? Related to this, what can we do to keep from being affected by the "negative energy" of others?

• In every course that I teach I offer practicum experiences where the trainees teach and learn from each other. This benefit of observing, being observed, and exchanging feedback is invaluable. You can do the same without professional guidance by going through the exercises in the book with a companion. I have tried to write the instructions clearly and completely so that a person unfamiliar with the concepts can become a fairly good guide for the person who at a given moment is taking the role of student.

• We used both EFT and TAT in our experiment. In this case, TAT was more effective (according to our measures). In the book I describe seven basic exercises and other secondary ones because in my experience it is useful to have options. Sometimes a technique will work well for one person, but not for another. This reminds me of the redundancy built into our brains which allows one part to take over the function of a damaged part, even though this substitute part was not intended to perform that function. In like manner, it appears to me that different approaches to healing are aimed in the same direction, but take different routes (neural, energetic, etc.), depending on many factors: the preference of the client, the issue, perhaps the beliefs of the practitioner. I grow suspicious when I hear a practitioner say about his or her chosen approach: "This is all you need to know and it will work for everyone", or imply that "This approach is better than any other one." My practical suggestion is this: if the healing strategy you are using is not working, or not as effectively as you would like, try something else from the book. This is a call for more collaboration and less competition.

• I will not follow up with this young man until I return to his country in a year or so. In the meantime, I do not know how he is faring. I am reminded of how often I hear of miraculous cures with no mention of whether or not the purported benefit endured over time, hence whether it was truly a "cure" or not. The importance of following up with those persons we presume to have helped remains a challenge for all of us, and is the issue most habitually neglected in the reports I hear about healing. We overstate our effectiveness when we give more attention to immediate results than to the long-term.

• I believe that the healing effects that we seek and report are objectively measurable. This does not mean that they are measurable *today* with available technology. Nonetheless, more and more devices are coming on the market. The software used to register cardiac coherence scores, for example, was invented only recently – thousands of years after the first use of the techniques that we still use to increase high cardiac coherence scores. In the meantime, I believe it makes sense to talk of the "subtle" energies that are still not detectable by modern technological instruments.

• The modest experiment I conducted with my students causes me to wonder about the many experiments I have *not* conducted, indeed the many that have not yet been done anywhere. I agree with a colleague who suggests that we are barely on the ground floor of a high rise, and with another who wonders if we have risen even to that level of knowledge and enlightenment.

• Speaking of experimentation: we need more true experiments, those that involve controlled groups, treatment of various groups simultaneously to see which method might be preferred for a given issue, and measurement with instruments that are recognized by professional and academic communities. I have noted some of the studies that encourage us to continue to use the exercises, but for the most part we still rely on case studies to justify our work, rather than more scientific empirical data.

• Nonetheless, I do not believe we need to suspend using the exercises until definitive scientific proof is available, just as we do not suspend doing most therapies (or coaching, or leadership development, or many other services) while awaiting a go-ahead from a laboratory. (As I finish this epilogue an email arrives from another country. A colleague, only recently exposed to the concepts underlying the exercises, took the book draft with him as he flew halfway around the world and he writes: "Read the book on my flights. Got to tell you that after flying more than a million miles I tried the jet lag procedures and for the first time I had no jet lag. Amazing. Was able to do some work with three people on a trauma team here, and they all noticed benefits almost immediately. Also amazing. The team is excited about doing a complete training"). This is "proof" enough for me.

I would like to recognize just a few of the people to whom I have looked for assistance in arriving at this (largely pre-scientific) point in my professional and personal life.

Thanks to all those who allowed me to include their photographs demonstrating the exercises. Langdon Foss [www.lllama.com] did all of the computer-generated illustrations. Thanks also to Sandi Dallas at Industrial Printers.

I have learned from many teachers, including clients who came to me for help and ended up teaching and inspiring me. Formal teachers have included Francine Shapiro, Fred Gallo, Greg Nicosia, Gary Craig, Tapas Fleming, Larry Nims, Donna Eden, David Feinstein, John Diamond, John Diepold, Asha Clinton, plus many others.

Special thanks are due to colleagues and team leaders around the world: in Argentina, Pablo and Raquel Solvey and María Elena Adúriz; in Austria, Margit Ganster-Breidler; in Brazil, Ecuador, and elsewhere, Esly Carvalho; in Colombia, Jhon Jairo Trejos Parra; in Costa Rica, Gabriela Segura Fonseca; in Ecuador, Santiago Jácome Ordóñez; in El Salvador, Atzimba Lemus; in Guatemala and many other training sites, Ligia Barrascout de Piedra Santa; in Indonesia, Doreen Biehle and Wolf Fernandez; in México, Ignacio Jarero, Lucina Artigas, and Jenny Roldan; in Panama, María Sang; in Peru, Luis Benitez; in Sri Lanka, Johanne Jayaratne; in Turkey, Emre Konuk and Ozlem Kaleli; and in Venezuela, Carlos Rivas. And thanks to many, many, other marvelous team members.

A list of persons to whom I am indebted in the United States would be too long so I mention only two names: thanks first to my bicycling buddy, frequent coauthor, and editor, Michael Galvin. And much gratitude and love to Nikki Brooker, my wife, editor, and life companion. Also, apologies to the many other individuals I did not acknowledge.

References

In the notes after each chapter and in Appendix A are the names of persons who have written more about the themes in this book. Here you can find the original sources for those writings. Web sites listed in Appendix A offer information on related topics.

Alman, B. and Lambrou, P. (1983). *Self-hypnosis: A complete manual for health and self-change*. San Diego: International Health Publications.

Anderson, B. (2000). *Stretching: 20th anniversary revised edition*.

Aspinwall, L. G. & Staudinger, U. M. (2003). *A psychology of human strengths: Fundamental questions and future directions for a positive psychology*. Washington, DC: American Psychological Association.

Auerbach, J E. (2001). *Personal and executive coaching: The complete guide for mental health professionals*. Venture, CA: Executive College Press.

Avery, D. H., & Eder, D. N. (2001). Dawn stimulation and bright light in the treatment of SAD: A controlled study. *Biological psychiatry, 50* (3), 205-216.

Baker, A.H., & Siegel, L.S. (2004). *Is emotional freedom technique (EFT) effective? An attempt to resolve conflicting conclusions between two recent laboratory studies*. Unpublished paper available from Harvey Baker: [harveybaker@fast.net]

Barrios-Choplin, B., McCraty, R., & Cryer, B. (1997). An inner quality approach to reducing stress and improving physical and emotional well-being at work. *Stress medicine, 13* (3), 193-201.

Bassett, C. A. L. (1995). Bioelectromagnetics in the service of medicine. In Blank, M. (Ed.) *Electromagnetic fields: biological interactions and mechanisms. Advances in Chemistry Series 250*. Washington, DC: American Chemical Society.

Bassett, C. A. L., Mitchell, S. N., & Gaston, S. R. (1982). Pulsing electromagnetic field treatment in ununited fractures and failed arthrodeses. *Journal of the American Medical Association, 247,* 623 – 628.

Bassman, L. E., & Uellendahl, G. (2003). Complementary/alternative medicine: Ethical, professional, and practical challenges for psychologists, *Professional psychology: Research and practice, 34* (3), 264-270.

Beck, A. (1967). *Depression: Clinical, experimental, and theoretical aspects*. New York: Harper & Row.

Beck, A. (1976). *Cognitive therapy and the emotional disorders*. New York: International Universities Press.

Benson, H. (1996). *Timeless healing: The power and biology of belief*. New York: Fireside Books.

Beutler, L. E., & Harwood, T. M. (2001). Antiscientific attitudes: What happens when scientists are unscientific? *Journal of clinical psychology, 57,* 43-51.

Blumenthal, J. M., Babyak, M.A., & Moore, K.A. (1999). Effects of exercise training on older adults with major depression, *Archives of internal medicine, 159,* 2349-2356.

Brennan, B.A. (1990). *Hands of light.* (Subtitled *A guide to healing through the human energy field* in earlier editions). New York: Bantam.

Brighton, D. T., Black, J., Friedenberg, Z. B., Esterhai, J. L., & Connolly, J. F. (1981). A multicenter study of the treatment of non-union with constant direct current. *Journal of Bone and Joint Surgery (America), 63A,* 1 – 13.

Burr, H.S. (1972). *Blueprint for immortality: The electric patterns of life.* Essex, UK: Saffran Walden.

Busch Lee, C., & Pinney, A. (2002). *So what! Now what? The coaching guide for leaders and managers.* Cascade, Colorado: Catalyst Consulting. [claudiabuschlee.com]

Callahan, R.J. (1985) *Five minute phobia cure.* Wilmington, DE: Enterprise.

Callahan, R. J. (1987) *Stop smoking now!* Indian Wells, CA: Callahan Techniques.

Callahan, R. J. & Callahan, J. (1996). *Thought field therapy and trauma: Treatment and theory.* Indian Wells, CA: Thought Field Therapy Training Center.

Callahan, R., J. & Perry, P. (1991). *Why do I eat when I'm not hungry?* New York: Doubleday.

Callahan, R. J. with Trubo, R. (2001). *Tapping the healer within.* Lincolnwood (Chicago), IL: Contemporary Books.

Carbonell, J. (1996). An experimental study of TFT and acrophobia. *The Thought Field, 2,* 1 & 6.

Carrington, P. (2001). *Annual energy psychology research update.* Presentation at the Third Annual International Comprehensive Energy Psychology Conference, San Diego, May 8-15.

Carrington, P., & Craig, G. (2000). Emotional freedom technique (EFT): A meridian based intervention for trauma. *Bridges.* Arvada, CO: The International Society for the Study of Subtle Energies and Energy Medicine.

Chambless, D.L., Baker, M.J., Baucom, B.H., Beutler, L.E., Calhoun, K.S., Crits-Christoph, P., Daiuto, A., DeRubeis, T., Detweiler, J., Haaga, D.A.F., Bennett Johnson, S., McCurry, S., Mueser, K.T., Pope, K.S., Sanderson, W.C., Shoham, V., Stickle, T., Williams, D.A., & Woody, S.R. (1998). Update on empirically validated therapies II. *The Clinical Psychologist, 51,* 3-15.

Chemtob, C.M., Tolin, D.F., van der Kolk, B.A., & Pitman, R.K. (2000). Eye movement desensitization and reprocessing in E. Foa, T. Keane, & M. Friedman (Eds.) *Effective treatments for PTSD: Practice guidelines from the International Society for Traumatic Stress Studies.* New York: Guilford Press, p. 139-155, 155, 333-335.

Childre, D., & Rozman, D. (2005). *Transforming stress: The HeartMath solution for relieving worry, fatigue, and tension.* Oakland, CA: New Harbinger.

Clinton, A. N. (2002). Seemorg Matrix Work. In Gallo, F. (Ed.) *Energy psychology in psychotherapy: A comprehensive source book.* New York: Norton.

Craig, G. (1998). *Steps toward becoming the ultimate therapist.* Sea Ranch, CA: Author.

Craig, G. (1999). *Emotional freedom techniques: The manual. Third edition.* Sea Ranch, CA: Author. See: [http://www.emofree.com/downloadEFTmanual.htm].

Cummings, N. A. (1999). Comment on L'Abate: Psychotherapist future shock. *Family journal: Counseling and therapy for couples and families, 7,* 221-223.

Czikszentmihaylyi, M. (2000). *Flow: The psychology of optimal experience.* New York: Harper & Row

Darby, D. (2001). *The efficacy of Thought Field Therapy as a treatment modality for individuals diagnosed with blood-injection-injury phobia.* Unpublished dissertation, Minneapolis, MN: Walden University.

Davidson, K., MacGregor, M.W., Stuhr, J., Dixon, K., & McLean, D. (2000). Constructive anger verbal behavior predicts blood pressure in a population-based sample. *Health psychology, 19,* 55-64.

Davidson, R.J., Kabat-Zinn, J., Schumacher, J., Rosenkranz, M., Muller, D., Santorelli, S.F., Urbanowski, F., & Harrington, A. (2001). Alterations in brain and immune function produced by mindfulness meditation. Submitted for publication.

Davis, M., Eshelman, E. R., & McKay, M. (2004). *The relaxation & stress reduction workbook (5th edition).*

DeBary, W. & Bloom, I (1999). *Sources of Chinese tradition, vol. 1.* New York: Columbia University Press.

Dennison, P. E., & Dennison, G. (1989). *Brain gym handbook.* Ventura, CA: Educational Kinesiology Foundation.

Diamond, J. (1979). *Your body doesn't lie* (Original title: *BK Behavioral Kinesiology*). New York: Warner.

Diamond, J. (1985). *Life energy.* New York: Dodd, Mead.

Diamond, J. (1988). *Life energy analysis: A way to cantillation.* Valley Cottage, NY: Archaeus.

Diepold, J. H. Jr. (2000). Touch and Breathe: An alternative treatment approach with meridian based psychotherapies. *Traumatology, 6,* 109-118. Also available at: [http://www.fsu.edu/~trauma/] *Electronic Journal of Traumatology,* 6(2).

Diepold, J.H.J., Britt, V., & Bender, S. S. (2004). *Evolving thought field therapy: The clinician's handbook of diagnosis, treatment and theory.* New York: Norton.

Dossey, J. (1993). *Healing words: The power of prayer and the practice of medicine.* San Francisco: Harper.

Durlacher, J. (1994). *Freedom from fear forever.* Tempe, Arizona: Van Ness,

Eden, D., with D. Feinstein. (1998). *Energy medicine.* New York: Jeremy P. Tarcher/Penguin Putnam, Inc.

Edwards, D. J. A., Dattilio, F. M., & Bromley, D. B. (2004). Developing evidence-based practice: The role of case-based research. *Professional psychology: Research and practice, 35* (6), 589-597

Everly, G. S. & Lating, J. M. (1990, 2nd edition). *A clinical guide to the treatment of the human stress response.* New York: Kluwer Academic/Plenum Publishers.

Everly, G. S. & Mitchell (1999) (2nd. Ed.). *Critical incident stress management: A new era and standard of care in crisis intervention*Ellicott City, MD: Chevron.

The Executive Coaching Forum (2001 or latest draft). *The executive coaching handbook.* Download at: [http://www.theexecutivecoachingforum.com]

Farrow, J. T. & Herbert, R. (1982). Breath suspension during the transcendental meditation technique. *Psychosomatic medicine, 44* (2), 133-153.

Feinstein, D. (2002). *Energy psychology interactive: A 40-hour course in the basics of energy psychology* (CD). Ashland, OR: [http://www.innersource.net].

Fernandez, I., Gallinari, E., & Lorenzetti, A. (2004). A school-based eye movement desensitization and reprocessing intervention for children who witnessed the Pirelli Building airplane crash in Milan, Italy. *Journal of Brief Therapy,* 2129-136.

Field, T. M. (1998). Massage Therapy Effects. *American Psychologist, 53* (12), 1270-1281.

Finney, M.L., Stoney, C. M., & Engbretson, T.O. (2002). Hostility and anger expression in African-American and European-American men is associated with cardiovascular and lipid reactivity. *Psychophysiology, 39,* 340-349.

Fitzgerald, C. & Berger, J. (2000) *Executive coaching.* Palo Alto, CA: Davies-Black Publishing

Fleming, T. (1999). *You can heal now: The Tapas acupressure technique (TAT).* Redondo Beach, CA: TAT International.

Fox, R. E. (2004). Towards creating a real profession of psychology: A misguided emphasis on science at the expense of social relevance. *The independent practitioner, Spring, 2004,* 58-61.

Fröhlich, H. (1968). Bose condensation of strongly excited longitudinal electric modes. *Physics Letters, 26A,* 402-403.

Furlan, R., & Piazza, D. (1993). Early and late effects of athletic training on neural mechanisms controlling heart rate, *Cardiovascular research, 27,* 482-488.

Gach, M.R. (1990). *Acupresure's potent points: A guide to self-care for common ailments.* New York: Bantam Doubleday Dell.

Gach, M.R., & Henning, B.A. (2004) *Acupressure for emotional healing.* New York: Bantam.

Gallo, F. (2000). *Energy diagnostic and treatment methods.* New York: Norton.

Gallo, F. (2005). (2nd ed.). *Energy psychology: Explorations at the interface of energy, cognition, behavior, and health.* Boca Raton, FL: CRC Press.

Gallo, F. P., & Vincenzi, H. (2000). *Energy tapping.* Oakland, CA: New Harbinger.

Gerber, R (2000). *Virbational medicine for the 21st century.* NY: Eagle Brook.

Goldsmith, M., Lyons, L., Freas, A., & Wither-spoon, R. (Eds.). (2002) *Coaching for leadership: How the world's greatest coaches help leaders learn.* San Francisco: Jossey-Bass.

Haggarty, J. M., Cernovsky, Z., & Husni, M. (2001). The limited influence of latitude on rates of seasonal affective disorder, *Journal of nervous and mental disease, 189* (7), 482-484.

Hargrove, R. (1995). *Masterful coaching.* San Diego, CA: Jossey-Bass/Pfeiffer. (Note: this is a series and includes the trainer's package, facilitator's package, participant workbook, observer assessment instrument, masterful coaching set, and the masterful coaching fieldbook.

Hartung, J.G., & Galvin, M.D. (2003). *Energy psychology and EMDR: Combining forces to optimize treatment.* New York: Norton.

Hays, K. F. (1999). *Working it out: Using exercise in psychotherapy.* Washington, DC: American Psychological Association Press.

Hays, K. E., & Brown, C. H., Jr. (2004). *You're on! Consulting for peak performance.* Washington, DC: American Psychological Association Press.

Herbert, J. D., & Gaudiano, B. A. (2001). The search for the holy grail: Heart rate variability and thought field therapy. *Journal of Clinical Psychology, 57,* 11207 – 1214).

Hibbeln, J. (1998). Fish consumption and major depression, *The Lancet 351,* 1213.

Hornstra, G., et al. (2000). Essential fatty acids in mothers and their neonates. *The American Journal of Clinical Nutrition, 71* (5 supplement), 1262S-1269S.

Hover-Kramer, D. (2000). Incorporating chakra and biofield concepts into energy psychotherapy. In F. Gallo (Ed.). *Energy psychology in psychotherapy.* NY: Norton.

Hover-Kramer, D. (2002). *Creative energies: Integrative psychotherapy for self-expression and healing.* New York: Norton.

Howard, P.J. (2000). *The owner's manual for the brain: Everyday applications from mind-brain research.* (2nd ed). Austin, TX: Bard Press.

Ironson, G., Freund, B., Strauss, J., & Williams, J. (2002). Comparison of two treatments for traumatic stress: A community-based study of EMDR and prolonged exposure. *Journal of Clinical Psychology, 58,* 128-133.

Jarero, I. (1999). El abrazo de la mariposa. Available at [http://www.amamecrisis.com.mx/ac1.htm]

Jarero, T., Artigas, L., Maurer, M., Lopez Cano, T., & Alcala, N. (1999). Children's post traumatic stress after natural disasters: Integrative treatment protocols. Poster presented at the annual meeting of the International Society for Traumatic Stress Studies, Miami, FL.

Johnson, C., Shala, M., Sejdijaj, X., Odell, R., & Dabishevci, K. (2001). *Journal of Clinical Psychology, 57,* 1237 - 1240.

Karlin, W.A., Brandolo, E., & Schwartz, J. (2003). Workplace social support and ambulatory cardiovascular activity in New York traffic agents. *Psychosomatic medicine,* 65 (2), 167-176.

Katula, J., Blissmer, B., & McAuley, E. (1999). Exercise intensity and self-efficacy effects on anxiety reduction in healthy, older adults. *Journal of Behavioral Medicine, 22,* 233-247.

Kendall, H. O., & Kendall, F. M. P. (1949). *Muscles—Testing and function.* Baltimore, MD: Williams and Wilkins.

Kilburg, R. R. (2000), *Executive coaching: Developing managerial wisdom in a world of chaos.* Washington, DC: American Psychological Association Press.

Kinlaw, D. C. *Coaching for commitment: Interpersonal strategies for obtaining superior performance from individuals and teams.* (Note: this is a series that includes the *coaching for commitment book, trainer's package, participant package, participant workbooks, coaching skill inventory,* and *the problem-solving questionnaire.)*

208

Koocher, G. P. (2004). Three myths about empirically validated therapies. *The independent practitioner, Spring 2004, 62-63*.

Korkmazler-Oral, & Pamuk, S. (2000, October). Group EMDR with child survivors of earthquakes in Turkey. Paper presented at the EMDR clinical applications with children: A cost-effective treatment tool, Westminster, England. (2002)

Lambrou, P., & Pratt, G. (2000). *Instant emotional healing: Acupressure for the emotions*. New York: Broadway Books.

Langman, L. (1972). The implications of the electro-metric test in cancer of the female genital tract. In Burr, H.S. (Ed.), (1972). *Blueprint for immortality: The electric patterns of life*. Essex, UK: Saffran Walden.

Lawson, A., & Calderon, L. (1997). Inter-examiner reliability of applied kinesiology manual muscle testing. *Perceptual and Motor Skills, 84*, 539-546.

Leisman, G., Ferentz, A., Zenhausern, R., Tefera. T., & Zemcov, A. (1995). Electromyographic effects of fatigue and task repetition on the validity of strong and weak muscle estimates in applied kinesiology muscle testing procedures. *Perceptual and Motor Skills, 80*, 963-977.

Leisman, G., Shamlaugh, P., & Ferentz, A. (1989). Somatosensory evoked potential changes during muscle testing. *Int'l. Journal of Neuroscience, 45*, 143-151.

Leonard, T. (1998) *The portable coach*. NY: Scribner

Leonoff, G. (1995). Successful treatment of phobias and anxiety by telephone and radio: A preliminary report on a replication of Callahan's1987 study. *The Thought Field*. Undated number. Indian Wells, CA: The Callahan Techniques.

Levin, P., Lazrove, S., & van der Kolk, B. (1999). What psychological testing and neuroimaging tell us about the treatment of posttraumatic stress disorder by eye movement desensitization and reprocessing. *Journal of anxiety disorders, 13*, 159 - 172.

Levitt, A., Joffe, R., & Kennedy, S. (1991). Bright light augmentation in antidepressant nonresponders, *Journal of Clinical Psychiatry, 52*, 8, 336-337.

Linde, K., Clausius, N., & Ramírez, G. (1997). Are the clinical effects of homeopathy placebo effects? A meta-analysis of placebo-controlled trials. *The Lancet, 350*, 835-843.

Litz, B. T., Bryant, R., Williams, L., Wang, J., & Engel, C. C. (2004). A therapist-assisted Internet self-help program for traumatic stress. *Professional Psychology: Research and Practice. 35*: 628-634.

Lombardo, M. M., & Eichinger, R.W. (2004). (4rd ed). *For your improvement: A guide for development and coaching for learners, managers, mentors, and feedback givers*. Minneapolis, MN: Lominger Limited, Inc.

Lopez, S. L. & Snyder, C. R. (Eds.). (2003). *Positive psychological assessment: A handbook of models and measures*. Washington, DC: American Psychological Association Press.

Luskin, F., & Reitz, M. (2002). A controlled pilot study of stress management training in elderly patients with congestive heart failure. *Preventive cardiology, 5* (4), 168-172.

McCabe, O. L. (2004). Crossing the quality chasm in behavioral health care: The role of evidence-based practice. *Professional psychology: Research and practice, 35* (6), 571-579

McCraty, R. (ed.). (2001). Science of the heart: Exploring the role of the heart in human performance. Boulder Creek, CA: Institute of HeartMath.

McCraty, R. (2005). The body's heart field. *Shift, December 2004 – February 2005,* 15-19. Petaluma, CA: Institute of Noetic Sciences.

McCraty, R., Barrios-Choplin, Rozman, D.,Atkinson, M., & Watkins, A.D. (1998). The impact of a new emotional self-management program on stress, emotions, heart rate variability, DHEA, and cortisol. *Integrative physiological and behavioral science, 33* (2), 151-170; and the *Pavlovian* Journal of Biological Science, *33,* 151-170.

Messer, S. B. (2004). Evidence-based practice: Beyond empirically supported treatments. *Professional psychology: Research and practice, 35* (6), 580-588.

Monti, D.A., Sinnott, D.C., Marchese, M., Kunkel, E.J.S., & Greeson, J.M. (1999). Muscle test comparisons of congruent and incongruent self-referential statements. *Perceptual and Motor Skills, 88,* 1019-1028.

Moyers, B. (1993). *Healing and the mind.* New York: Doubleday.

Myss, C., & Shealy, C.N. (1988). *The creation of health: The emotional, psychological, and spiritual responses that promote health and healing.* New York: Three Rivers Press.

Nambudripad D.S. (1993). *Say Goodbye to Illness.* Buena Park, CA: Delta.

Nicosia, G. (1999). *Test Dx: Thought Energy Diagnostic and Treatment Procedures (Manual for thought energy synchronization therapy training).* Pittsburgh, PA: Author.

Oschman, J. L. (2000). *Energy medicine: The scientific basis.* Edinburgh: Churchill Livingstone.

Paffenbarger, R. S., Lee, I. M., & Leung, R. (1994). Physical activity and personal characteristics associated with depression and suicide in American college men, *Acta psychiatrica scandinavica supplementum, 377,* 16-22.

Perkins, B. & Rouanzoin, C. (2002). A critical evaluation of current views regarding eye movement desensitization and reprocessing (EMDR): clarifying points of confusion. *Journal of Clinical Psychology, 58,* 77-97.

Pert, C. (1999). *Molecules of emotion.* New York: Scribner's.

Pert, C. (2000). *Study guide to Your body is your subconscious mind,* two audiocassettes. Boulder, CO: Sounds True.

Peterson, C. & Seligman, M. E. P. (2004). *Character strengths and virtues: A handbook and classification.* Co-published by the American Psychological Association and Oxford University Press.

Physicians Desk Reference for Herbal Medicines. (2000). (2nd ed.). Montvale, NJ: Medical Economics Press.

Pignotti, M., & Steinberg, M. (2001). Heart rate variability as an outcome measure for Thought Field Therapy in clinical practice. Journal of Clinical Psychology, 57, 1193-1206.

Pomeranz, P (1987). *Scientific basis of acupuncture*. New York: Acupuncture textbook and atlas.

Pressman, M.R., & Orr, W.C. (2004). *Understanding sleep: The evaluation and treatment of sleep disorders*. Washington, DC: The American Psychological Association.

Rama, Swami, Ballentine, R., & Hymes, A. (1998). *Science of breath: A practical guide.* Honesdale, PA: The Himalayan Institute Press.

Rechlin, T., & Weis, M. (1994). Are affective disorders associated with alternation of heart rate variability? *Journal of Affective Disorders, 32,* 4, 271-275.

Reilly, D., Taylor, M., Beattie, N., Campbell, J., McSharrie, C., & Aitchison, T. (1994). Is evidence for homeopathy reproducible? *The Lancet, 344,* 1601-1606.

Rosenman, R. & Friedman, M. (1974). *Type A behavior and your heart.* New York: Knopf.

Rubik, B. (1995). "Can Western Science Provide a Foundation for Acupuncture?" *Alternative therapies magazine* (September, *1*, 4).

Sakai, C., Paperny, D., Mathews, M. Tanida, G, Boyd, G., Simons, A., Yamamoto, C., Mau, C., & Nutter, L. (2001). Thought field therapy clinical application: Utilization in an HMO in behavioral medicine and behavioral health services. *Journal of Clinical Psychology, 57,* 1215-1227.

Schoninger, B. (2004). *TFT in the treatment of speaking anxiety.* Unpublished doctoral dissertation. Cincinnati, OH: Union Institute.

Seligman, M. E. P. (1990). *Learned optimism.* New York: Knopf.

Seligman, M. E. P. (2002). *Authentic happiness.* New York: Free Press.

Seligman, M. E. P. & Czikszentmihaylyi, M. (2000). Positive Psychology: An Introduction. *American Psychologist, 55,* 5-14.

Selye, H. (1974). *Stress without distress.* Philadelphia: Lipincott.

Selye, H. (1976). *Stress in heart disease.* Boston: Butterworth.

Servan-Schreiber, D. (2004). *The instinct to heal: Curing stress, anxiety, and depression without drugs and without talk therapy.* Rodale. Originally published in French, *Guerir l'anxiete et la depression sans medicaments ni psychanalyse* (2003, Paris: Editions Robert Laffont).

Seto, A., Kusaka, C., & Nakazato, S. (1992). Detection of extraordinary large bio-magnetic field strength from human hand. *Acupuncture and Electro-Therapeutics Research International Journal, 17,* 75 - 94.

Shapiro, F. (2001). *Eye movement desensitization and reprocessing: Basic principles, protocols, and procedures* (2nd ed.). New York: Guilford.

Stoll, A. L. (2001). *The omega-3 connection: The groundbreaking omega-3 antidepression diet and brain program.* New York: Simon & Schuster.

Stoney, C.M., & Engebretson, T.O. (2000). Plasma homocysteine concentrations are positively associated with hostility and anger. *Life sciences, 66,* 2267-2275.

Stys, A., & Stys, T. (1998). Current clinical applications of heart rate variability. *Clinical cardiology, 21,* 719-724.

Suarez, E.C., Harlan, E., Peoples, M.C., & Williams, R.B., Jr. (1993). Cardio-vascular and emotional responses in women: The role of hostility and harassment. *Health psychology, 12,* 459-468.

Swingle, P., Pulos, L., & Swingle, M. K. (May, 2001). Effects of a meridian-based therapy, EFT, on symptoms of posttraumatic stress disorder in auto accident victims. Paper presented at the annual meeting of the association for comprehensive energy psychology, Las Vegas, NV. Correspondence: Paul G. Swingle, PhD, 630-1190 Melville St., Vancouver, BC V6E 3W1 CANADA

Taylor, S. (2002). *The tending response.* New York: Hold.

Taylor, S. (2000). Biobehavioral response to stress in females: tend-and-befriend, not fight-or-flight. *Psychological Review, 107* (3), 411-429.

Teeguarden, I. M. (1996). *A complete guide to acupressure.* Tokyo: Japan Publications.

Thie, J. (1994). *Touch for health: A practical guide to natural health with acupressure touch and massage.* Marina del Rey, CA: DeVorss.

Tsuji, H., Vendtti, F., Manders, E.S., Evans, J.C., Larson, M.G., Feldman, D., & Levy, D. (1994). Reduced heart rate variability and mortality risk in an elderly cohort. The Framington heart study. *Circulation* 90, 2, 878-883.

Van Raalte, J. L. & Brewer, B. W. (2002) *Exploring sport and exercise psychology (2nd edition).* Washington, DC: American Psychological Association Press.

Veltheim, J. (1999). *The bodytalk system: The missing link to optimum health.* Sarasota, FL: Parama.

Vernejoul, de, P., Albare, de, P., Darras, J.C. (1985). Etude des meridiens d'acupuncture oar les traceurs radioactifs. [Study of the acupuncture meridians with radioactive tracers.] *Bull. of the academy of national medicine* (Paris), *169*, 1071-1075.

Wells, S., Polglase, K., Andrews, H.B., Carrington, P., & Baker, H.B. (2003). Evaluation of a meridian-based intervention, emotional freedom techniques (EFT), for reducing specific phobias of small animals. *Journal of Clinical Psychology, 59,* 9, 943-966.

Walther, D.S. (1988). *Applied Kinesiology: Synopsis.* Pueblo, CO: Systems DC.

Wampold, B. E., & Bhati, K. S. (2004). Attending to the omissions: A historical examination of evidence-based practice movements. *Professional psychology: Research and Practice, 35* (6), 563-570.

Wilber, K. (2000). (2nd ed.). *A brief history of everything.* Boston: Shambhala.

Wilber, K. (2000). (2nd ed.). Sex, ecology, spirituality: The spirit of evolution. Boston: Shambhala.

Wilber, K. (2001). *No boundary: Eastern and western approaches to personal growth.* Boston: Shambhala.

Williams, M. B. & Poijula, S. (2002). *PTSD workbook: Simple effective techniques for overcoming traumatic stress symptoms.* Oakland, CA: New Harbinger.

Williams, P. & Davis. D. (2002). *Therapist as life coach: Transforming your practice.* NY: Norton.

Wilson, S.A., Becker, L.A., & Tinker, R.H. (1995). Eye movement desensitization and reprocessing (EMDR) treatment for psychologically traumatized individuals. *Journal of Consulting and Clinical Psychology, 63,* 928-937.

Wilson, S. A., Tinker, R.H., Becker, L. A., & Logan, C. R. (2001). Stress management with law enforcement personnel: A controlled outcome study of EMDR versus a traditional stress management program, *International journal of stress management, 8* (3), 179-200.

Wilson, S. A., Tinker, R.H., Hoffman, A., Becker, L.A., & Marshal, S. (2000). *A field study of EMDR with Kosovar-Albanian refugee children using a group treatment protocol.* Paper presented at the annual meeting of the International Society for the Study of Traumatic Stress, San Antonio, TX, November.

Wolpe, J. (1969). *The practice of behavioral therapy.* New York: Pergamon Press.

Zaccaro, S. J. (2001) *The nature of executive leadership: A conceptual and empirical analysis.* Washington, DC: American Psychological Association Press.

Zanarini, M.C., & Frankenburg, F.R. (2003). Omega-3 fatty acid treatment of women with borderline personality disorder: A double-blind, placebo-controlled study. *American Journal of Psychiatry, 160,* 167-169.

Zimmerman, J. (1990). Laying-on-of-hands healing and therapeutic touch: A testable theory. *BEMI Current, Journal of the Bio-Electro-Magnetics Institute, 2,* 8 –17.

Appendix A:
Resources, professional help,
and additional information

This appendix is for readers who would like to learn more about the exercises and topics in the chapters, who are curious in general about complementary and alternative medicine and psychology, or who would like a referral so they can continue their personal work with a professional. Subsequent editions will have more information about resources outside of the USA. Some of the information I include next was also mentioned earlier in the book.

The organization plan for the appendix begins with the seven exercises that have been described in chapters 1 through 5. EFT and the tapping shortcuts are discussed together as they come from the same energy tradition. Next there is additional information about the techniques suggested for sleep problems and jet lag (chapter 6), then for energy balancing and enhancement (chapter 7) and for performance enhancement (chapter 8). In chapter 9 I covered three professions, so I make comments specific to each regarding psychotherapy, medicine, and coaching. Additional exercises introduced in chapters 7 and 8 then follow. There is no additional information to be found in this appendix relevant to chapters 9 and 10. The appendix ends with comments about alternative and complementary medicine and psychology. Because of the nature of chapter 10, I already included advanced information there.

This plan produces a list of 13 topics that may be of special interest to the reader:

1. breathing (chapters 1 through 5)
2. TAT (chapters 1 through 5)
3. EFT and the tapping shortcut, both based on acupuncture points (chapters 1 through 5)
4. cardiac coherence (chapters 1 through 5)
5. the Butterfly Hug (chapters 1 through 5)
6. physical activity (chapters 1 through 5)
7. sleep and jet lag solutions (chapter 6)
8 energy balancing and enhancement (chapter 7)
9. performance enhancement (chapter 8)
10. psychotherapy (chapter 9)
11. medicine (chapter 9)
12. coaching (chapter 9)
13. complementary and alternative medicine

1. Breathing

This is exercise #1 in chapters 1 through 5, and is also referred to in chapters 7 and 8. It is mentioned first because it is so basic, and yet is often taken for granted and neglected as a healing resource.

Practitioners of hatha yoga have noted the connection between breathing and heart rate, and believe that if a person has perfect breath, he or she will have perfect health. Some yogi masters reportedly have been able to manage their breathing to such an extent that they can reduce their heart rate to a few beats per minute. One such yogi, Swami Rama, demonstrated control of his heart rhythm under laboratory-controlled conditions and, with the collaboration of two noted American physicians, has written of the resulting research findings. Their book (Rama, Hymes, & Ballantine, 1998) is one example of the science of breathing. About three-fourths of their book, by the way, is dedicated to scientific research, and in only about a fourth are specific breathing exercises described (an example is diaphragmatic breathing). Chapters include "Respiration and the chest: The mechanics of breathing;" "Nasal functioning and energy;" and "Portal to higher awareness: The science of breath." The theme of this latter chapter suggests that optimal breathing may be the missing key to both physical/emotional health and the experience of higher states of consciousness.

All of the approaches and techniques mentioned in this book have some connection with optimal breathing. An additional and useful approach that employs conscious breathing techniques and one that I have not yet mentioned is the BodyTalk system of John Veltheim (1999). Veltheim believes that a full breath cycle is important in treatment, and to ensure that treatment lasts. More information is available on the internet: [www.bodytalksystem.com].

Some of the methods mentioned in this book utilize specific forms of healing breath work. A good example is the breathing exercise described on page 153 and used for energy balancing. There are many other breathing exercises that are particularly potent in healing, but also somewhat risky because of the strong emotion they can elicit. Examples of the kind of breath work that requires professional guidance are those used during allergy elimination procedures. See the references under allergy treatment on page 227 for further information.

2. TAT

Tapas Fleming's Tapas Acupressure Technique (TAT) is exercise #2 in chapters 1 through 5. TAT is also mentioned in chapters 7 through 10. You may review the TAT pose and instructions on pages 28 to 35.

The point at the inside of the eye, on either side of the bridge of the nose, is the acupuncture point known as bladder-1. It is the first of 67 points that run from this site up and over the top of the head, then down along either side of the spine, ending on the outside of the little toe.

The meridian is traditionally associated in medical acupuncture with bladder functioning. In psychologically-related acupressure it is associated with trauma, as well as other emotions that accompany traumatic memories such as frustration.

TAT is consistent with an observation that many psychotherapists have made: the vast majority of problems that patients bring into the psychotherapy clinic have their origins in unresolved traumatic memories. If we were to choose only one of the 361 meridian points as the most valuable treatment for a wide variety of psychological problems, it would be this first point of the bladder meridian. Tapas also notes that all of the meridians converge in some way at this point of the bladder meridian.

The finger on the forehead is said by Tapas to stimulate energy on the frontal cortex, where clear judgment, sound reasoning, conscience, and other higher human functions are mediated in the brain. This point is also called the third eye by some, or the location of the head chakra. It is also the site of a concentration of receptor molecules described by Pert (2000).

The hand on the back of the head is said to stimulate visual memory. Generally, people who choose to work on traumatic memories begin by identifying a picture or image of the memory, and in this way TAT is again consistent with more traditional psychology and psychotherapy.

Tapas Fleming offers trainings in her approach. I have attended several and have consistently found her to be a sensitive, astute, and effective therapist. For further information: [http://www.tat-intl.com].

3. EFT and the tapping shortcuts

EFT is exercise #3 and the tapping shortcuts are #4 in chapters 1 through 5, and are also mentioned in chapters 7 through 10. You may review the figure of the EFT meridian points on page 38. I discuss these two exercises together because meridian theory is the basis for both of these techniques. Meridian theory is also the basis for acupuncture. It is thought that there are 14 meridians, each with a certain number of energy points for a total of 361 points on the 14 meridians. In acupuncture all the meridians and meridian points are used, depending on the problem. Needles are used to stimulate the points.

For EFT and the tapping shortcuts, and for other psychological uses of the meridians, all of the meridians are generally used but only a few of the 361 points are stimulated. And instead of using needles to stimulate the points, we generally recommend tapping or touching on the points with the fingers.

Let me offer a brief history of the two exercises I have described. I begin with the tapping shortcuts because these preceded the invention of EFT historically.

What I call "**tapping shortcuts**" in the book are similar to the "algorithms" of a therapy approach called Thought Field Therapy (TFT). Psychologist Roger Callahan invented TFT after learning from Australian physician John Diamond (1979, 1985, 1988) that specific meridians seemed to be associated with specific thoughts and emotions. Callahan independently found that for most psychological problems, stimulating only one point on each meridian seemed sufficient to stimulate the entire meridian line. Hence, he identified 14 key points in TFT, one for each meridian. He found that he could work with his patients even more economically by stimulating only a few points instead of all 14, depending on the problem. For example, he found that tapping only three of the key meridian points instead of all 14, and that tapping those three points in a particular order, would reduce symptoms of anxiety. He called these specific points and their prescribed order an "algorithm". (For a review of the anxiety shortcut, see pages 88-89. Note that I added a few more points to the three that Callahan recommended.)

The shortcuts or algorithms allow you to be specific and efficient in your work. This approach is also somewhat complex because you are required to memorize a different shortcut or algorithm for each different problem. To use a car repair metaphor, this would be akin to beginning with an initial diagnosis, and then attending only to those parts needing to be tuned or replaced.

Callahan and his partners teach the TFT system around the world and market technology to diagnose energy disruptions via analysis of a patient's voice resonance (see the R.J. Callahan references). There is preliminary scientific support for the effectiveness of TFT with phobias and other anxiety disorders (Darby, 2001; Schoninger, 2004).

For more information: [Callahan Techniques®/TFT: 800-359-2873, http://www.tftrx.com]

James Durlacher is one of the pioneers in meridian-based therapy, and practices a version of energy therapy that is similar to TFT: Durlacher: 800-529-8836; [http://www.freedomfromfearforever.com/].

Greg Nicosia (1999) is also a trainer of energy psychology who weaves quantum physics and astronomical calculations into his training courses: Thought Energy Synchronization Therapies: 412-683-8378, [http://www.thoughtenergy.com].

John Diepold, Victoria Britt, and Sheila Bender (2004; Diepold, 2000) teach touching instead of tapping in their meridian-based therapy courses, hence the name Touch-and-breathe. They are called the DBB Group: [http://www.tftworldwide.com].

EFT (Emotional Freedom Techniques), the second of the exercises based on meridian theory, was invented to eliminate the diagnosis and need for different algorithms. Gary Craig, the inventor of EFT, recommends tapping all 14 key meridian points for every presenting problem. The same points are tapped over and over for stress, anger, trauma – no matter the problem. In the car repair metaphor, EFT is akin to taking your car into the shop and having all of the parts replaced. You will be replacing some parts unnecessarily, but you can skip the diagnosis and not have to understand the nature of the problem in order to resolve it. It is less elegant but more simple and direct than the shortcuts, which is why thousands of persons around the world study and use this uncomplicated and effective treatment.

Support for the effectiveness of EFT with phobias can be found in Carrington (2001), Wells and colleagues (2003), and Baker & Siegel (2004). As an example of a study of EFT with trauma victims, see Swingle and colleagues (2002). For more information: USA: Emotional Freedom Technique: [http://www.emofree.com].
    In Britain: [http://members.aol.com/TickhillHealth], or [TLlewellyn@aol.com].

Other meridian-based approaches

Some practitioners believe that treatment can be more effective if we utilize more than the limited number of meridian points that Callahan and Craig espouse. Steve Reed, for example, teaches all of the 361 points so that if the ones being stimulated do not produce the desired effect, additional points can be tried. With Steve's permission I reproduce in figure 49 on page 219 one of the meridian graphs he uses in his courses. The graph is of the bladder meridian. You can see that it includes the bladder-1 point used in TAT (at the insides of the eyes), and both bladder-1 and bladder-2 used in EFT and the tapping shortcuts.

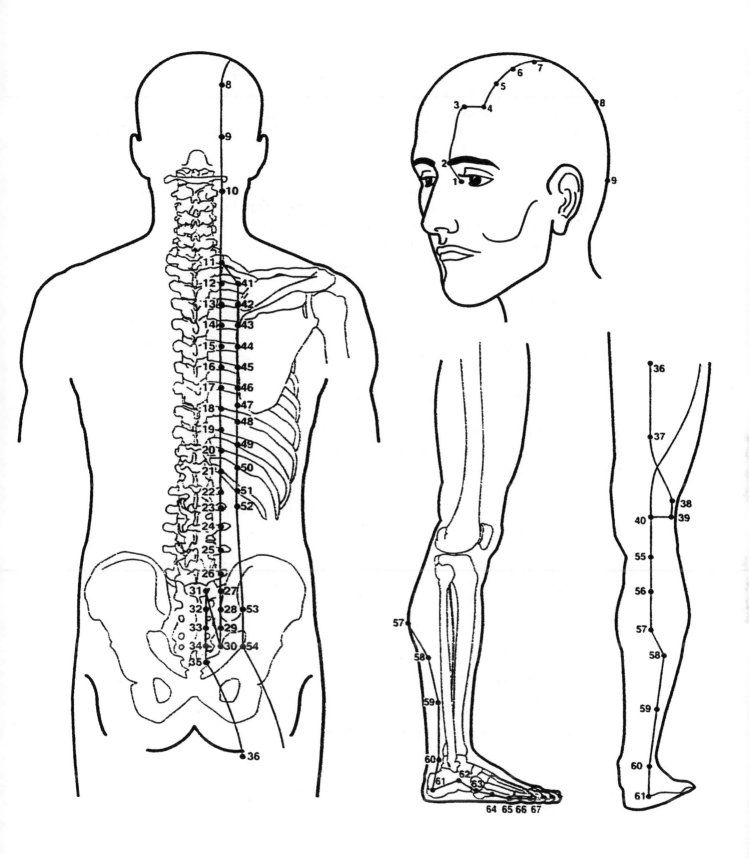

Figure 49: **Bladder meridian** (From REMAP, reproduced with permission)

219

The meridian charts are available on Steve's site at [http://www.remap.net]. For further information on what the REMAP process is, information about trainings and individual consultations, and related materials, contact Reed Eye Movement Acupressure Psychotherapy (REMAP), (972) 997-9955, Richardson, TX; [http://www: psychotherapy-center.com].

Fred Gallo also uses more than minimal meridian points recommended in TFT and EFT in his EDxTM approach. I first learned energy psychology from Fred, and recommend his approach and trainings with enthusiasm. For further information see especially the second edition of his classic energy psychology book (Gallo, 2005) and Energy Diagnostic and Treatment Methods: [http://www.energypsych.com].

Other resources

The organization most effective in promoting and researching energy psychology is the Association for Comprehensive Energy Psychology (ACEP), which can be accessed at:

800-915-3606 x21, [http://www.energypsych.org].

For an overview of the field of energy psychology, DVDs and self-help guides and programs are available from David Feinstein (2002). Also consult his website: [http://www.innersource.net].

The pioneers in the use of meridian theory for psychology problems generally began their studies in applied kinesiology. The International College of Applied Kinesiology has a website: [http://www.icakusa.com].

For names of persons trained in meridian-based therapy, consult the Institute for Meridian Psychotherapy and Counseling list. Send a blank e-mail to [IMPC.Forum-subscribe@listbot.com]

Another practitioner list is Energy Field, Healing and Power Therapy-tm e-Study Group List, moderated by Phil Friedman, Ph.D., [EFHPT101@aol.com] or PilF101@aol.comf, [http://www.philly.digitalcity.com/friedmanphilip].

Still another list is the Energy Therapy Home Page: [http://home.att.net/-tom.altaffer/index.htm].

Acupressure applications of meridian points can be found in Gach (1990), and Gach & Henning (2004).

4. Cardiac coherence

The software for measuring cardiac coherence to which I referred in the text is manufactured by heartmath, a registered trademark of the Institute of Heartmath. The Institute is a nonprofit corporation with a focus on the scientific evidence for the value of maintaining optimal heart coherence. For further information on scientific findings refer to the information website: [http://www.heartmath.org].

This group also markets a wide range of techniques and products under a commercial website: [[http://www.heartmath.com]; 1-800-450-9111; Email: [info@!heartmath.com];

The principles of heart coherence have been applied to stress and anxiety management; anger and rage reduction; business and athletic performance; the development of a sense of calm, confidence, and creativity; and ways to use the intelligence of the heart to respond gracefully to change, crisis, and challenges. As this book goes to printing, research plans can be accessed on the heartmath.org website. One example: federal (U.S.) funding in the amount of $1 million was awarded to the Institute of HeartMath to measure the impact of a heartmath program to reduce test anxiety and other emotional stress in various school districts across the United States. Preliminary results indicate that students can be taught to improve problem-solving, focusing, listening skills; to reduce test anxiety; and to learn better as evidenced by gains of 50% or more over the average math and reading proficiency scores of a test school district. Implications for improvements in self-esteem and performance in later life are also discussed [http://heartmath.org/education/testedge/why.php].

Works by R. McCraty mentioned in the references are recommended. Rollin McCraty is director of research of the Institute of HeartMath. Also see the relevant chapters in the excellent book by Servan-Schreiber (2004).

The concept of heart coherence may become more comprehensible if one reads the work of Candice Pert (1999, 2000). One of the six sites on the human body where receptor molecules congregate is in the area of the heart, and one can speculate that the techniques designed to enhance heart coherence produce their effect by stimulating the functioning of those receptor molecules (receptor molecules are related to peptide functioning).

To raise this to another level, it may be interesting to the reader to review figure 47 on page 197 and notice the overlap among the heart coherence techniques, the receptor sites, and the ancient chakras. A further speculation is that strategies based on the tradition of the chakra may also produce their effect by stimulating receptor molecules.

For readings on this topic, see Dorothea Hover-Kramer (2000, 2002). Also refer to Asha Clinton (2002) for information on Seemorg Matrix workshops.

5. The Butterfly Hug

This technique is based on Eye Movement Desensitization and Reprocessing (EMDR), a powerful brief therapy recommended by government and professional organizations around the world (see for example Chambless and colleagues, 1998; Chemtaub and others, 2000; Ironson and colleagues, 2002; and Perkins & Rouanzoin, 2002). The Butterfly Hug is an EMDR adaptation that is generally safe for self-use according to most clinicians who have used it.

EMDR is generally taught to and used by professional psychotherapists only. If for any reason you have tried the Butterfly Hugh or any of the other exercises in the book and find them insufficient, or if you simply wish to work with a professional psychotherapist for any problem, you can consult the following organizations:

> USA: EMDR Institute, 831-372-3900; [http://www.emdr.com].
> USA: EMDR International Association, 512-451-5200; [http://www.emdria.org].
> EMDR Europe: [http://www.emdr-europe.net].
> In Mexico and other Latin American countries:
>   [http://www.amamecrisis.com.mx/ac1.htm]
> In Argentina: [http://www.emdr.org.ar].

Additional information can be found at:
> EMDR News: [http://www.emdrnews.com].
> EMDR Portal: [http://www.emdrportal.com].
> David Baldwin's Trauma Information Pages: [http://www.trauma-pages.com].

Instead of giving my impression of EMDR from my clinical and research work, I will quote from Vanessa Spady who wrote the following letter to *Newsweek* magazine (December 20, 2004, Letters) regarding her experience as an EMDR client:

> I was surprised to find no reference to eye-movement desensitization and reprocessing in your article on posttraumatic stress disorder ("Battling the Effects of War"). EMDR is an amazing nonpharmaceutical resource for immediate relief of the anxiety, panic and long-term stress created from traumatic events. Eleven years ago I was in my bank when it was taken over by two men with assault weapons. They grabbed employees and customers, creating hysteria, panic and trauma for all of us. The shock of that had not fully set in when the Northridge earthquake hit while I was sound asleep on the first night in my new house, only four miles from its epicenter. To describe me as shellshocked would be entirely apt. After months of increasing restlessness and a diminishing ability to function on a day-to-day level, I sought talk therapy. Luckily for me, my therapist was also trained in EMDR. When certain anxiety-triggering events shut me down, she suggested a session of EMDR. In the less than 50 minutes we spent doing it, I

processed and released stress, anxiety, fear and confusion that talk alone would have taken years to uncover. I was able to relive the events without the crippling emotions and find a way out of the eddy of panic and anxiety that had become the increasing norm. No drugs, no long-term care, no rehab. Just that one-hour session, and "normal" was something I could recognize again.

6. Physical activity

As noted earlier in the book, studies have been cited that point to the value of physical activity in reducing stress (van Raalte & Brewer, 2004) and depressive symptoms (Blumenthal and colleagues, 2000; Paffenbarger and colleagues, 1994).

7. Sleep and jet lag solutions

First consult the references at the end of chapter six, page 145. Many devices are available that purportedly reproduce the cellular energy frequency necessary for health and well-being. One reported to correct insomnia is the Alpha-Stim 100, a registered electromedicine stimulator manufactured by Electromedical Products International, Inc. Information on research support for the stimulator is available: [http://www.alpha-stim.com], Email: [alpha-stim@epii.com].

8. Energy balancing and enhancement

Pages 147 to 155 summarize the energy and brain balancing techniques I have found to be most useful. Another effective approach to energy balancing is Braingym. For further information, see the Denison & Denison (1989) citation in the reference section.

9. Performance enhancement

Many executive and life coaches are skilled in specific techniques for performance enhancement. See the coaching section below for references.

10. Psychotherapy

It is worth repeating that if the exercises do not produce the result you desire, you may seek professional assistance. Psychotherapy is licensed by the states in the US. Many psychiatrists (though not all) limit their treatment to pharmaceuticals. Psychologists, social workers, and professional counselors in the US tend to provide psychotherapy treatment. Other providers who may become licensed are marriage and family therapists, and pastoral counselors. Always check the credentials, experience, skills, experience, and track record of someone you plan to consult professionally. Licensing is considered to be evidence that the licensed person has met only "minimal" standards of training. Many persons without a psychotherapy degree or a professional license provide excellent psychotherapy.

Not all psychotherapists have been trained in the brief treatment techniques described in this book, and some that have learned the exercises may be inexperienced in their use. If you wish to consult with a professional for the purpose of learning the exercises better, ask both if the person knows about what you are referring to, and whether the person agrees with what you are seeking. I have at times referred a client to a practitioner in another state or country only to learn later that the professional was on a specific practitioner list but did not practice the approaches that the list implied.

11. Coaching

The only source I know of for research on the impact of coaching is the Center for Creative Leadership: [httl://www.ccl.org]. (In the interest of transparency, I will mention that I have been on the CCL adjunct staff for 15 years.) I offer next a sampling of coaching services and training programs. While I know some of these trainers and would recommend them if asked, I do not endorse any one listed. Interested persons are encouraged to contact these and other resources through the Internet and decide for themselves which program might be a good fit.

Catalyst Consulting, Cascade, CO USA: [http://www.claudisbuschlee.com]

Coachville offers extensive training for persons interested in becoming professionally certified coaches [http://www.Coachville.com]

CoachWorks is a group of coaches available at:
[http://www.CoachWorks.com or www.LegacyLeadership.com]

College of Executive Coaching, 897 Oak Park Blvd #271, Pismo Beach, CA USA, offers coach training for mental health and other professionals:
[http://www.executivecoachcollege.com]

(For 15 years I have worked as an executive coach in the same organization as my sometimes co-author, Michael Galvin): [http://www.DrGalvin.com]

The Global Consulting Partnership: [http://www.clinical-to-consulting.com]

Kate Hays, author of *You're On! Consulting for peak performance*: Email:
[The_performing_edge@compuserve.com]

[http://www.innovativeleader.com]

The Institute for Life Coach Training offers programs for mental health professionals transitioning into coaching: [http://www.lifecoachtraining.com]

International Journal of Coaching in Organizations. C/O Professional School of Psychology, 9912 Business Park Drive, Suite 170, Sacramento, CA 95827: Email:
[mazien@ijco.info]

Leadership Development Specialists & Executive Coaching (TLS Associates) is located in Rochester, NY USA:
[http://www.TLSassociates.com]

Leadership University: [http://www.leadu.com/path]

Metro Media offers a teleclass on marketing a coaching practice: Email: [learn@metrocoaching.net]

MentorCoach offers coach training for mental health professionals: [http://www.mentorcoach.com]

The National Institute for the Clinical Application of Behavioral Medicine sponsors various on-line coaching training courses: [http://www.nicabm.com]

The Professional School of Psychology offers a Certificate in Executive Coaching. PSP, 9912 Business Park Drive, Suite 170, Sacramento, CA 95827: [mazien@ijco.info]

Reencuadre of Mexico City offers international coaching certification through the International Society of Neurosemantics (NLP-based training): [http://www.reencuadre.com]

Right Management Consultants offer coaching and are located at 1818 Market St., 33rd floor, Philadelphia, PA USA. [http://www.right.com]

Phillippe Rosinski is a coach trainer and facilitator in Brussels, Belgium: [http://www.philipperosinski.com]

SuccessPartner, LLC/Executive Coaching & Consulting is located in Denver, CO USA: [leslie@successpartner.com]

Syzergy is a group that offers coaching out of Australia: P.O. Box 950, Surfers Paradise, Qld, Australia, 4217
Email: [Christine@syzergy.biz]

12. Medical personnel

The National Center for Complementary and Alternative Medicine has a website: [http://www.nccam.nih.gov]

The White House Commission on Complementary Alternative Medicine also has a website: [http://www.whccamp.hhs.gov/finalreport.html].

13. Complementary and alternative medicine and psychology (CAMP)

It is awkward to separate the following into either medicine or psychology, as there is such mind-body overlap in the work done by those who practice in these professions. Psychologists notice improvement in patients' physical symptoms as a function of psychological improvement, and medical personnel are aware of the influence of psychological factors on medical problems. Herbs and other nutritional supplements can assist in reducing depressed and anxious feelings, and homeopathy has been shown to benefit various emotional and psychological complaints. This information is provided as a sampling of available resources in complementary and alternative medicine and psychology CAMP). About 2 out of 3 persons living in the US use CAMP resources.

Acupuncture

Meridian theory underlies acupuncture and helps to comprehend exercises #2 (TAT), #3 (EFT), and #4 (tapping shortcuts) in chapters one through five. For overviews of Chinese acupuncture and meridian theory, see Debary & Bloom (1999) and Pomeranz (1987). Internet information on theory and research is also available. Here are three examples among many:

[http://www.emofree.com/research/meridianexistence.htm]

[http://www.Peacefulmind.com]

[http://www.LAtimes.com/features/health/la-he
        acupuncture4apr04,1,3798014.column?coll=la-headlines-health]

Acupressure

Exercises #2 through #45 are more consistent with acupressure than acupuncture, as needles are not used. Examples of other acupressure applications can be found in Gach (1990), Gach and Henning (2004), and Teeguarden (1996).

Allergy treatment:

Sandi Radomski [SandiRadom@aol.com], [http://www.AllergyAntidotes.com]

Nambudripad Allergy Elimination Technique: [http://www.naet.com], [714-523-8900

Jaffe-Mellor: [http://www.jmt.jafmeltechnique.com]; Email: [jmtseminars@juno.com]

Other associations and organizations that may be of interest include these:

American Association of Naturopathic Physicians: [http://www.naturopathic.orh]
The American Herbalists Guild: [http://www.americanherbalistsguild.com]
American Holistic Health Association: [http://www.ahha.org]
American Holistic Medical Association: [http://www.molisticmedicine.org]
American Institute of Homeopathy: [http://www.homeopathusa.org]
Bastyr University: [http://www.bastyr.edi/]
Bioenergetic analysis: [http://www.bioenergetic-therapy.com]
Body-mind centering: [http://www.bmcassoc.org]
Center for Mind-Body Medicine: [http://www.cmbm.org]
The Council on Naturopathic Education: [http://www.cnme.org/]
ETox (energy toxins), two websites by Don Elium: [http://www.eToxResearch.com],
        [http://www.eToxAutism.com]
HBLU: [http://www.jaswack.com]
[http://andrewhahn@andrewhahn.com]
Healing Touch: See Brennan (1987), in the references
Institute for Healing in Society and Medicine: [http://www.healinginmedicine.org]
The Institute of Noetic Sciences: [http://www.noetic.org]; Email:
        [IONResearch@noetic.org]
International College of Applied Kinesiology: [http://www.icakusa.com]. See also
        Walther (1988) in the references.
International Society for the Study of Subtle Energies and Energy Medicine:
        [http://www.issseem.org]
The International Society of Orthomolecular Medicine:
        [http://www.orthomed.org/isom/isom.htm?1]
The National Center for Complementary and Alternative Medicine,
        [http://www.nccam.nih.gov]
The National Center for Homeopathy: [http://www.homeopathic.org/find.htm]
The National Certification Commission for Acupuncture and Oriental medicine:
        [http:///.www.nccaom.org]
National College of Naturopathic Medicine: [http://www.ncnm.edu/intro.html]
The Southwest College of Alternative Medicine:
        [http://www.scnm.edu/college/future/index_future.html]
Three-in-one: [http://www.onebrain.com]
Touch for Health. See Thie (1994) in the references.
The White House Commission on Complementary Alternative Medicine
        [http://www.whccamp.hhs.gov/finalreport.html].

Also see Myss & Shealy (1998) as an example of medical intuition.

Index

This is an abbreviated index and includes only main topics covered in the text, and only the first author, or the first two authors, of an article or book cited.

233